TIMELESS
BEADWORK
DESIGNS

CYNTHIA RUTLEDGE

New York

My bounty is as boundless as the sea, my love as deep;
the more I give to thee, the more I have, for both are infinite.

—William Shakespeare, *Romeo and Juliet*

To my soul mate, Mark. You are the wind beneath my wings.

All my love, Cynthia

LARK
New York

An Imprint of Sterling Publishing
1166 Avenue of the Americas
New York, NY 10036

Project illustrations by Bonnie Brooks
Project photography by Lynne Harty
Materials photography by Chris Bain
Author photograph by Mark Rutledge
p. 2: stone cabochons courtesy of Joe Jelks of Horizon Mineral
Art Resource: Alfredo Dagli Orti: p. 176; RMN-Grand Palais: p. 62; Scala: p. 52; Scala/White Images: p. 92;
AKG-images: p. 77; Bridgeman Images: © Towneley Hall Art Gallery and Museum, Burnley, Lancashire: p. 168;
Courtesy Wikimedia Foundation: Academy of Fine Arts Vienna: p. 41; Charlottenburg Palace: p. 152; J. Paul Getty Museum: p. 132;
Mauritshuis The Hague: p. 34, 69; Metropolitan Museum of Art: p. 141; Royal Collection of Belgium: p. 120; Stadel: p. 20;
Yale Center For British Art: p. 108

ISBN 978-1-4547-0875-9

Distributed in Canada by Sterling Publishing
c/o Canadian Manda Group, 664 Annette Street
Toronto, Ontario, Canada M6S 2C8
Distributed in the United Kingdom by GMC Distribution Services
Castle Place, 166 High Street, Lewes, East Sussex, England BN7 1XU
Distributed in Australia by Capricorn Link (Australia) Pty. Ltd.
P.O. Box 704, Windsor, NSW 2756, Australia

For information about custom editions, special sales, and premium and corporate purchases,
please contact Sterling Special Sales at 800-805-5489 or specialsales@sterlingpublishing.com.

Manufactured in China

2 4 6 8 10 9 7 5 3 1

larkcrafts.com

CONTENTS

FOREWORD

Cynthia started her beading journey in 1993 in southern California, and I had my chance to teach off-loom bead weaving at Penland School of Crafts in western North Carolina, 2400 miles away. Little did we know at the time that we would become good friends and enjoy the opportunities of sharing what we both love with others— off-loom bead weaving.

As time moved forward, our paths, or I should say work, would cross within the same publications: *Beaded Amulet Purses* (1994) by Nicolette Stessin and *Creative Bead Jewelry* by Carol Taylor (1995), and in my book *Creative Bead Weaving*, published in 1996. The amulet purse titled Garden Urn already shows Cynthia's attention to detail and the integration of other materials that complement the beadwork.

It wasn't until 2002 that we finally connected, face to face, for a period of time that allowed a friendship to blossom. For the next 10 years at the Beads on the Vine retreat we would teach and enjoy each other's company. Cynthia always impressed me with her creativity, her good nature, and her willingness to share her knowledge. So, when she asked me to write the foreword for her book I was more than honored.

Cynthia has taught thousands of students, nationally and internationally, and they line up for her classes. Her popularity is due to several things: her effervescence and her ingenious class projects, her color sense, and her engineering ability when shaping within the confines of a stitch.

This book, *Timeless Beadwork Designs*, takes you on a journey of creative feelings. It is not just about the finished work, but about how Cynthia got there. It opens up new pathways to seeing what might be if one were able to remove the translucent veils that blind creativity. Cynthia lifts that boundary. She uses historical paintings as jumping blocks to inspire her work and show you the way.

There is a direct and obvious inspiration for the first project, Renaissance Cameo Necklace. The painting *Portrait of a Young Woman* shows a cameo pendant, and the project is a cameo pendant—simple enough. Cynthia could have left it as just a pendant, but her muse took it further and incorporated a beautiful chain made up of knitted wire tubing and beaded end caps and clasps.

And then we have the Queen's Lace Bracelet. Cynthia removed herself from the obvious and chose the lace as a guide for her inspiration. The bracelet is fit for a queen and would have completed Queen Louise's ensemble perfectly.

You don't have to copy a painting; you just need to feel it, to allow yourself the right to your inspiration. Cynthia is showing you the way. Her projects reflect her thoughts, and in doing the projects, the connection becomes clear.

Each of the inspired pieces is accompanied with detailed instructions and so many wonderful illustrations you won't have any problems completing it. You will be amazed by the simplicity of her "step-up/step-down" method for odd-count peyote, and you will enjoy the many different ways to bezel a crystal or pearl. The way Cynthia constructs her pieces is a learning experience all its own.

So take this book and learn how to see and feel your creative path through Cynthia's inspired creations. You will not be disappointed!

I will leave you with a quote by author Charlotte Perkins Gilman (1860–1935) that seems appropriate to this beautiful book: "To be surrounded by beautiful things has much influence upon the human creature: to make beautiful things has more."

Happy creating,
—*Carol Wilcox Wells*

INTRODUCTION

I can't imagine designing without the muse of history. I marvel at what wonders, created by people, have been left behind for those in the future to enjoy. These treasures and wonders of the world are a window into the past. Maybe that is why I love to travel to distant places, why I love museums to distraction, and why my work wouldn't have its creative soul if I didn't have this passion.

Two great things happened in my life at about the same time, and who knew that they would enrich my life to the extent that they have. I started beading in the early 1990s, and during that same time, my husband, Mark, and I started doing eighteenth-century reenacting for the year 1757 with a national living history group. We portray a physician and his wife from the American colonies. In-depth historical research and hard work are part of reenacting, in order to portray our characters to the best of our ability. As we researched everything from garments to tents, we started documenting and gathering tons of materials.

Some of the best documentation materials are paintings from the period. Paintings document diverse lifestyles, from those of the very wealthy to the poorest of the poor. Still-life paintings show us everyday items used at table, as in *A Richly Laid Table with Parrot* (Jan Davidsz de Heem, c. 1650). Portraits show hairstyles, jewelry, garments, and accoutrements of the sitter, as in the portrait *Princess de Broglie* by Jean-August-Dominique Ingres (c. 1851–83). Some paintings just steal your heart, as does *The Girl with the Pearl Earring* by Johannes Vermeer (c. 1665).

This book is the result of my inspiration to design and bead, using as my muse famous paintings dating from the late 1400s to the early 1900s. A wide range of artists' styles and compositions, together with diverse color palettes and subject matter, have made these paintings among my favorites. To design a piece of beadwork to go with each painting has been a very humbling but rewarding experience. The masters who created these priceless works of art have left us in awe of their abilities. I wanted to create beadwork that, in a small way, was a tribute to their amazing skills, and to thank them for the richness they have added to my life.

One of the great things about using paintings for inspiration is to study how color is used. The wonderful artists who painted them were truly masters of color. Even if you are not a designer, try building a color palette around a famous painting for your next project. You will be amazed at how this exercise in color theory will help with your own color sensibility.

Each of the 15 new designs in this book uses multiple techniques and beautiful materials to create a timeless style of jewelry that never goes out of fashion. Elegant earrings, necklaces, bracelets, and a brooch make up this collection of work. Each design has two colorways (one has three) to give you a lot of options when either working from my color palettes or striving to design your own.

The jewelry designs in this book are there to inspire you to bead with passion. Finding what inspires you to create is a glorious experience. My path to being an artist has always been driven by my desire to create something that is beautiful. I bead for myself, to satisfy my desire to create, to feed my soul. That others admire my work is a gift. If they see something in my work that appeals to them, that calls to them, then I am blessed indeed, as maybe they can glimpse the part of me that is just following my heart. What the painter Van Gogh said of art is very true for designing with seed beads: "What is done in love is done well."

—*Cynthia Rutledge*

GETTING STARTED

Skill Levels

Intermediate: Designs suited to seed beaders who have a working knowledge of the basic stitches described for the design and are ready to add new techniques to their repertoire.

Intermediate Advanced: Designs suited to the seed beaders who are comfortable with the basic stitches and are ready to raise their skill level by learning new techniques.

Advanced: Designs suited to seed beaders who are proficient in the basic stitches and are comfortable with detailed designs. These designs are for those who are ready for a creative and technical challenge.

Basic Materials

For the Love of Beads!

Was it the shape, or the color? That they were tiny and you could make things out of them? I will never know, but once I laid my eyes on seed beads, they stole my heart. For many years my motto was "There is no bead I do not need!"

Seed beads: I started beading using Czech seed beads, but I prefer Japanese seed beads in 15° and 11°, as the holes are a bit larger. I use both Toho and Miyuki seed beads. The color selections these days are amazing, with all kinds of finishes available in many sizes. But my love affair with 15°s began a long time ago, and they are my favorite size.

Cylinder (tubular) beads: I was already beading at the time Miyuki came out with Delica beads. I instantly was attracted to them. When stitched they had so much structure, like building a peyote stitch brick wall! I prefer the 11° size as they work well with the size 15° and 11° seed beads that I use to design.

Note: My studio has always stocked the same color in at least three sizes, giving me more options when designing, so when you purchase your beads, make a plan to have 15°s, 11°s, and cylinder beads in the same color. These three sizes of beads work really well together. One thing to remember on bead sizes: the larger the number, the smaller the bead.

Pearls: Symbols of purity, virtue and modesty, pearls have been harvested for more than 4,000 years, and I find them a beautiful addition to my designs. In most cases, I use Swarovski crystal pearls and Czech glass pearls. These beauties come in rounds, cabochon shapes, drops, and more, and add an elegant touch to beadwork. The finish on high-quality faux pearls is really durable and realistic. Plus, they are available in a lot of beautiful colors at a reasonable price.

Natural and cultured pearls are a fabulous addition when strung for a necklace. When shopping, look for the highest quality you can afford. The highest quality pearls reflect almost a mirror image when viewed, but are very expensive. I usually choose a good-quality strand that is free of inclusions.

Glass beads: This category is virtually inexhaustible, from fire-polished beads to all shapes and sizes of pressed glass. The hardest thing to decide here is what to use! In this book, I have used fire-polished beads and beautiful faceted rondelles, as both shapes are readily available and come in many colors and sizes.

Crystals: I use crystals with a bit of reserve, but I do love the little 2-mm round ones. Unfortunately most of the colors have been discontinued. Luckily, the Swarovski crystal and crystal AB colors are still available, so I enjoy them a lot. They lend a little touch of sparkle without being overdone.

Cubic zirconia (CZ) stones and teardrops: I love these beauties! I use and stock CZs that are made mostly from zirconium dioxide and corundum. Laboratory-created synthetic and corundum gemstones are loupe clean, highly faceted, and scratch resistant. This material is very hard and optically flawless, offering a beautiful elegance to beadwork. I work with many sizes. Some are so small they have to be hand set into a metal setting, while some can be beaded around on their own. Either way, the bar was raised in my work when I started using them, and I have never looked back.

CZs come in many shapes, and sizes. I use round faceted, pears, ovals, cushion cuts (like throw pillows), trillions, and top-drilled teardrops.

Carved and Hand-Painted Cameos, Intaglios, Porcelain Transfers, and Cabochons

My grandmother always wore a small cameo with her pearls, and I thought it was so elegant! There are many types of cameos; the most common are the hand-cut shell cameos from Italy and the agate cameos from Germany. I scour thrift stores and antique stores for old ones that are waiting to be repurposed. They also are available online through auction sites. Look for high-quality carving and for one that speaks to you.

Intaglios are cameos in which the image is etched or carved into the surface of gemstones or glass. Swarovski makes some lovely ones out of glass. Antique ones may be found online through auction sites and at times in antique stores.

Hand-painted cameos are usually from Russia and are painted on onyx. They are colorful and a beautiful addition to beadwork. Available at online auction sites and at some bead shows.

Porcelain transfers are porcelain bases with a thin photographic "skin" on top, or else they have been hand painted. They are usually an inexpensive alternative to the higher-quality cameos, but are a lot of fun to incorporate into beadwork.

Stone cabochons are always a beautiful addition to beadwork. They can be used as a substitute for cameos. Look for high-quality work. Well-cut and well-finished cabochons are a pleasure to work with and add color and texture to beadwork.

Findings

If I were only going to say one thing about findings, it would be to buy the best you can afford. There's nothing worse than seeing a beautiful piece of beadwork with a badly made, cheap clasp attached to it, or a lovely brooch with an ugly pin back slapped on the back! Search out and find good quality.

Settings: I use round 6-prong gold-filled and sterling flat-bottomed settings. These little guys let me put CZs into my beadwork without having to bezel them with beadwork first. Some are so tiny that if you try to bezel them with beads, they would just disappear. I use 2-mm, 3-mm, 4-mm, 6-mm, and 10-mm CZs and settings in my work.

Ear wires, clasps, cup chains, spacers, and pin backs: Using great-quality findings adds to the overall look of your beadwork. I use sterling and vermeil findings and spacers from Bali and absolutely beautiful clasps and ear wires from Ezel Findings. Ezel also makes great cup chains, as they have realized that in order to stitch down the cup chain without your thread showing, you need extra holes. Miyuki makes a series of findings, including the best pin backs I have ever used. They come in two sizes and are well worth having in hand. The pin back has little holes along the top and bottom edges of the pin back for ease in stitching it down to beadwork. I stitch it down with seed beads. Fabulous!

Brass cuff blanks: There are times when beadwork needs a helping hand. When it comes to making bangles and cuff-style bracelets, I use raw brass cuff blanks. These are available in different lengths and widths.

Beader's Supply Kit

My students always want to know what supplies and tools I carry in my beading kit, so for the first time, here's the complete list.

With a well-stocked kit, you will have everything you need at hand when you sit down to bead or prepare to head for a workshop. I use this kit in my studio, and it travels with me to all of my workshops. I even take it camping! Whether you pack your beading kit in a beautiful basket, tote bag, zippered travel bag, or a toolbox, having your beading supplies always on hand lets you bead in your comfort zone, knowing that you are prepared!

Needles, thread, and wax

Beading needles: size 10 (2 lengths), size 11 (2 lengths), size 12 (2 lengths), size 13 (2 lengths), and 15 long, all in their own needle cases, labeled. I use Tulip, John James, and Pony brand beading needles.

1 plastic box containing 12 bobbins (12 colors) of nylon thread (I use One-G Assortment pack)

1 small chunk of microcrystalline beading wax in a plastic bag

Scissors and thread burner

1 small pair of good-quality sharp scissors

1 pair of Teflon-coated craft scissors

1 pair of craft scissors

1 thread burner

Jewelry tools

1 flush wire cutter

2 pairs of jewelry chain-nose pliers

1 small diamond file

Measuring tools

1 6-inch (15 cm) ruler

1 12-inch (30.5 cm) fold-up ruler

1 measuring tape

1 step gauge or Hedebo gauge (this embroidery tool looks like a small ring mandrel and is a very useful tool for tubular beading projects)

Beading supplies

1 baby's toothbrush for cleaning wax off of beads

1 beading awl (I like Tulip brand)

1 small beading dish (plastic)

1 small bead scoop

2 small color wheels (regular and tonal)

1 rubber needle puller

1 small pincushion

1 folding mesh trash can (available at container supply stores)

1 pad of small stick-on removable notes (such as Post-Its) and tabs

A few glass-headed straight pins

1 package plastic bags, 1½ x 2 inches (3.8 cm x 5 cm)

1 pen

1 pencil

Magnification, beading surface and lighting

1 pair head-mounted MagEyes magnifiers

1 pair of magnifying readers

1 small bead board (I used Bead On It!)

1 extension cord

1 traveling task light

Knitted jewelry wire mesh

I use SilverSilk Capture and SilverSilk Leather. I love the look of mixed mediums, and these two products are a lot of fun to work with and offer many design opportunities. A machine-knit tubular copper mesh is knit around a ball chain for the Capture and around smooth round leather for the latter. Capture has a soft hand, and the Leather has a sturdy hand.

Threads

I always tell my students to use the thread that they are most comfortable with for a pleasant beading experience. My thread of choice is One-G manufactured by Toho, and K.O. by Kobayashi Co., Ltd. They are similar in weight and are available in many colors. I prefer my thread to match or at least blend with my beads. I wax my thread to keep it well conditioned.

I occasionally use FireLine, a nylon fishing line (made by Berkley, but available in most bead stores and online shops), for sewing on snaps and when using crystals, if I can't protect them otherwise. But I do not care for the "dirtiness" of the thread. If the thread isn't stripped of its coating, it changes the look of the beadwork. I do wax FireLine once it has been stripped of the coating for less slip. I place the thread between the folds of a paper towel. Pressing the thread into the paper towel, I then drag the thread through to remove the coating. This is only needed for the "smoke" color. It comes in different weights, and now in colors. I say, "Use what you like!"

Preparing thread: Most beading threads are made from nylon fibers that are bonded together. A conditioned thread is a happy thread, so you will want to wax it to help cut down on fraying. My choice is microcrystalline wax, as it smoothes the fibers of the thread, and adds a slight tackiness, which aids in adding structure to my beadwork.

To wax, thread the needle, then place the thread on top of the wax about an inch away from the eye of the needle.

Holding the thread down on top of the wax with your thumb, pull the thread (not the needle) through between your thumb and the wax to coat the thread.

I always prepare my thread before starting to bead and along the way if it isn't behaving, except if I need to weave a new thread into the beadwork. It is best to weave the thread in un-waxed, then wax the thread when you are ready to begin stitching, otherwise as you weave in the thread you will end up with waxy beads.

Needles

There are many different beading needles available. They commonly are available in two lengths and five sizes. The larger the needle size, the smaller the needle. For years I have used Pony brand beading needles as they are inexpensive and readily available, but when Tulip brand beading needles (from Japan) became available, it was hard to not use only them. They are my needles of choice. They are smooth and flexible with an eye that is easily threaded from both sides. They resist bending and breaking and last a long time, so they are well worth the expense.

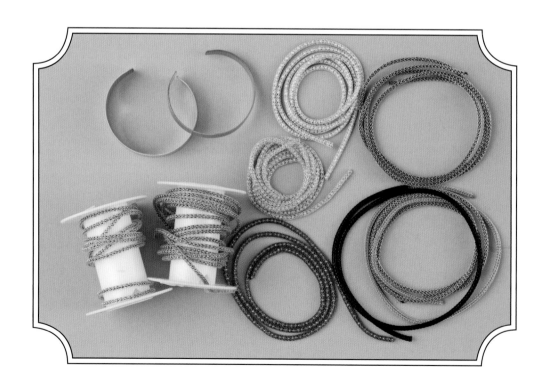

Basic Stitches

LADDER STITCH AND HERRINGBONE STITCH

The look of the herringbone stitch reminds me of herringbone fabric. It can be worked flat or tubular, even flat circular, and is fun when used free-form.

Ladder stitch

I start herringbone with a ladder stitch (Figure 1) row for ease in beginning this interesting stitch. This ladder stitch is the set-up round for herringbone and brick stitch. It can be a bit fiddly to get started, but straightens out once you begin the next row or round. I used this approach to begin the herringbone neck chain for Necklace of Dancing Circles.

Beads 1 and 2: String 2 beads. Sew up through the first bead strung to begin a ladder. Sew down through the second bead; adjust the tension so that the beads are held taut.

Bead 3: String 1 bead. Sew down through the second bead; adjust the tension. Sew up through the bead just added; adjust the tension.

Bead 4: String 1 bead. Sew up through the third bead; adjust the tension. Sew down through the bead just added; adjust the tension.

Repeat the instructions for adding beads 3 and 4 until you reach the desired length.

Figure 1. Ladder stitch and turnaround.

Herringbone stitch

Once you have a ladder row (even number of beads), you can work herringbone flat or zip the ladder into a tube by sewing the last ladder bead added to the first ladder bead.

If working flat: String 2 beads. Sew down through the next bead on the ladder and up through the following bead. Repeat to the end of the row, then tuck and turn to step up (see Tuck and turn on p. 18). Continue in this manner for the desired length (Figure 2).

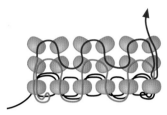

Figure 2. Flat herringbone stitch: Adding two rows of stitches.

If working tubular as will be done in Necklace of Dancing Circles project: Create your ladder row with an even number of beads (Figure 3). Connect the last bead to the first bead with one more ladder stitch (Figure 4). Work in herringbone as discussed above (Figure 2) until you reach the first stitch added in this round. Step up through 2 beads, one from the previous round and one from this round (Figure 5). Continue in this manner until you reach the desired length (Figure 6).

Figure 3. Start of tubular herringbone stitch.

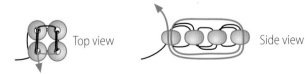

Figure 4. Start to make the tube by connecting (zipping) last and first beads.

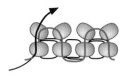

Figure 5. Step up to prepare to add the next round.

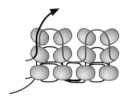

Figure 6. Step up to prepare to add the next round.

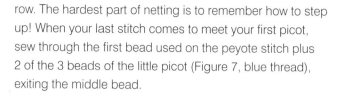

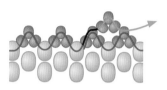

Figure 7. Adding picots to create netting.

row. The hardest part of netting is to remember how to step up! When your last stitch comes to meet your first picot, sew through the first bead used on the peyote stitch plus 2 of the 3 beads of the little picot (Figure 7, blue thread), exiting the middle bead.

For subsequent rows: String 3 beads and sew through the middle bead of the next picot, creating a net. Repeat around until your last stitch meets the first. Step up through the first 2 beads added to exit the middle bead of the picot.

As the circle gets bigger, the count or the bead size will eventually have to change. I usually work nets with odd numbers of beads, as this gives you a center bead from which to work the next round. Also, the number of beads that you have to step up through will change, as you need to exit the middle bead of a net (in most cases) to create the next round.

Peyote Stitch

A friend of mine told me that she considered peyote stitch to be the mother of all stitches. Maybe that is why this stitch is my go-to or comfort-zone stitch. There are many ways to manipulate this stitch, as you will see once you check out the projects in *Timeless Beadwork Designs*, but here are a few of the basics.

Peyote stitch/starting flat—even and odd count

I begin both flat even-count and flat odd-count a bit differently than you might expect. My even-count rows start with an odd number of beads; my odd-count rows start with an even number. This is explained in the text that follows.

Netting

This lacy stitch is easy to work and looks beautiful in many applications. I mostly use netting to add texture and embellishment. The open "holes" allow for the addition of set CZs, pearls, and crystals, which are a beautiful touch on many of my designs—for example, An Elegant Ladies' Brooch.

I also made a beautiful necklace chain (vertical netting) for The Key to Unlocking the Past, so you will have quite a few opportunities to experiment with this lovely stitch in this book.

I usually work netting off tubular peyote stitch, so my first row of netting is often from a stitch-in-the-ditch row (p. 12) added around the circumference of a beaded tube, such as in my Florentine Rosette Cuff.

From a piece of tubular even-count peyote stitch, move the thread to exit the row to which you wish to add netting. With 3 beads on the needle for each stitch, sew through the next bead on the peyote stitch in the same row (Figure 7, red thread), stitching-in-the-ditch and creating a tight net, which are called **picots**. Continue in this manner around the

Even-count flat peyote stitch

String an odd number of beads (Figure 8). Half of the even number will be for Row 1, the other half will be for Row 2, and the remaining bead is the first bead for Row 3.

Figure 8. String on an odd number of beads for even-count peyote stitch.

Without a bead on the needle, skip the last 2 beads strung and sew back through the third bead, creating the first stitch for Row 3 (Figure 9); adjust the tension. *With 1 bead on the needle, skip the next bead and sew through the one after that; adjust the tension. Repeat from * to the end of the row (Figure 10). The tail thread and the working thread exit at the same bead.

Figure 9. Skip the last two beads and sew back through the third bead from the end.

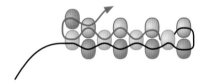

Figure 10. With one bead on the needle, skip the next bead and sew through the one after that. Repeat to the end of the row.

To start the next row and beyond, *place 1 bead on the needle and sew through the closest "high" bead on the previous row (the last bead you added). Repeat from * to the desired length.

Odd-count flat peyote stitch

String an even number of beads. For example, if I string 8 beads (Figure 11), 4 beads will be for Row 1, 3 beads for Row 2, and 1 bead for Row 3. Here's how I do it.

Without a bead on the needle, skip the last 2 beads strung and sew through the third bead from the end, creating the first stitch for Row 3 (Figure 12); adjust the tension. *With 1 bead on the needle, skip the next bead and sew through the one after that (Figure 13); adjust the tension. Repeat from * to the end of the row. There will be 1 bead left over on the tail thread. Place a bead on the needle, sew through the bead that has the tail thread exiting it, from the end side; adjust the tension and your hold on the beadwork.

Figure 11. String an even number of beads to start odd-count flat peyote stitch.

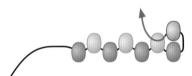

Figure 12. Skip the last two beads strung and sew back through the third bead from the end.

Figure 13. With one bead on the needle, skip the next bead and sew through the one after that. Repeat across the row. Sew through the bead with the exiting tail thread. With a bead on the needle step-up.

From here, I prefer to work odd-count flat peyote stitch using a technique I call step-up/step-down peyote stitch. This is a great technique, as it eliminates the need for adding a "homeless" bead, thread turnarounds and thread catches, which is why most beaders hate odd count! The step-up/step-down technique is determined by the number of stitches called for in each project, so it's not illustrated here. You'll see it in my projects, including the Time in Motion Ring. However, once you do some practicing, you'll see why I include it in my instructions. The advantages this technique offers are many, and once you learn it, you will never go back to the old ways.

Tubular even-count peyote stitch with a step up

Many of my projects in this book use this technique—for example, Byzantine Pearl Cuff. Tubular peyote stitch is just flat peyote stitch going around in a circle! One thing it does have is a step-up point, meaning that when the last stitch added meets the first, you run into what looks like three little stairs. Bead up to it; then for the last stitch, place a bead on the needle, skip the lowest bead of the three, and then sew through the middle and topmost bead (Figures 14 and 15). The row is complete.

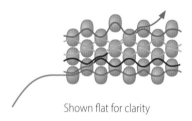

Shown flat for clarity

Figure 14. Stepping up in tubular peyote stitch.

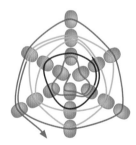

Expanded for clarity

Figure 15. Overhead view of tubular peyote stitch, showing step up.

Zip flat to tubular or flat to circular

I use this technique a lot, especially for bezel work, as I did in Earrings for the Dutch *Mona Lisa*. Approaching a bezel flat lets you change the count of beads in it if needed. I also feel that the overall tension is better if I begin this way. It is easy!

Make a strip of even-count flat peyote stitch to the desired length. Both tail and working threads exit the same Row 2 bead (Figure 16).

Place a needle onto the tail thread. Wrap the strip around your finger or a step gauge. With the longer thread, sew through the closest bead on Row 3, the next bead on Row 2, and the next bead on Row 3. With the tail thread, sew through the closest bead on Row 1, the next bead on Row 2, and the next bead on Row 1 (Figure 16, blue thread).

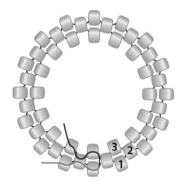

Figure 16. Zipping a flat piece of peyote stitch to tubular or flat circular peyote stitch.

Either pull the work up to form a tube or flatten the work to begin flat circular. Both approaches will now have a step up!

Counting rows in peyote stitch

Peyote stitch is a bit different to count, but still easy once you know what to look for. If the beadwork is a strip, I count all beads along one edge *plus* all of the beads in the ridge next to the edge (Figure 17), as shown in the Labyrinth Bracelet.

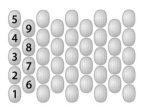

Figure 17. Counting rows in a strip of peyote stitch.

If the work is tubular, I count the same way as if it were flat, picking two ridges of beads that are next to each other, counting both and adding the numbers together.

If the work is flat circular, I count from the innermost row toward the outer edge at a diagonal (Figure 18). It looks like a pinwheel, but is easy to see that way.

Figure 18. Counting rows in flat circular peyote stitch.

Zipping a strip together (beginning to the end)
This technique is great for making a tube of beadwork out of a piece of flat even- or odd-count peyote stitch, as in Amalie's Pearl Necklace.

Wrap the ends of a strip of peyote stitch, even- or odd-count, around so the ends just touch. The high and low beads should fit together like the teeth on a zipper. If you see spaces where beads should be, stitch another row, then test it again. This should be seamless.

Step 1: Sew into a bead on the beginning of the strip. Sew out through the bead in the same position on the other end of the strip. Then sew back through the bead at the beginning of the strip (Figure 19, red thread).

Step 2: Holding the beadwork edges together, sew through the next bead on the opposite side, then through the next bead on the beginning side (blue line in Figure 19). Continue in this manner to the other end.

Repeat Step 1 on this edge to complete the zip (Figure 19, green thread).

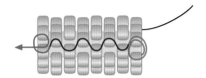

Figure 19. Zipping the ends of a peyote stitch strip together.

Edge-stitching
This simple technique does a great job in covering up the thread path on the outside edges of peyote stitch, as I did in An Elegant Ladies' Brooch. Weave the thread over to exit an edge bead of the peyote stitch. I usually use 15° seed beads for this technique, as the size fits nicely along the edge. String 1 edge bead. Tuck the needle under the closest edge thread between 2 edge beads of the peyote stitch, pull needle through, and tighten tension. The new bead sits on top of a bead on the peyote stitch. Continue in this manner to cover all edges, as needed (Figure 20).

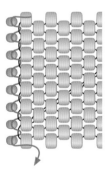

Figure 20. Adding edge-stitching on a peyote-stitch strip.

Stitch-in-the-ditch peyote stitch

This is a great technique for embellishing or changing the direction and shape of your beadwork.

Move the thread to the row from which you want to work. Put 1 bead (green in Figure 21) on the needle and sew through the next bead on the same row the thread is exiting, creating a stitch-in-the-ditch bead. This bead sits on the beadwork and is great for branching off in many directions, as I've done in my Pearl Inlay Earrings.

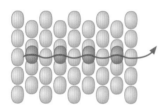

Figure 21. Stitch-in-the-ditch off of peyote stitch.

This technique is always handy for adding picot embellishment. Use the same technique as above, but with 3 beads on the needle for each picot. Play with combinations of beads to get the look you want, but try not to make a stitch that shows too much thread. If that happens, think about changing the size of the beads being used to fill the ditch between those 2 beads.

Increasing in peyote stitch

Increasing is a way to add shape to peyote stitchery. The basic increase takes 2 rounds to complete. The number of increases within the round will depend on the design, but the approach for each increase is the same. Whether starting the increase from a 3-bead start or off a tube of peyote stitch, this technique allows for shaping. The Necklace of Dancing Circles project is all about creating flat circular discs in varying sizes, using increasing.

Round 1. Two beads in place of one: Work peyote stitch while placing 2 beads in the space that would normally only have one at intervals around (green beads and red thread in Figure 22). Snapping those 2 beads down into the space causes the beadwork to roll out a little bit. I prefer to divide the increases evenly for a better shape. How close they are to each other depends on the desired shape.

Round 2. One bead in between two: Work peyote stitch and, as you approach the 2 beads of the Round 1 increase, put a bead on the needle, sew through the first bead of the increase, put a bead on the needle, and sew through the second bead of the increase, snapping this bead down into place (Figure 22, blue thread). Put a bead on the needle and continue stitching. This round takes beadwork back to regular stitching, but for every increase completed, you have gained a new stitch.

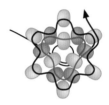

Figure 22. Increasing in flat circular peyote stitch.

Two-row decrease in peyote stitch

The reverse of increasing is decreasing; decreasing removes stitches from the round. I use multiple variations, but in this book I have used two types. The beautiful beaded cones on Version #1 of the Renaissance Cameo Necklace really show how decreasing helps to shape beadwork. This decrease takes 2 rounds to complete and is a fast decrease.

Round 1. The skip: The decreases for this technique need to be spaced evenly, and cannot be right next to each other. Work peyote stitch and at intervals create a skip by sewing through the next bead from the previous round and then through the next bead on the round that you are working (Figure 23). The number and placement of the skips determine the shape that is created. Be mindful of step-up points.

Figure 23. The skip in two-row decrease for peyote stitch.

Round 2. One over the skip: Work peyote stitch and when you come to the skip, place 1 bead on the needle and sew through the closest bead from the previous row (Figure 24), adjusting the tension. Continue in this manner, making sure to step up.

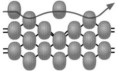

Figure 24. One over the skip for 2-row decrease in peyote stitch.

Four-row decrease in peyote stitch

This version of decreasing is a slower process, shapes the beadwork more gently, and takes four rounds to complete. I used this technique for the clasp area of the Labyrinth Bracelet.

Round 1. The skip: Work in peyote stitch as for Round 1, the skip (Figure 25).

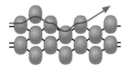

Figure 25. The skip in four-row decrease in peyote stitch.

Round 2. Place 2 over the skip: Work peyote stitch and when you come to the skip, place 2 beads on the needle, jump over the skip, and sew through the closest bead on the previous round, thus placing 2 over the skip (Figure 26). Continue in this manner, making sure to step up.

Figure 26. Place 2 over the skip in four-row decrease in peyote stitch.

Round 3. Treat 2 as 1: Work peyote stitch and when you come to "place 2 over the skip," place a bead on the needle and sew through the 2 beads as if they were 1 bead, treating 2 as 1 (Figure 27). Continue around in this manner, making sure to step up.

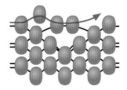

Figure 27. Treat 2 as 1 in four-row decrease in peyote stitch.

Round 4. Place 1 over 2: Work peyote stitch and when you come to the "treat 2 as 1" beads that are sitting low in the work, place 1 bead on the needle and sew through the closest bead from the previous row, adjusting the tension (Figure 28). Continue in this manner around making sure to step up.

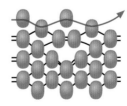

Figure 28. Place 1 over 2 in four-row decrease in peyote stitch.

Right-Angle Weave (RAW)

I use this stitch mostly in its many variations, since the basic stitch shows a lot of thread. Two variations appear in The Queen's Lace Bracelet and the necklace chain for Amalie's Pearl Necklace. Here I show the basic stitch so you can get familiar with the thread path. One thing to remember when moving your thread through this stitch is this: Do not cross thread junctions. This is a circling stitch and your thread needs to follow that path or it will be unsightly.

To make a basic sample, let's say that we are going to make it 5 units wide (Figure 29).

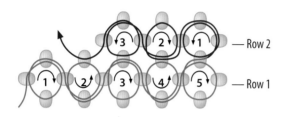

Figure 29. Creating units for the basic right-angle weave.

Row 1

Unit 1: String 4 beads, and pass through the first 3 beads again to form the first unit.

Unit 2: String 3 beads; pass through the bead the thread is exiting on Unit 1, and then sew through 2 beads on Unit 2.

Unit 3: String 3 beads, pass through the bead the thread is exiting on Unit 2, and then sew through 2 beads on Unit 3.

Unit 4: Repeat the instructions for Unit 2.

Unit 5: Repeat the instructions for Unit 3, but only sew through 1 bead to exit a top bead of Unit 5.

Row 2

Unit 1: String 3 beads, pass through the bead the thread is exiting on Row 1, unit 5, then sew through 3 beads to exit the inside side bead of this unit.

Unit 2: Sew through the top bead of Row 1, Unit 4. String 2 beads and sew through the side bead of Unit 1. Sew through 2 beads to exit the side bead of Unit 2.

Unit 3: String 2 beads, sew through the top bead of Row 1, Unit 3. Sew through the side bead of Unit 2 plus 2 beads to exit a side bead on Unit 3.

Unit 4: Sew through the top bead of Row 1, Unit 2. String 2 beads and sew through the side bead of Unit 3, the top bead of Row 1, Unit 2 and 1 bead of this unit to exit a side bead.

Unit 5: String 2 beads, sew through the top bead on Row 1, Unit 1, the side bead on Unit 2 and the top bead of this unit.

Row 3 begins from here. The thread path is a series of figure eights that alternate direction for each stitch. Continue stitching in this manner to the desired length. Since this is just a sample, play until you are comfortable, then head for one of my designs in the book.

Basic Knots

I don't use knots very often, but there are certain stitches and techniques that really benefit from this approach. There are four knots that I find invaluable to learn, and they are all a great addition to your beading skills repertoire.

Slipknot and Bookbinder's Knot

These great knots are perfect for adding a new thread to the end of an old thread when working right-angle weave, netting, herringbone, and St. Petersburg chain. Steps 1 through 3 make a slipknot that is great for temporarily holding multiple threads together, such as in the netted necklace for The Key to Unlocking the Past. Steps 1 through

7 make the bookbinder's knot, which works great for right-angle weave and its many variations.

Step 1: Wrap the thread around 2 fingers to form a loop, leaving a 6-inch (15 cm) tail (Figure 30).

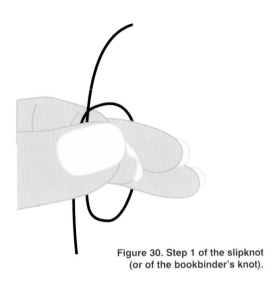

Figure 30. Step 1 of the slipknot (or of the bookbinder's knot).

Step 2: Pinch the loop; remove your fingers from the center of the loop. Reach through the loop and begin to pull a bit of thread through the loop (Figure 31).

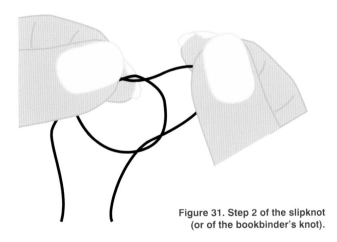

Figure 31. Step 2 of the slipknot (or of the bookbinder's knot).

Step 3: Tighten the slipknot while making the loop smaller (Figure 32).

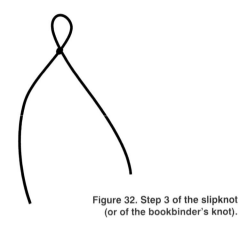

Figure 32. Step 3 of the slipknot (or of the bookbinder's knot).

Step 4: Slip the slipknot over the end of the old thread, placing the loop as close to the where the old thread is exiting as possible (Figure 33).

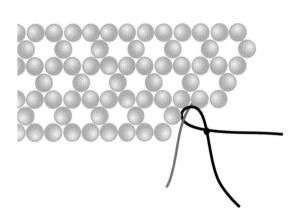

Figure 32. Step 4 of the slipknot; place the loop of the slipknot very close to where old thread is exiting.

Step 5: Pick up the old thread in your nondominant hand (left shown in Figure 34), holding it tightly with your middle finger, ring finger, and pinky finger. Pick up both ends of the new thread, with one end between the thumb and forefinger of the nondominant hand and the other end in the first two fingers of your dominant hand.

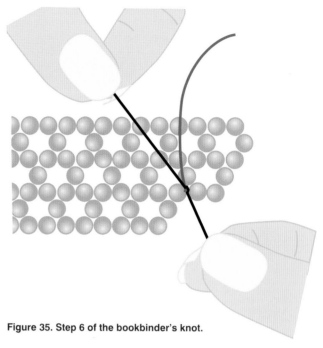

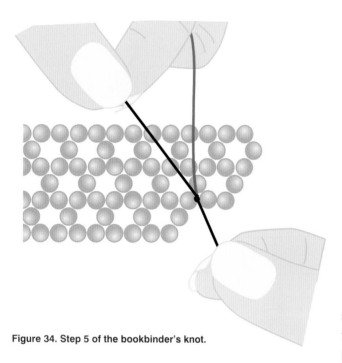

Figure 34. Step 5 of the bookbinder's knot.

Figure 35. Step 6 of the bookbinder's knot.

Step 6: Hold the old thread tight while pulling on the ends of the new thread, making the slipknot as small as possible and keeping the slipknot close to the bead that the old thread is exiting. Release the old thread and pull tightly on the ends of the new thread until you hear a little snap or a pop (Figure 35).

Step 7: Weave off the old thread and the tail of the new thread. Wax the new working thread. Move the thread in position and continue stitching.

Half-Hitch Knot

Sometimes, when reinforcing a strung component or weaving off within stitches such as netting, this knot makes quick work of securing threads. I used this technique to secure threads in the clasp connector of Victorian Garland Necklace. Simply tuck the needle under the strung thread, between 2 beads; pull through, leaving a small loop; pass the needle through the loop and pull tight. If you decide to use this knotting technique, make multiple half-hitches at intervals to be secure (Figure 36).

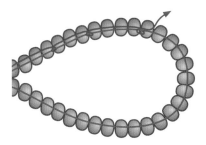

Figure 36. Making half-hitch knots.

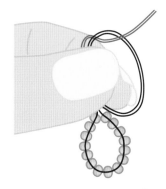

Figure 38. Step 2 of the overhand knot.

Overhand Knot

Basically, this is a pearl knot made without using tools, and it's a great knot for tying beads into a circle.

Step 1: Center the beads on the thread; then lower your thumb and forefinger down the thread, holding on tightly right above the ring of beads (Figure 37).

Step 3: Start pulling the threads away from you (red thread) until the loop fits the end of your forefinger (Figure 39). Rock the 2 threads back towards you (Figure 40), lowering the knot down to the top of the loop of beads; put your thumb back into place (Figure 41); pull on the two threads until it knots (Figure 42).

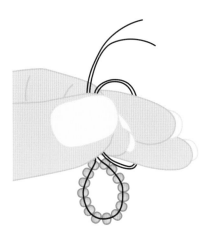

Figure 37. Step 1 of the overhand knot.

Step 2: Make a generous loop around 2 fingers, tucking the thread between the thumb and forefinger; remove the 2 fingers from the loop; pass the ends of the thread through the loop (Figure 38).

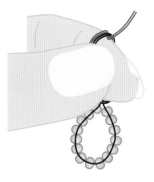

Figure 39. Step 3 of the overhand knot, A. Fit threads to forefinger.

Figure 40. Step 3 of the overhand knot, B. Rock thread ends back to you.

Figure 41. Step 3 of the overhand knot. Hold loop with thumb and forefinger.

Stopper Bead

I rarely use a stop bead, but at times it will come in handy when you need to keep beads from sliding off your thread. All you do is sew through the first strung bead again to keep it in place (Figure 45). The necklace chain for The Key to Unlocking the Past, the Florentine Rosette Cuff, and the Byzantine Pearl Cuff use a stop bead to secure long strands of seed beads. Don't forget to disconnect the stop bead if you plan on using it in your beadwork!

Figure 42. Step 3 of the overhand knot. Pull the two threads until there is a knot.

Figure 45. Tying on a stop bead at the start of a strand.

Step 4: Separate the 2 threads and pull (Figures 43).

Figure 43. Step 4 of the overhand knot. Pull the two threads.

Tuck and turn

I use this technique when I need to decrease on a beaded edge or in some cases when the thread is just going the wrong direction! For the Labyrinth Bracelet I used it for decreasing along an edge of flat peyote stitch to shape the central component base. For An Elegant Ladies' Brooch, I used this technique to move the thread in creating the sides of the brooch.

The thread needs to exit the beadwork where you want to make the turn. Tuck the needle under thread between the bead where the thread is exiting and the bead right next door. Pull the excess thread through and tighten. Sew back through the bead just exited to continue stitching (Figure 46).

Step 5: Weave the ends of the thread into your work so the knot is hidden (Figure 44).

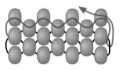

Figure 44. Step 5 of the overhand knot.

Figure 46. Tuck and turn lets you turn your thread around.

RENAISSANCE CAMEO NECKLACE

A CUSTOM-BUILT BEZEL FOR A BEAUTIFUL CAMEO is the focal point of this design. My flat peyote-stitch bezel technique creates a customized bezel to fit the circumference of any size cameo. I give you instructions here for two slightly different styles. Embellished simply and elegantly, the pendant in Version #1 hangs from metal braided cording, clasped with beaded pearl buttons. In Version #2 it dangles from a strand of natural pearls, closed with a delicate vermeil S-hook. Either way, this design is a classic.

Version #1

{ HISTORICAL PERSPECTIVE }

In the days before photography, hand-painted or carved cameos and intaglios (which are similar but worked in reverse so that the image is cut into the surface) were a way to preserve the likenesses of loved ones, kings and queens, mythological creatures, and fictional characters.

Carved from gemstones, shell, or ivory, or painted onto gemstone or vellum (the best-quality "paper" of the time, made from animal skin), likenesses were little works of art used as tokens of love, affection, and regard. They were reminders of loyalty to the crown, of love lost and found, and of the intimacy of family.

Sandro Botticelli's muse, Simonetta Vespucci, was renowned for being the greatest beauty of her age. The exact nature of their relationship is unknown, but Botticelli featured her in many of his most famous paintings. A prominent member of Florentine aristocracy during the Renaissance, Simonetta is shown here in the painting *Portrait of a Young Woman* wearing a beautiful cameo necklace, bezeled in gold with a series of gold cables.

The philosopher Plato had some thoughts about muses. He said that the art produced by someone uninspired, no matter how technically skilled, inevitably pales in comparison to the masterpieces made by someone moved by the artistic inspiration—and madness—brought on by a muse. Don't confuse ability with creativity!

Portrait of a Young Woman by Sandro Botticelli

Dimensions

Either version can be extended or shortened as desired.

Version #1: 18 inches (45.7 cm) long*

Version #2: 16½ inches (41.9 cm) long*

Techniques

Braiding

Peyote stitch, flat, even count

Peyote stitch, flat, odd-count technique, step up/step down

Peyote stitch, tubular, even count with decreasing

Stitch-in-the-ditch

Skill Level

Version #1: Intermediate advanced

Version #2: Intermediate

Materials, Version #1

1 beautiful contemporary or antique cameo, or a hand-painted or image-transfer cabochon, 1⅛ x 1⅝ inch (3 x 4 cm or larger), in shell, onyx, or porcelain

2 g higher-metallic antique silver 15° seed beads (A)

2 g bronze lustered amber 15° seed beads as an optional accent (B)

2 g higher-metallic white gold AB 11° cylinder beads (C)

2 g bronze lustered amber 11° seed beads (D)

1 g higher-metallic antique rhodium 11° seed beads (E)

8 cream 3-mm crystal pearls

1 cream 6-mm crystal pearl

2 cream 8-mm crystal pearls

3 twenty-inch (50.8 cm) pieces of 3-mm SilverSilk Capture (color: fall–brown/gold), longer if desired*

Double-sided craft tape, any width

Dark beige nylon beading thread

12 inches (30.5 cm) of 28-gauge gold-toned craft wire

* SilverSilk Capture is a 3-mm tube of knitted wire with a ball chain running up the center. It's sold by the yard or packaged in 1-yard (91.4 cm) lengths. However you buy the product, just remember that you need 3 pieces.

Materials, Version #2

1 beautiful contemporary or antique cameo, or a hand-painted or image-transfer cabochon 1⅛ x 1⅛ inch (3 x 4 cm or larger), in shell, onyx, or porcelain

1 strand, 16 inches (40.6 cm) long of 9–mm or 10-mm natural pearls, crystal pearls, or Czech glass pearls

2 g higher-metallic rose gold AB 15° seed beads (A)

1.5 g higher-metallic rose gold AB 11° cylinder beads (C)*

3 higher-metallic rose gold AB 11° seed beads (D)

Double-sided craft tape, any width

Gold nylon beading thread

4 feet (1.2 m) of nylon thread for stringing the pearl necklace

1 vermeil S-hook clasp with soldered jump rings

No B accent 15° seed beads are used in this necklace.

Tools

2 size 12 beading needles

1 size 13 beading needle
(may be needed when embellishing)

1 glass-headed straight pin or size 10 beading needle (Version #1)

1 tapestry needle #24

1 rubber band (Version #1)

Step gauge (optional, but helpful)

Small Teflon-coated craft scissors

Flush wire cutter

Measuring tape

Beader's supply kit (p. 5)

Version #2

Instructions

Prepare the Cameo

A little help from double-sided craft tape will make the bezeling process a lot easier. Use Teflon-coated craft scissors to cut a thin strip of tape about twice as wide as the thickness of the cameo. Center the strip along the edge of the cameo, leaving the plastic coating attached; press the tape to the side of the cameo. Continue cutting and adding tape (don't overlap it) until the circumference of the edge has tape all around it as in Figure 1.

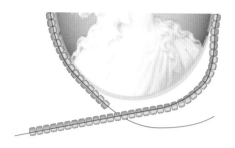

Figure 2

Row 3: Leaving a 2-foot (61 cm) tail, and without a bead on the needle, skip the last 2C strung, and sew back through the third C, making the first peyote stitch (p. 9 and Figure 3, end of red thread); adjust the tension.

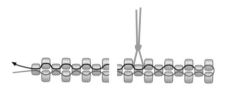

Figure 3

Figure 1

Bezel

This technique for creating a bezel may be used for any size cameo or cabochon. Since cameos are made from different mate rials and have different thicknesses, exact round-per-round instructions are impossible. With that said, I will show you how to create a perfect bezel without knowing the count. Flat, even-count peyote stitch is used to begin the bezel. Once the count is on track, the strip gets zipped into tubular peyote stitch around the circumference of the cameo.

Rows 1 & 2: Using 6 feet (1.8 m) of prepared thread (p. 6), string enough C beads that, when pushed together on the thread and wrapped around the circumference of the cameo, the beads go all the way around and overlap about ¼ to ⅜ inch (6 mm to 1 cm), as in Figure 2.

Work one row of flat peyote stitch, using 1C in each stitch (Figure 3, blue thread). *Note:* If you have a floating C bead left on the tail, remove it. Tighten the strip of peyote stitch.

Mark center top: Before the beadwork gets attached to the cameo, we need to mark the center top. Using 6 inches (15.2 cm) of thread on a different needle, sew through a single C bead on Row 2 about 1 inch (2.5 cm) from the starting end of the strip. Fold the thread in half. Remove the needle and tie the ends of the thread together to form a tailor's tack; trim (Figure 3, green thread).

Add the beadwork to the edge of the cameo: Peel the plastic coating (if applicable) off the double-sided craft tape, avoiding touching the tape. Press the bead marked with a tailor's tack at center top on the cameo; press the short end of the strip against the tape along the edge of the cameo. Continue pressing the long end of the strip around the circumference of the cameo, bringing the end of the strip around to meet the beginning. The strip needs to end with both threads exiting a single bead (Figure 4).

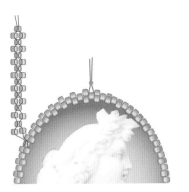

Figure 4

Holding the beadwork stable around the outside edge of the cameo, loosen or tighten the beadwork, and add or remove beads to get a good fit. There shouldn't be any gaps between the beads, and there shouldn't be any space between the edge of the cameo and the beadwork. Once you're satisfied that the strip is snug around the outer edge of the cameo, remove the unwanted beads and place a needle onto the tail thread. You'll now work in tubular peyote stitch (p. 10) and even count.

Zip the strip ends together: Using the working thread, zip the ends of the strip together by sewing through the first C added on Row 3, the next C on Row 2, and the next C on Row 3 (p. 11 and Figure 5). Using the tail thread, complete the zipping by sewing through the closest C on Row 1, the next C on Row 2, and the next C on Row 1 (Figure 5).

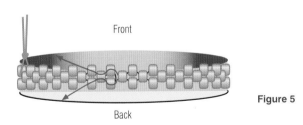

Front

Back

Figure 5

Position the 2 threads: The tail thread needs to be in Row 3 (topmost row), close to the front of the cameo; the longer thread in Row 1 (lowest row) should be closest to the bottom. If necessary, adjust the threads now.

Note: All subsequent rounds will require stepping up (p. 10) at the end of each round. As you work, make sure that the tailor's tack stays at center top.

Round 4, for the back of the bezel: Press the beadwork tight against the tape. Using the longer thread, work tubular peyote stitch, using 1C in each stitch; step up into the first C added in this round (p. 10 and Figure 6, red thread).

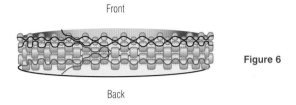

Front

Back

Figure 6

Rounds 5 & 6, for the front of the bezel: Using the shorter thread, work two rounds of tubular peyote stitch, using 1B in each stitch if you're making Version #1, or 1A if you're making Version #2; step up into the first bead added in each round (Figure 6, blue thread).

Note: Make sure that the bead marked with the tailor's tack is still at center top. What if it has moved? Gently push the beadwork around to bring it back into position. I call this technique "bead massage."

Tip: If you're having problems controlling tension, try this technique: At the end of a round, without a bead on the needle, sew forward 1 stitch and pull tight.

Getting a custom fit: Turn the beadwork over to look at the back of the cameo. Is the last round of C beads ever so slightly sticking up above the back edge of the cameo, as shown in Figure 7? If so, move on to Round 7. If not, work tubular peyote stitch, using 1C in each stitch, for one or more rounds on the back; step up at the end of each round. Now does the beadwork look like Figure 7? If so, proceed to Round 7.

Figure 7

Rounds 7, 8 & 9, for the back of the bezel: Using the longer thread, work three rounds of tubular peyote stitch, tightly, using 1A in each stitch; step up into the first A added in each round (Figure 8, red thread).

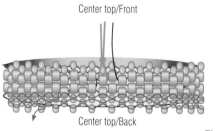

Center top/Front

Center top/Back

Figure 8

Create the Bail

Step-up/step-down peyote stitch is a technique that I use to create a flat, odd-count strip without thread catching, turnarounds, or figure eights, as in traditional techniques.

Row 1: Move the longer of the 2 threads into position as in Figure 8, blue thread. Stitch-in-the-ditch as follows (p. 12). With 1C on the needle, sew through the C bead marked with the tailor's tack; with 1C on the needle, sew through the next C on the bezel for a total of 2C added in this row (Figure 9, red thread). Cut off the tailor's tack once you've double-checked that the bail will be centered.

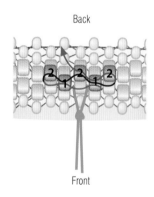

Back

Front

Figure 9

Row 2: Work flat peyote stitch using 1C in each stitch, make 1 stitch; using 1C, make 1 stitch and step down through the first C added on Row 1 and the closest C on the bezel (Figure 9, blue thread). String 1C and step up through the closest 2C (Figure 9, green thread).

Note: Row 2 is now complete, but the thread is not at the beginning of the row. This is the trick, so, with that said, step-up/step-down flat odd-count peyote stitch begins now!

Rows 3 & 4: *Row 3:* Using 1C in each stitch, make 1 stitch (Figure 10, red thread). *Row 4:* Using 1C, make 1 stitch and step down (Figure 10, blue thread). *Back to Row 3:* Using 1C, make 1 stitch (Figure 10, green thread). *Back to Row 4:* Using 1C, make 1 stitch (Figure 10, green thread). The V in the beadwork is what I call "V for victory." This is the end of the progression, so pay attention. Using 1C, make 1 stitch and step down (Figure 11, red thread), then *turn around* (Figure 11, blue thread).

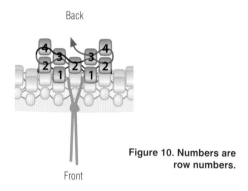

Back

Front

Figure 10. Numbers are row numbers.

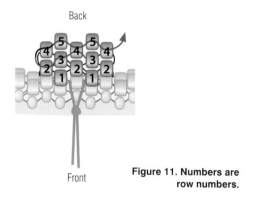

Back

Front

Figure 11. Numbers are row numbers.

Row 5: Using 1C in each stitch, make 2 stitches (Figure 11, green thread).

Note: As the strip is being extended, Row 2's first step down is now made on the strip, and the step down and turn-around technique will alternate sides.

Repeat Rows 2, 3, 4, and 5 until the beadwork measures 1⅜ inches (3.5 cm) long (41 rows) for Version #1, or 1⅜ to 1½ inches (3.5 to 3.8 cm) long (45 rows) for Version #2, depending on the diameter of the pearls. Both versions need to have the strip end with Row 5's 2 stitches (Figure 11, green thread).

Zip the end of the strip to the back of the bezel
Roll the strip to the back of the bezel, nestling the last row on the strip into the spaces between beads on the bezel. Where to zip will depend on how many rounds of cylinder beads you created. I like to zip to the last round of cylinder beads or the second round of 15°s on the back of the bezel (Figure 12, either C beads zippered to C beads or C beads zippered to the A beads marked with red dots).

Figure 12

Back

Step 1: Sew through the first C or A on the bezel to start the zipping; sew back through the C bead just exited on the strip; sew back through the same C or A on the bezel (Figure 12, red thread); adjust the tension.

Step 2: Sew through the next C on the last row on the strip; sew through the next C or A on the bezel; sew through the next C on the last row of the strip; sew through the next C or A on the bezel (Figure 12, blue thread).

Step 3: Sew back through a C bead on the strip on the second-to-last row; sew back through the same C or A bead just exited on the bezel (Figure 12, green thread), finishing the zip. Adjust the tension.

Edge-stitch the bail
A simple edging adds the finishing touches to the bail. Using 1B for Version #1 or 1A for Version #2, tuck the needle under the closest piece of thread on the edge of the

strip (p. 11 and Figure 13); adjust the tension. Repeat along this side of the strip.

Figure 13

Back

Move the thread into the closest C on Row 1 of the strip; string 3A for Version #1 or 3B for Version #2 and sew through the last C bead on Row 1 of the strip, forming a picot (Figure 14). Weave the thread forward through the next C on the strip and the next C on the bezel (Figure 14).

Figure 14

Front

Tuck the needle under the closest piece of thread on the second edge of the strip; repeat edge stitching the bail along this side of the strip. Weave off and trim the shorter of the two threads.

Embellish the Edge of the Bezel
The pendant is beautiful already, but a simple picot edging detail adds just enough to make it even more special.

Move the remaining thread into a C bead on the bezel, as close to the bail as possible, 5 rounds back from the front (Figure 15, beginning of red thread path). Be careful, as this area is getting tight and beads could break.

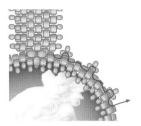

Figure 15

It's now time to count. With the thread in position, count the number of spaces between 2 Cs on the round that the thread is exiting.

If the count is odd, follow the instructions in this paragraph. If it's even, skip to the next paragraph. String 3B (if you're making Version #1) or 3A (for Version #2) and sew through the next C on the same round the thread is exiting, stitching-in-the-ditch and forming a picot; weave forward 1 stitch by sewing through a C bead on a round above or below the round you're working on, then through the next C bead on the same round you just exited, weaving around this next ditch (Figure 15). Continue around the bezel in this manner. Weave off the thread and trim.

If the count is even, string 3B (if you're making Version #1) or 3A (for Version #2) and sew through the next C on the same round the thread is exiting, stitching-in-the-ditch and forming a picot; weave forward 1 stitch by sewing through a C bead on a round above or below the one you're working on, then through the next C bead on the same round you just exited, weaving around this next ditch (Figure 15). But before you continue, we have to work out the numbers.

My count was 48 for Version #2. Since we're placing a picot every other stitch, and we want a picot at center bottom and picots on either side of the bail, we have to make an adjustment. It's easy. Since the picots are going into every other space, divide your count by 4 (mine was 12). I placed 12 picots along one side of my pendant. So for your count, figure out your math; then create the number of picots needed to get within one stitch of center bottom (Figure 16, red thread).

Sew through the closest C on the round below; string 3D and sew through the next C bead on the same round, forming a picot (Figure 16, beginning of blue thread path). Sew through a C bead on the round above, placing the thread back onto the round that gets the rest of the picots (Figure 16, end of blue thread path).

Figure 16

So how did the 11° picot help with the embellishing on the pendant? Hold up the pendant. You know that the center bottom stitch is different, but see how the eye just flows right past it? Awesome! Continue placing the balance of the picots up the other side of the bezel. Weave off the thread and trim.

Necklace Strap, Version #1
Prepare the SilverSilk Capture: Cut 6 inches (15.2 cm) of 28-gauge wire and thread it onto a tapestry needle. On your work surface, even up one end of each of the 3 SilverSilk cords.

Wire-wrap the ends: Sew through all 3 of the SilverSilk cords, just shy of the cut ends, leaving a 1½ inch (3.8 cm) tail. Fold the long portion of the wire around the back of the 3 cords (Figure 17). *Note:* Don't squeeze the 3 ends too tightly as they need to lie flat.

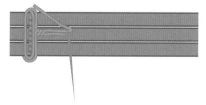

Figure 17

Sew through the 3 ends again, in about the same place. Wrap around the front; continue to wire-wrap until secure, ending by twisting the tail end of the wire to the working end, and trim (Figure 17).

Braid the cords: Attach the wired end of the 3 cords to a solid work surface—a nail on the wall, for example—or whatever is stable. You'll need a rubber band. This is a 3-strand braid; here we go!

Holding all 3 cords, pass the right-hand cord over the middle cord, tighten; pass the left-hand cord over the middle cord, tighten. Pass the right-hand cord over the middle cord, tighten; pass the lef-hand cord over the middle cord, tighten (Figure 18).

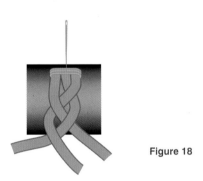

Figure 18

Continue in this manner until you can't braid any farther. Wrap a rubber band around the ends to keep the braid from unwinding (Figure 19).

Figure 19

Prepare the other end of the braided cord: The rubber-banded ends will need to be cut and the ends wire-wrapped as for the first end. However, first try on the braided cord necklace to decide on the desired length, being mindful that the cones, buttons, beaded jump rings that connect the buttons, and the button connector will add almost 3 inches (7.6 cm) to the length.

To make a necklace with a finished length of 18 inches (45.7 cm), the braided cording, from wired end to wired end, needs to be 15 inches (38.1 cm) long; adjust as desired. Push a pin or needle through all 3 cords at the point that needs to be wired (Figure 20).

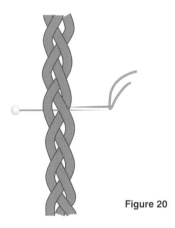

Figure 20

Thread a tapestry needle with 6 inches (15.2 cm) of 28-gauge wire. Wire-wrap the end of the braided cording as you did previously, right at the pin marking. Remove the pin. Then cut off the unwanted cording close to the wire-wrapping, matching the look of the other cut end (Figure 21).

Figure 21

Cones at the ends of the cording

Beaded cones add the perfect finishing touch to the ends of the braided cording. Make two cones as follows.

Rows 1 & 2: With 3 feet (91.4 cm) of prepared thread, string 21D, leaving a 1-foot (30.5 cm) tail.

Row 3: Without a bead on the needle, skip the last 2D strung and sew back through the third D to begin flat peyote stitch; using 1D in each stitch, make 9 stitches for a total of 10D added in this row.

Zip the ends: Put a needle onto the tail thread. Wrap the beadwork around your finger or around a step gauge. Using each of the threads, zip the ends together. Remove the beadwork from your finger or gauge and tighten (Figure 22).

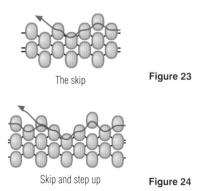

Figure 22

Round 4: Work tubular even-count peyote stitch and, using 1D in each stitch, make 10 stitches. Step up into the first D added in this round.

Round 5, 4-row decrease and the skip: Work tubular peyote stitch and, using 1D in each stitch, make 4 stitches. Without a bead on the needle, sew through the next D from Row 3 and the next D from Round 4, creating the skip (p. 13 and Figure 23). Using 1D in each stitch, make 4 stitches; then skip and step up (Figure 24).

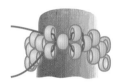

The skip   **Figure 23**

Skip and step up   **Figure 24**

Round 6, 2 over the skip: Work tubular peyote stitch and, using 1D in each stitch, make 3 stitches; with 2D, sew through the closest D on Round 5, placing 2 over the skip (Figure 25). Using 1D in each stitch, make 3 stitches; with 2D, place 2 over the skip and step up (Figure 26).

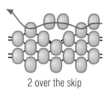

2 over the skip   **Figure 25**

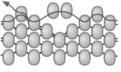

2 over the skip and step up   **Figure 26**

Round 7, treat 2 as 1: Work tubular peyote stitch and using 1D in each stitch, make 2 stitches; with 1D, sew through the 2D over the skip, treating 2 as 1 (Figure 27; using 1D in each stitch, make 3 stitches; with 1D, sew through the 2 over the skip, treating 2 as 1; using 1D make 1 stitch. Step up into the first D added in this round (Figure 28).

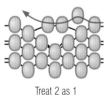

Treat 2 as 1   **Figure 27**

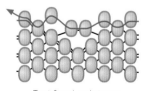

Treat 2 as 1 and step up   **Figure 28**

Tip: The decreases are going to shape the cones on their sides, so squeeze the shapes as shown in Figure 29.

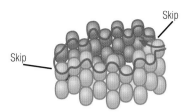

Figure 29

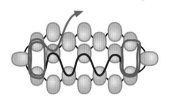

Figure 32

Round 8, 1 over 2: Work tubular peyote stitch and, using 1D in each stitch, make 2 stitches; using 1D, sew through the next D on Round 7, placing 1 over 2 at the corner (Figure 30). Using 1D in each stitch, make 3 stitches. Using 1D, sew through the next D on Round 7, placing 1 over 2 at the corner. Using 1D, make 1 stitch; step up into the first D added in this round.

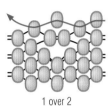

1 over 2   **Figure 30**

Round 9: Work tubular peyote stitch and, using 1D in each stitch, make 8 stitches; step up into the first D added in this round.

Row 10: Move the thread forward to exit the first D bead on Round 9, past a corner (Figure 31, red thread). Work flat peyote stitch and, using 1D in each stitch, make 3 stitches (Figure 31, blue thread).

Figure 31

Zip the ends of the cone shape together

Step 1: Sew through the closest D bead on the opposite side (Round 9) of the cone. Sew back through the same D bead just exited; then sew back through the opposite D bead (Round 9), as shown in Figure 32 with red thread; adjust the tension.

Step 2: Sew through the last D added on Round 10 to begin the zipper, then sew through the next D on Round 9. Keep zipping across the top of the cone, adjusting the tension as you go (Figure 32, blue thread).

Step 3: To secure the last 2 stitches, circle the thread around them as in Step 1 directly above (Figure 32, green thread). Move the thread into the first D added on Row 10 to position the thread for the bead loop (Figure 32, end of green thread path).

Add the bead loop to each cone: String 1B, a 3-mm pearl, 7B, a 3-mm pearl, and 1B; skip the next D (Row 10) on the same row where the thread is exiting at and sew through the one after that (Figure 33, red thread). String 1B, then sew back through the closest pearl, through the 7B, and through the next pearl. String 1B, and sew through the first D added on Row 10 (Figure 33, blue thread). Rework to secure the loop; weave off this thread and trim. Shape the loop nice and round by pushing the end of a pencil, pen, or step gauge through it.

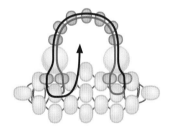

Figure 33

Attach a cone to one end of the braided cording

Step 1: Place a needle onto the thread attached to one of the cones. Move the thread up one round (Row 2) away from the open end. Position the cone onto 1 end of the braided cording, covering the wire-wrapped end and aligning the decreases on the cone with the outer edges of the braided cord (Figure 34).

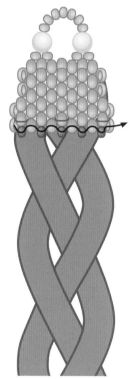

Figure 34

Step 2: Push the needle through the beadwork and the braided cording, exiting on the other side of the cone; sew through a D bead that is close by and tighten. Make sure that most connections are made below the wire-wrapped portion of the braided cording for a secure attachment (Figure 34, red thread). Repeat this technique in different places until the connection is tight.

Step 3: Weave the thread to exit a D bead on Row 1 of the cone (Figure 34). Work tubular peyote stitch and, using 1A bead in each stitch, make 10 stitches (Figure 34, blue thread). Weave off the thread and trim. Don't attach the other cone yet.

Add the pendant to the braided cording: Slide on the pendant over the unfinished end; repeat Step 3 to attach a cone to the other end of the braided cording.

Beaded Buttons

Beaded buttons are a beautiful and functional detail. Two buttons and a connector allow the necklace to be opened comfortably by either a right- or left-handed wearer.

Rows 1 & 2: With 2 feet (61 cm) of prepared thread, string 23C, leaving a 6-inch (15.2 cm) tail.

Row 3: Without a bead on the needle, skip the last 2C strung; sew through the third from last C; adjust the tension. Work flat peyote stitch using 1C in each stitch; make 10 stitches for a total of 11C added in this row.

Zip the strip into tubular peyote stitch: Place a needle onto the tail thread. Wrap the beadwork around your finger or around a step gauge. Using each of the threads, zip (stitch) the ends together (Figure 35). Remove the beadwork from your finger or gauge and tighten.

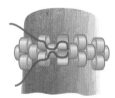

Figure 35

Add the 8-mm pearl to the button

Step 1: Set the tube of beadwork down on your work surface with the long thread up and in a C bead on Row 3; string one 8-mm pearl and place it into the center of the tube, aligning the hole in the pearl with the C bead that the long thread is exiting.

Step 2: Look across the opening and find the opposite C bead (Row 2); sew through that C bead, back through the pearl, and back through the C bead that the thread was exiting for this technique (Figure 36); tighten.

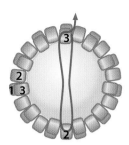

Figure 36

Rounds 4 & 5: Work tubular peyote stitch, and using 1E in each stitch, make 11 stitches in each round; step up at the end of each round (Figure 37, red thread).

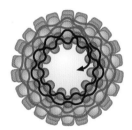

Figure 37

Rounds 6 & 7: Work tubular peyote stitch and, using 1A in each stitch, make 11 stitches in each round; step up at the end of each round (Figure 37, blue thread).

Add the beaded loop to the button

Step 1: Using the longer thread, string 1A, one 3-mm pearl, 5A, one 3-mm pearl, and 1A; look directly across the opening of the button and find the 3 opposite A (Figure 38). Sew through the first A on Round 7, the next A from Round 6, and the next A from Round 7 (Figure 38, red thread).

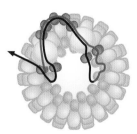

Figure 38

Step 2: String 1A; sew back through the closest 3-mm pearl, through 5A, and through the next 3-mm pearl. String 1A; sew through the same A on the button from which the thread is exiting—this is where my technique is different from the traditional approach (Figure 38, blue thread). Rework the loop to secure. Weave off the tail thread and trim.

Step 3: Move the working thread through the beadwork to exit any E bead on Round 4 (Figure 39, beginning of red thread). String 1A, 1E, and 1A; then stitch-in-the-ditch by sewing through the next E on Round 4; pull tight, thus creating a picot. Repeat around the button for a total of 11 picots (Figure 39, red thread).

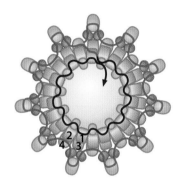

Figure 39

Step 4: Move the thread to exit a C bead on Row 1 (Figure 39, beginning of blue thread). Work tubular peyote stitch and, using 1B in each stitch, make 11 stitches (Figure 39, blue thread). Weave off the thread and trim.

Repeat all steps for second button.

Attach the button to the loop on the cone end of the necklace:
With 1 foot (30.5 cm) of prepared thread, string 15B. Sew down through the loop on a cone end and up through the loop on a button. Then even up the ends of the thread. Use an overhand knot (p. 17) to tie the beads into a ring and tighten. Rework, then weave off both threads and trim (Figure 40, red thread). Repeat to make a second loop (Figure 40, blue thread).

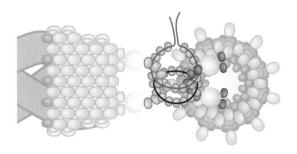

Figure 40

Attach the second button to the loop on the second cone, at the other end of the necklace.

Create the button connector: With 2 feet (61 cm) of prepared thread, string 33D, leaving a 6-inch (15.2 cm) tail; sew through the 33D again to form a ring (Figure 41, red thread). String one 6-mm pearl and 33D (Figure 41, blue thread). Then sew through the 33D just added to form a ring; sew back through the pearl (Figure 41, green thread). Test the fit over a button, adjust the count if necessary, weave through both loops to secure the thread, and then trim. Weave off the tail thread and trim.

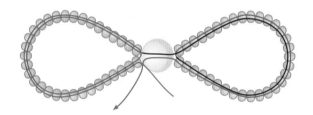

Figure 41

Necklace Strap, Version #2 (with Pearls)

Place a needle onto 4 feet (1.2 m) of prepared thread in a color that blends with the pearls. String 13A and center them on the thread. String on one of the soldered jump rings from the S-hook clasp. Overhand knot the beads into a ring around the jump ring (Figure 42); tighten the knot. Rework the loop to secure.

Figure 42

Remove the needle; place the needle over both ends of the thread, then wax. String the desired number of pearls to make your necklace strap. On the other end, string 13A and the other jump ring from the clasp; sew through half of the A beads to form a ring; tighten it. Sew through the rest of the A beads (Figure 43, red thread) plus 3 pearls (Figure 43, blue thread).

Figure 43

Where the needle is exiting, make a half-hitch knot (p. 16) around the base thread; secure it by making a loop and tucking the needle through the loop (Figure 43, blue thread); pull tight, then pass the thread through 3 more pearls and repeat. Continue until you're close to the other end and the thread is secure; then trim.

EARRINGS FOR THE DUTCH *MONA LISA*

A BRILLIANT TRILLION-SHAPED CZ is captured within a simple peyote-stitch bezel and embellished with glass pearls. The crystal pearl drop has a beautiful beaded cap, which adds just the right touch of classical elegance.

Version #1

{ HISTORICAL PERSPECTIVE }

In the seventeenth century, pearls were extremely important status symbols and prized possessions. They were worn as jewelry or incorporated into embroidery on clothing. The luminescent quality of pearls has been well represented in fine art.

The introduction of glass pearls into Venice in the thirteenth century allowed the burgeoning middle-class population to afford to own faux pearls, starting a fashion craze!

Johannes Vermeer must have enjoyed the look of pearls on canvas, since eight of his paintings include a woman wearing a drop-shaped or tear-shaped pearl earring. But it is *The Girl with the Pearl Earring* (c. 1665) that is considered Vermeer's masterpiece. The young girl, wearing a turban and a faux pearl earring, looks over her shoulder in such an intimate way; she has the ability to draw your eyes to hers effortlessly. It remains my favorite painting.

The Girl with the Pearl Earring by Johannes Vermeer

Dimensions

2¼ inches (5.7 cm) long

Techniques

Netting

Peyote stitch, flat, even count

Peyote stitch, tubular, even count

Stitch-in-the-ditch

Skill Level

Intermediate

Materials, Version #1

2 Moxie Universe 12-mm trillion CZs (custom coated)

1.5 g bronze lustered amber 15° seed beads (A)

0.5 g teal-lined crystal 15° seed beads (B)

1.5 g higher-metallic copper 11° cylinder beads (C)

1 g bronze lustered amber 11° seed beads (D)

54 light peach/gold 2-mm glass pearls

24 gold 3-mm crystal pearls

2 jade 12-mm crystal pearls

1 pair gold-filled ear wires

Gold nylon beading thread

Materials, Version #2

2 Moxie Luna 12-mm trillion CZs (custom coated)

1.5 g metallic brown iris 15° seed beads (A)

0.5 g matte metallic dark bronze 15° seed beads (B)

1.5 g metallic steel iris 11° cylinder beads (C)

1 gram metallic brown iris 11° seed beads (D)

54 green satin 2-mm glass pearls

24 matte green 3-mm crystal pearls

2 platinum 12-mm crystal pearls

1 pair gold-filled ear wires

Dark brown nylon beading thread

Tools

2 size 12 beading needles

1 beading awl

1 pair jewelry chain-nose pliers

Beader's supply kit (p. 5)

Version #2

Instructions

Bezels for the Trillions

A simple bezel using flat, even-count peyote stitch makes a tight connection around the 12-mm trillion. Make two bezeled trillions, one for each earring.

Rows 1 & 2: Using 3 feet (94.1 cm) of prepared thread (p. 6), string on 33C, leaving a 10-inch (25.4 cm) tail.

Row 3: Without a bead on the needle, skip the last 2C strung; sew back through the third to the last C strung, making the first peyote stitch (p. 9 and Figure 1, red thread); adjust the tension. Work flat peyote stitch, using 1C in each stitch, for a total of 16C added in this row (Figure 1, blue thread).

Figure 1

Zip: Place a needle onto the tail thread; wrap the strip around your finger; and, using the working thread, zip (stitch) the ends of the strip together (p. 11) by sewing through the first C added on Row 3, the next C on Row 2, and the next C on Row 3 at the beginning of the strip (Figure 2, red thread).

Figure 2

Using the tail thread, sew through the closest C from Row 1, the next C from Row 2, and the next C from Row 1 at the beginning of the strip (Figure 2, blue thread); adjust the tension. The beadwork will now be worked in tubular peyote stitch (p. 10) and the count is 16 high and 16 low.

Round 4, for the top of the bezel: Using the tail thread, work flat peyote stitch, using 1A in each stitch, snugly, for a total of 16A added; step up through the first A added in this round (p. 10 and Figure 2, green thread); weave off the tail thread tightly in the top 2 rounds, and trim.

Wipe off the stone; place it into the beadwork so that the flat faceted side is touching Round 4 (Figure 3).

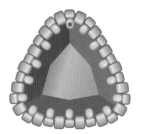

Figure 3

Rounds 5 & 6, for the back of the bezel: Using the remaining thread, work 2 rounds of tubular peyote stitch, using 1A in each stitch, for a total of 16A added in each round; step up into the first A added in each round (Figure 4, red and blue threads). Work tightly so that the stone doesn't fall out!

Figure 4

Center up a corner: Take a look at the front of the stone and bezel. In order to center up the 2 bead loops that have to be added, we need to make sure that we have an A bead, from Round 4, centered on one of the three corners of the trillion (Figure 3, A bead with the red dot). If you don't have it, massage the bezel around until you do.

Round 7. Stitch-in-the-ditch: Move the thread into an A bead on Round 5 (first round of A beads stitched on the back), as shown in Figure 5. Using *1C in each stitch, stitch-in-the-ditch (p. 12) by sewing through the next A on Round 5; repeat from * for a total of 16C added. Step up into the first C added in this round (Figure 5, red thread).

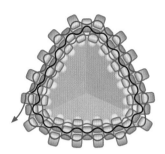

Figure 5

Rounds 8 & 9. Add a point protector: Work 2 rounds of tubular peyote stitch, using 1C in each stitch, for a total of 16C added in each round; step up into the first C added in each round (Figure 5, blue and green threads).

Add the pearl embellishment

Before we begin, find the A bead on Round 4 (front) that is most centered with a corner (Figure 3, A bead with the red dot); move the thread into position on Round 8 as in Figure 6 (blue arrow).

Center corner

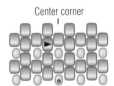

Figure 6

Step 1: String twenty-five 2-mm glass pearls (Figure 7); weave through the first 4 pearls added in this step to both form a ring and hold its shape (Figure 7, red thread).

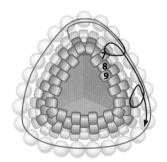

Figure 7

Step 2: Find a C bead on Round 7 (stitch-in-the-ditch round on the back) that aligns with a pearl; move the thread into position (Figure 7, end of red thread path); sew through the C bead; sew back through the pearl just exited (Figure 7, blue thread); tighten. Weave through pearls to the next alignment and repeat Step 2 around the ring of pearls. You should be able to make about 10 connections.

Add the loops

Add the top loop of CZ bezel: If necessary, close the loop on each ear wire tightly, using a pair of pliers.

Move the thread out of the pearl ring; using the centered A bead on Round 4 as a guide, weave the thread to exit a C bead on Round 7, matching the position shown on Figure 8, beginning of the red thread path. String 11A; string the ear wire over the A beads; skip the next 2C on Round 7; sew through the next C bead on Round 7 as shown in Figure 8, red thread; adjust the tension.

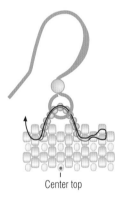

Figure 8

Center top

Check that the ear wire faces forward and the loop is centered over the centered A bead on Round 4 (front). If all is well, turn the thread around; rework the loop to secure (Figure 8, blue thread); keep the thread.

Add the bottom loop of the bezel: Looking at Round 4 on the front of the bezel, find the center bottom A bead (Figure 9, A bead with the red dot). Using this bead as a guide, weave the thread to exit a C bead on Round 7, matching up to Figure 9, beginning of red thread path.

String 13A; skip the next 2C on Round 7, sew through the one after that (Figure 9, red thread); adjust the tension and check that the loop is centered (Figure 9). If so, turn the thread around; rework the loop to secure (Figure 9, blue thread), weave off the thread, and trim.

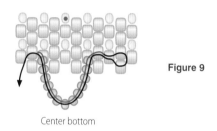

Figure 9

Center bottom

Create the Pearl Drops

A beautiful netting technique is used to create the elegant pearl cones for the 12-mm pearl drops. Make 2 pearl drops.

Round 1: With 3 feet (91.4 cm) of prepared thread, string 6D, leaving a 10-inch (25.4 cm) tail; knot into a ring; sew through the closest D bead (Figure 10, red thread).

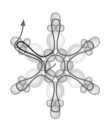

Figure 10

Round 2: *String one 3-mm pearl, 1A, 1D, and 1A; pull them down to the ring of beads; skip the A, D, and A just added; sew back through the pearl and the next D on Round 1 (Figure 10, blue thread). Repeat from * 5 more times; step up by sewing through the first pearl added and the first A and D added in this round, as shown in Figure 10, green thread.

Round 3: With the working thread, *string 1A, one 3-mm pearl, and 1A, and sew through the next D from Round 2; repeat from * 5 more times; tighten (Figure 11, red thread). Hold on tight and rework this round to secure, exiting any A before a pearl on Round 3 (Figure 11, end of red thread path).

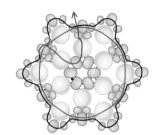

Figure 11

Round 4: *String 1A, 1D, and 1A; skip the closest pearl from Round 3; sew through the next A (Round 3), D (Round 2), and A (Round 3); tighten. Repeat from * 4 more times, then string 1A, 1D, and 1A and exit through the next A from Round 3, for a total of 6 picots added in this round (Figure 11, blue thread). Weave the thread to exit any D bead on Round 1 (Figure 11, green thread); sew through the closest pearl and the closest A added on Round 2 (Figure 11, purple thread).

Add the 12-mm pearl: Put a needle onto the tail thread; sew through the closest D bead from Round 1 to get away from the knot. Push the thread to the inside of the cone; string one 12-mm pearl and 3D; skip the 3D, sew back through the pearl and into the opposite D bead on Round 1; weave through 2D on Round 1 (Figure 12); rework the pearl addition again; weave off this thread and trim.

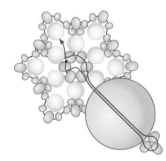

Figure 12

Round 5: Using the remaining thread, *string 1B and sew through the next A to form a picot; sew back through the pearl and the closest D on Round 1; repeat from * 5 more times, exiting any D bead on Round 1 (Figure 13).

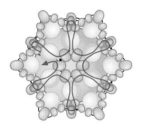

Figure 13

Add the bead loop to drop pearl cap: With the thread in a D bead on Round 1, string 1A, one 2-mm pearl, 7A, one 2-mm pearl, and 1A; sew through an opposite D bead on the ring; string 1A, step up through the closest 2-mm pearl, and sew through the 7A and the next pearl; string 1A; sew through the same D, from the opposite side, to complete the loop (Figure 14). Rework the loop to center and secure, then weave off the thread and trim.

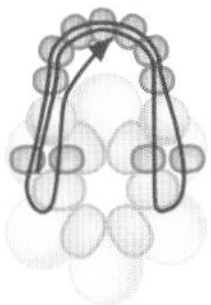

Figure 14

Attach the drop pearl cap to the trillion bezel with beaded jump rings: Using 1 foot (30.5 cm) of prepared thread, string 15A and center them on the thread; feed the end of the thread without the needle through the loop on the trillion; with the needle end of the thread, sew through the loop on the pearl dangle (Figure 15, red thread).

Figure 15

Overhand-knot (p. 17) the beads into a tight jump ring. Place a needle onto the other end of the thread. Weave off with one thread going one direction around the jump ring and the other thread going in the other direction; trim. Use an awl to round out the shape of the jump ring.

Make a second beaded jump ring that catches the bottom loop of the trillion and the loop of the pearl drop (Figure 16).

Repeat from the beginning to create the second earring.

Figure 16

THE KEY TO UNLOCKING THE PAST

A THREE-DIMENSIONAL, PEYOTE-STITCHED KEY is the focal point of this design.
Bezel a beautiful CZ in beadwork; then attach it to a beaded shaft and tip it with a
pearl embellishment, which is a creative approach to making the bit end.
The necklace technique is unusual but makes for a great necklace cording.

Version #1 (left), Version #2 (right)

{ HISTORICAL PERSPECTIVE }

The earliest known locking device is around 4,000 years old, so the key has played a major role in securing our valuables from the time of ancient civilizations to the present day. The earliest keys were made of wood, iron, or bronze, and in most cases were worn on the person. At the time of Jan Davidsz de Heem's painting *A Richly Laid Table with Parrot,* around 1650, keys were being made for locking writing desks and bedside tables, armoires, liquor boxes, document boxes, linen cabinets, and tea and sugar cabinets. This painting shows a locking liquor cabinet on a well-laid table—a feast fit for a king!

A Richly Laid Table with Parrot by Jan Davidsz de Heem

Detail from Version #1

Detail of keys from painting

Dimensions
Necklace: 33¼ inches (84.5 cm) long
Key: 2¾ inches (7 cm) tall

Techniques
Netting
Peyote stitch, flat, even count
Peyote stitch, tubular, even count
Stitch-in-the-ditch

Skill Level
Intermediate advanced

Materials, Version #1
1 salsa flare 14-mm antique cushion-cut briolette CZ
15 g metallic brown iris 15° seed beads (A)
1 g matte metallic dark bronze 15° seed beads (B)
3 g metallic steel iris 11° cylinder beads (C)
1 g matte metallic dark bronze 11° seed beads (D)
2 platinum 3-mm crystal pearls
1 platinum 6-mm crystal pearl
Dark brown nylon beading thread
1 round toothpick

Materials, Version #2
1 amethyst 14-mm antique cushion-cut briolette CZ (custom coated)
15 g purple fuchsia gold metallic iris 15° seed beads (A)
1 g matte metallic dark bronze 15° seed beads (B)
3 g matte metallic grey dusk gold iris 11° cylinder beads (C)
1 gram matte metallic dark bronze 11° seed beads (D)
2 light gold 3-mm crystal pearls
1 light gold 6-mm crystal pearl
Dark beige nylon beading thread
1 round toothpick

Tools
2 size 12 beading needles
Flush wire cutter
1 pencil
Basic beader's kit (p. 5)

Instructions

The basic key has three parts: the bow, or portion of the key that is held; the shaft, which is the part of the key that enters the lock; and the bit, which is the section of the key that activates and deactivates the locking device.

The Bow: Bezel the CZ

Rows 1 & 2: Using 3 feet (91.4 cm) of prepared thread (p. 6), string 41C beads, leaving a 10-inch (25.4 cm) tail.

Row 3: Without a bead on the needle, skip the last 2C strung and sew back through the third-to-last C strung, making the first peyote stitch (p. 8 and Figure 1, red thread); adjust the tension. Work flat peyote stitch using 1C in each stitch, for a total of 20C added in this row (Figure 1, blue thread).

Figure 1

Zip the ends of the strip together to create tubular peyote: Place a needle onto each thread end. Wrap the strip around your finger, a step gauge, or thread burner; with the working thread, sew through the closest C on Row 3, the next C on Row 2, and the next C on Row 3 (p. 10 and Figure 2, red thread).

Figure 2

With the tail thread, sew through the closest C on Row 1, the next C on Row 2, and the next C on Row 1 (Figure 2, blue thread). Remove the strip from the armature and tighten. The count is now 20 high and 20 low.

Round 4, for the front of the bezel: Using the tail thread, work tubular peyote stitch, using 1B in each stitch, for a total of 20B added; step up through the first B added in this round (p. 10 and Figure 2, green thread); weave off the tail thread, tightly, in the top 2 rounds and trim.

Wipe off the CZ; then place it onto the beadwork (Figure 3).

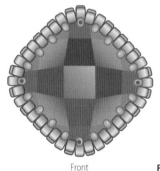

Front   **Figure 3**

Round 5, for the back of the bezel: Using the remaining thread, work tubular peyote stitch, using 1A in each stitch, for a total of 20A added; step up into the first A added in this round (Figure 4, red thread).

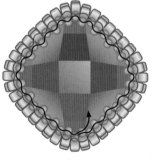

Back   **Figure 4**

Position 4, centered beads on the front of the bezel: Before the bezel gets tightened too much, we need a B bead, from Round 4 on the front, positioned in each corner of the bezel

(Figure 3, B beads marked with red dots). If you don't have them in place, adjust the beadwork now.

Round 6, for the back of the bezel: Work tubular peyote stitch, using 1A in each stitch, for a total of 20A added; step up into the first A added in this round (Figure 4, blue thread). Work tightly so that the CZ is snug within the bezel.

Create the Bail

A shaped flat peyote stitch bail (the loop connection to the necklace) adds interest and detail to the key.

Step 1: Move the thread into Row 1. Positioning the thread as shown in Figure 5, beginning of red thread path, turn the thread around by sewing through the closest C bead (from Row 3).

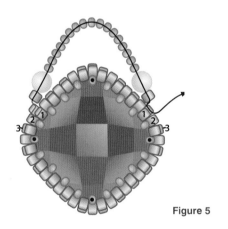

Figure 5

Step 2: String 1C, one 3-mm pearl, 17B, one 3-mm pearl, and 1C. Sew through a C bead on Row 3 of the bezel as shown in Figure 5, blue thread. Turn and sew through the closest C bead on Row 1 of the bezel (Figure 6, beginning of red thread path); tighten.

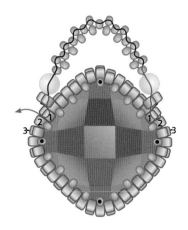

Figure 6

Step 3: With 1C, sew through the closest pearl and 1B on the bail (Figure 6, red thread); work flat peyote stitch and, using 1B in each stitch, make 8 stitches, ending the last one by sewing through the closest pearl (Figure 6, blue thread). With 1C, sew through the closest C bead on Row 1 (Figure 6, green thread).

Step 4: Sew through the closest C bead on Row 3, the closest C on the bail, and the closest pearl plus 1A (Figure 7, red thread). * Stitch-in-the-ditch (p. 12) on the front of the bail, using 1A in each stitch and sewing through the next B bead on the bail; repeat from * 7 more times. End by sewing through the closest pearl and 1C on the bail (Figure 7, blue thread).

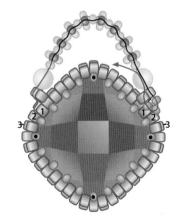

Figure 7

Step 5: String 3B; sew through the closest C and pearl on the bail to form a picot (Figure 7, green thread). Reinforce the bail in the front to tighten, exiting through the closest pearl and 1 of the C beads on the bail. String 3B; sew through the C on the bail next to the C where your thread is exiting to form a picot. Weave off the thread in the back of the bail and trim.

Create the Shaft of the Key

Zip a flat, even-count peyote stitch strip around a toothpick, forming a sturdy armature for the shaft of the key.

Rows 1 & 2: With 4 feet (1.2 m) of prepared thread, string 33C, leaving an 18-inch (45.7 cm) tail.

Row 3: Without a bead on the needle, skip the last 2C strung and sew back through the third-to-last C strung, making the first peyote stitch (refer to Figure 1, red thread); adjust the tension. Work flat peyote stitch, using 1C in each stitch, for a total of 16C added in this row (refer to Figure 1, blue thread).

Rows 4–16: Work flat, even-count peyote stitch, using 1C in each stitch, for a total of 16 rows (p. 9 and Figure 8).

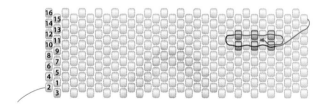

Figure 8

The Bit

A tidy little peyote stitch technique creates the perfect bit.

Round 1: Before starting, we must move the thread. Using the working thread, weave through the strip to exit as in Figure 8, red thread. Work stitch-in-the-ditch, using 1C in each stitch for 3 stitches. Turn the thread around (Figure 8, blue thread) and work stitch-in-the-ditch, using 1C in each stitch for 3 stitches; turn the thread around again and step up through the starting C bead on the strip and the first C bead added in this round (Figure 8, green thread).

Round 2: Work tubular peyote stitch using 1C in each stitch, make 2 stitches (Figure 9, red thread); with 1C on the needle, sew through the closest stitch-in-the-ditch C bead around the corner (Figure 9, blue thread). Using 1C in each stitch, make 2 stitches (Figure 9, green thread); with 1C on the needle, step up through the closest stitch-in-the-ditch C bead around the corner and the first C added in this round (Figure 9, purple thread). The count is now 6 high and 6 low.

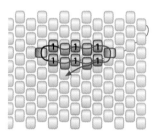

Figure 9

Rounds 3–6: Even though the beadwork looks like a buttonhole, the beadwork is still even-count tubular peyote stitch. Work 4 rounds of tubular peyote stitch, using 1C in each stitch, for a total of 6 stitches in each round; step up at the end of each round (Figure 10, numbered rounds).

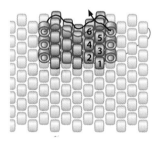

Figure 10

Round 7: Work tubular peyote stitch, use 1C to make 1 stitch; weave through the next C from Round 5 and the next C from Round 6; using 1C, make 1 stitch (Figure 10, red thread); using 1C, make 1 stitch; weave through the next C from Round 5 and the next C from Round 6; using 1C, make 1 stitch and step up (Figure 10, blue thread).

Finish the bit: Sew through the next C bead on Round 6 and the next C on Round 5 (Figure 11, red thread); sew through the opposite C bead on Round 5 on the other side; sew back through the same C just exited (Figure 11, blue thread); tighten. Weave the thread off the bit, through the strip, and exit any C bead on the closest edge of the beadwork (Figure 11, black thread).

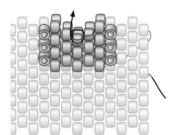

Figure 11

Continuing with the Shaft

Prepare the toothpick armature: Using a pair of flush cutters, cut the tip off one end of a toothpick. Lay the toothpick along the length of the strip of beadwork. Using a pencil, mark the length to match the strip. Cut the other end of the toothpick so that both ends are now flush with the beadwork.

Zip the strip into a tube: Place a needle onto the tail thread and roll the strip around the toothpick. Sew through the closest C on Row 16; sew back through the same C bead just exited on Row 2; sew back through the same C bead on Row 16 (p. 11 and Figure 12, red thread). Continue zipping by sewing through the next C on Row 1, then the next C on Row 16, to the end of the row (Figure 12, blue thread). End by sewing the last C on Row 1 to the last C on Row 15 (Figure 12, green thread). Weave the thread back through the shaft to exit any C bead on the opposite edge (Figure 12, black thread).

Figure 12

Add the decorative end to the shaft: Place a needle onto the working thread that is exiting a C bead on the edge, down by the bit.

Round 1: *Work edge-stitching (p. 11) using 1A in each stitch, tuck the needle under the closest piece of thread on the edge, then adjust the tension. Repeat from * 7 more times for a total of 8A added; step up through the first A added in this round (Figure 13, red thread; which has been enlarged for clarity).

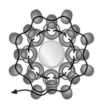

Figure 13

Round 2: *Working tubular peyote stitch using 1A for each stitch, sew through the next A from Round 1; repeat from * 7 more times, stepping up through the first A added in this round (Figure 13, blue thread). This round will want to roll out.

Rounds 3–5: Work 3 rounds of tubular peyote stitch using 1C in each stitch; make 8 stitches in each round. Step up through the first C added in each round (Figure 14). The beadwork will want to cup up on these rounds.

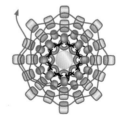

Figure 14

Attach the 6-mm pearl: Sew through the closest C bead on Round 4 (Figure 15, beginning of red thread path). String one 6-mm pearl and sew through the matching C bead on the opposite side of Round 4; sew back through the pearl and back through the same C bead and the next C bead on Round 3 (Figure 15, red thread).

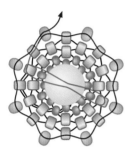

Figure 15

Round 6: Work tubular peyote stitch and, using 1D in each stitch, make 8 stitches; step up through the first D added in this round (Figure 15, blue thread). Weave off this thread and trim.

Attach the shaft to the bottom of the bow: Butt the top of the shaft up against the bottom of the bow (Figure 16), aligning to a B bead with a red dot, making sure that the bit is straight and on the lower right-hand side. Using the remaining thread, sew the shaft discreetly and securely to the bow by sewing each of the C beads on the edge of the shaft to whatever beads on the bit work (Figure 16). Weave off the thread in the bow and trim.

Figure 16

The Embellished Collet

A tubular button-shaped collet camouflages the connection of the shaft to the bow and also adds a bit of embellishment.

Rows 1 & 2: With 2 feet (61 cm) of prepared thread, string 20C, leaving an 8-inch (20.3 cm) tail. Wrap the string of beads around the top of the shaft, rethread through half of the beads, and tighten (Figure 17).

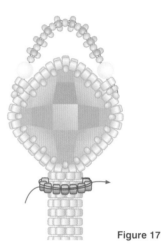

Figure 17

Round 3: Work tubular peyote stitch and using 1C in each stitch, make 10 stitches; step up through the first C added in this round (Figure 18).

Figure 18

Rounds 4 & 5, for the bottom of the shape: Add a needle to the tail thread. Using the tail, work 2 rounds of tubular peyote stitch with 1A in each stitch and 10 stitches in each round; step up through the first A added in each round. Keep the collet up by the bottom of the bow (Figure 18, red thread). Weave off this thread and trim.

Round 6, for the top of the collet: Work tubular peyote stitch, using 1A in each stitch, make 10 stitches; step up through the first A added in this round (Figure 18, blue thread).

Round 7: Spin the collet around so that a C bead from Round 3 is aligned with the side of the bow and the thread is exiting an A bead from Round 6, as shown in Figure 19.

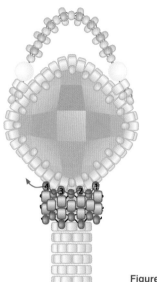

Figure 21

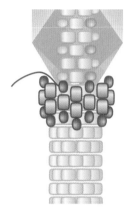

Figure 19

Work tubular peyote stitch and, using 1A in each stitch, make 4 stitches. Weave through the next C from Round 3 and the next A from Round 6, creating a notch. Using 1A in each stitch, make 4 stitches; weave through the next C from Round 3 and the next A from Round 6 and the first A added in this round, creating the second notch. Readjust the collet to place the notches along the lower sides of the bow (Figures 20 and 21), and tighten.

Sew the collet to the bow: Discreetly sew the front of the collet to the front of the bow and the back of the collet to the back of the bow in a couple of places; work tightly.

Embellish the collet: Weave the thread forward through the next A from Round 6 and the next A from Round 7 (Figure 22, beginning of red thread path). String 3B; make 1 peyote stitch, forming a picot. Weave forward through the next A on Round 6 and the next A on Round 7.

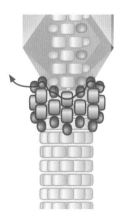

Figure 20

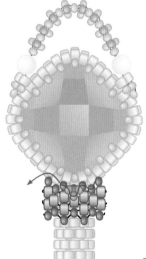

Figure 22

String 2B, 1D, and 2B, and sew through the next A on Round 7, straddling the notch in the corner (Figure 23). Weave forward through the next A on Round 6 and the next A on Round 7.

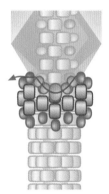

Figure 23

String 3B; make 1 peyote stitch to form a picot (Figure 22). Weave forward through the next A on Round 6 and the next A on Round 7. String 2B, 1D, and 2B, and sew through the next A on Round 7, straddling the notch in the corner (Figure 23). Weave off the thread and trim.

The Necklace Chain

This unique chain-style necklace is actually 2 chains that interlock with one another as they are being made. It takes a lot of 15° beads and a lot of thread. Clean off your beading surface so you have plenty of room to work.

Part 1 of making necklace chain

Step 1: Cut two pieces of thread 5 feet (1.5 m) long. Holding the threads together on one end, make a slipknot (p. 14) about 6 inches (15.2 cm) from the end; tighten it.

Step 2: One thread will do the stringing and the other thread will do the netting. Place a needle onto one of the threads, wax the thread, then string 6 inches (15.2 cm) of A beads. Push them down to the slipknot; make a stopper bead out of the last bead strung (p. 18) by rethreading through it without splitting the thread (Figure 24, red thread).

Figure 24

Tip: Don't ever crisscross the threads or your netting will be a mess! Figure out a comfortable way to hold the first thread. I wrap the first thread around the index finger of my left hand, and then hold the connection in my right hand.

Step 3: Place a needle onto the second thread, wax it, then sew through the first A bead strung on the first thread. Pick up and hold the first thread while you string 5A onto the second thread. Skip 5A on the first thread and sew through the sixth A bead (Figure 24, blue thread); tighten. Repeat this technique until you run out of beads.

Step 4: When you've run out of beads, disconnect the stopper bead on the first thread. String 6 inches (15.2 cm) of A; bring them down to the last netting stitch and make the last A strung the new stopper bead.

Repeat Steps 3 and 4 until you have 34 inches (86.4 cm) of bead chain, or the desired length (but whatever length you choose, bear in mind the necklace doesn't have a clasp so it has to fit over your head). When you've reached the right length, remove all but 5A from the first thread, and add 5A to the second thread (Figure 25, exiting green and orange threads).

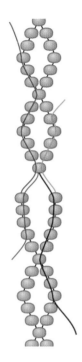

Figure 25

Step 5: Straighten out the neck chain and pin the ends of the chain to your work surface. (I use needles.) The chain cannot be twisted! Disconnect the slipknot at the beginning of the chain and tighten up the connection. All threads will be used to zip the neck chain together. Don't twist the chain or make thread path turnarounds.

Step 6: The beginning threads weave off through netting at the end of the necklace and the ends of the threads get woven off in the beginning of the netting. Working with one thread at a time, sew through the chain for about 1 inch (2.5 cm), with each thread exiting in different nets and not in A beads that are shared (Figure 25, red, blue, green, and orange threads). Pull on all 4 threads to tighten.

Step 7: Each of the threads will need to be woven off, using half-hitch knots (p. 16). Using one of the threads, tuck the needle through the loop of the net the thread is exiting; start pulling the thread through as you tuck the needle through the loop that has been made by the thread. Tighten by pulling on the thread and making sure that the knot is placed right where the thread was exiting the netting (Figure 26, red thread). Continue to weave and make half-hitch knots in the first thread, making sure to not cross over on the netting, until secure. Trim. Repeat Step 7 for the other 3 remaining threads, and trim.

Figure 26

Part 2

This portion of the necklace is made much like the first part, except the netting is worked in and out of the first chain's nets. It's a bit fidgety at first, so take your time and bring your patience to the table!

Step 1: Cut 2 pieces of thread 5 feet (1.5 m) long; holding the threads together on one end, make a slipknot about 6 inches (15.2 cm) from the end; wax thread. Tighten it.

Step 2: Put a needle on one of the threads and string 6 inches (15.2 cm) of A. Push them down to the slipknot; make a stop bead out of the last bead strung (Figure 27, red thread; for clarity, the illustration shows two different colors of beads).

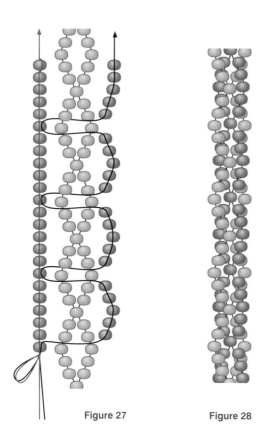

Figure 27   **Figure 28**

Step 3: One thread will do the stringing and the other thread will do the netting. With the second thread, sew through the first bead strung on the first thread (Figure 27, beginning of blue thread path).

Step 4: With the second thread, sew through one of the net openings of the first necklace chain; make sure that the first thread is on the left side of the first necklace chain and the second thread is on the right side of the first necklace chain (Figure 27, beginning of blue thread path).

Step 5: Pick up and hold the first thread while you string 5A onto the second thread. Point the needle through the hole on the next net on the first necklace chain; skip 5A on the

first thread and sew through the sixth A. Tighten gently. Pass the second thread back through the same net on the necklace chain. Tighten (Figure 27, blue thread).

Repeat the process, adding beads to the first thread as needed. When you get back to the beginning, end each thread with 5 beads. Repeat Part 1, Steps 5–7, weaving in all four threads and making half-hitch knots along the way. Trim the ends (Figure 28).

Attach the Key to the Chain

Two simple beaded jump rings make the connection to the necklace chain.

Cut 1 foot (30.5 cm) of thread and string 25A, leaving a 6-inch (15.2 cm) tail. Loop through the bail and around the chain; using an overhand knot (p. 17), tie the beads into a ring. Weave the thread in the ring to reinforce and trim off excess. Repeat one more time (Figure 29).

Figure 29

FLORENTINE ROSETTE CUFF

A BEAUTIFUL PEARL-AND-GLASS ROSETTE takes center stage on a beaded cuff. Rosettes consist of a circular arrangement of leaves or petals around a central component. Based on stylized flower designs, they have been used as sculptural ornaments on objects since antiquity. My beaded version can be used for earrings, a pendant, or in this case, attached to a peyote-stitch-covered brass cuff blank. The result is a contemporary approach to a timeless design.

Version #1

{ HISTORICAL PERSPECTIVE }

Agnolo Bronzino's commissioned portrait of Maria de' Medici, the eldest daughter of Cosimo I de' Medici, Grand Duke of Tuscany, resides in the palace of her family name, which was designed and built to house an extensive collection of fine art, both acquired and commissioned. The palace is now the home of the Uffizi Gallery, one of the oldest (opened to visitors in 1765) and most famous art museums in the Western world.

    The allure of this beautiful painting is in the details. As a bead artist, I was of course drawn to the fabulous pearl necklace, the gold and cameo earrings, and the lovely gem-encrusted tiara. But the fine aspects of the clothing are what have continued to capture my eye. The exquisite embroidery embellishment on the rich velvet in the gown reminded me of stylized rosette shapes. I kept coming back to the color palette—the darkest of greens, the softness of the pearl shades, the embroidery design with the alluring touch of aqua or teal, and the whisper of lace.

Portrait of Maria de' Medici by Agnolo Bronzino

Dimensions
Rosette, 1½ inches (3.8 cm) in diameter

Techniques
Edge-stitching
Netting
Peyote stitch, flat, even count
Peyote stitch, tubular, even count
Stitch-in-the-ditch

Skill Level
Intermediate

Materials, Version #1
3 g bronze lustered amber 15° seed beads (A)
0.5 g matte green gold iris 15° seed beads (B)
0.5 g matte olive 15° seed beads (C)
10 g 24-karat red/gold iris (D)
3 g matte green gold iris 11° seed beads (E)
0.5 g bronze lustered amber 11° seed beads (F)
0.5 g olive metallic color-lined aqua 11° seed beads (G)
16 aquamarine Picasso finish 4 x 6 mm faceted Czech gemstone rondelles
19 platinum 3-mm crystal pearls
1 platinum 12-mm crystal pearl
1 brass cuff blank, ½-inch (1.3 cm) wide*
Dark beige and dark brown nylon beading thread
Double-sided craft tape, 1 inch (2.5 cm) wide
10 x 3 inches (25.4 x 7.6 cm) plastic kitchen wrap

Materials, Version #2
3 g dark brown iris 15° seed beads (A)
0.5 g matte teal metallic iris 15° seed beads (B)
0.5 g gold metallic bronze 15° seed (C)
10 g dark steel metallic iris (D)
3 g matte forest green metallic iris 11° seed beads (E)
0.5 g dark brown iris 11° seed beads (F)
0.5 g gold metallic bronze 11° seed beads (G)
16 copper/teal 4 x 6 mm faceted Czech gemstone rondelles
19 bronze 3-mm crystal pearls
1 bronze 12-mm crystal pearl

1 brass cuff blank, ½-inch (1.3 cm) wide*

Dark brown nylon beading thread

Double-sided craft tape 1 inch (2.5 cm) wide

10 x 3 inches (25.4 x 7.6 cm) plastic kitchen wrap

Cuff blanks come in different lengths, between 5¾ and 7 inches (14.6 and 17.8 cm); the best choice is a cuff that can be shaped around the wrist for a comfortable fit and a 1-inch (2.5 cm) opening. Once the beadwork has been added, the inside measurement of the cuff blank will diminish by about ½ inch (1.3 cm), so plan accordingly.

Tools

3 size 12 beading needles

1 size 13 beading needle (may be needed when embellishing)

Step gauge (optional, but helpful)

Fine-point black permanent marker

Small Teflon-coated craft scissors

Measuring tape

Beader's supply kit (p. 5)

Version #2

Instructions

Shape the brass cuff blank: In most cases, the cuff blank will need to be shaped a bit as it's too round. We need a slightly flattened top and an oval shape with the openings about 1 inch (2.5 cm) apart.

Add double-sided tape to the cuff: Measure the length of the cuff; mark the center on the outside and inside with a permanent marker. Using Teflon-coated scissors, cut between 7 and 9 inches (17.8 and 22.9 cm), depending on the size of the blank, of double-sided craft tape. Stick a tiny bit of one end of the tape to something to hold it; cut the tape right up the center to make two ½-inch (1.3 cm) wide strips.

Press one end of the tape along the center mark at the top of the cuff; continue to press the tape along the length of the cuff, keeping it centered. Fold the tape around the end of the cuff; continue pressing it along the inside of the cuff. Using the remaining strip of tape, repeat the process for the other side of the cuff, trimming off any tape that overlaps underneath (Figure 1).

Figure 1

Peyote-Stitch Strip

Even-count flat peyote stitch completely covers a brass cuff blank.

Rows 1 & 2: Using 6 feet (1.8 m) of prepared thread (p. 6), string 11D; center the beads on the thread.

Row 3: Without a bead on the needle, skip the last 2D added and sew through the third D making the first stitch; adjust the tension. Work flat peyote stitch (p. 8), using 1D in each stitch, for 4 stitches. Roll up the tail thread to use later.

Rows 4 to the end: Work flat peyote stitch, using 1D in each stitch; make 5 stitches in each row for a total of 2 inches (5.1 cm). Keep both threads and set aside.

Make the Rosette

A peyote peyote stitch–bezeled pearl forms a beautiful center for the rosette.

Rows 1 & 2: Using 4 feet (1.2 m) of prepared thread, string 33D, leaving a 10-inch (25.4 cm) tail.

Row 3: Without a bead on the needle, skip the last 2D added and sew through the third D making the first stitch; adjust the tension. Work flat peyote stitch, using 1D in each stitch, to make 15 stitches, for a total of 16D added in this row.

Zip the ends of the strip: This technique turns flat peyote stitch to tubular (p. 10). Place a needle onto the tail thread. Wrap the strip around your finger, a step gauge, or your thread burner. With the longer thread, sew through the closest D on Row 3, the next D on Row 2, and the next D on Row 3 (Figure 2, blue thread). With the tail thread, sew through the closest D on Row 1, the next D on Row 2, and the next D on Row 1 (Figure 2, red thread). Remove the beadwork from the armature and tighten.

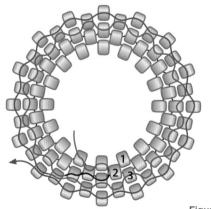

Figure 2

Rounds 4 & 5: Using the working thread, work 2 rounds of tubular peyote stitch (p. 10) using 1D in each stitch; make 16 stitches in each round. Step up through the first D added in each round (Figure 2, green and purple threads).

Add the pearl: Place the tube of beadwork you just created onto your work surface with the tail thread up. Using the tail thread, sew through the closest D bead on Row 2 of the bezel (Figure 3, beginning of red thread path). String one 12-mm pearl and sew through the opposite D bead on Row 2, as shown in Figure 3, red thread. Sew back through the pearl and into the same D bead the thread is exiting (Figure 3, blue thread); tighten. Reinforce this connection; then move the thread to exit the closest D bead on Row 1.

Figure 3

Round 6: Using the tail thread at the top of the pearl bezel, work tubular peyote stitch using 1D in each stitch for 16 stitches; step up through the first D added in this round (Figure 4 shows numbered rounds). Weave off the tail thread and trim.

Figure 4

Rounds 7–9: Using the remaining thread, work 3 rounds of tubular peyote stitch using 1D in each stitch; make 16 stitches in each round. Step up through the first D added in each round (Figure 4).

Add the support: Turn the pearl component upside down on your work surface. Fold the plastic wrap in half lengthwise; repeat until the wrap is a skinny rope. Fold the rope in half, twist it, and push it in along the edges around the pearl to fill the tube of beadwork (Figure 5). Trim off the excess.

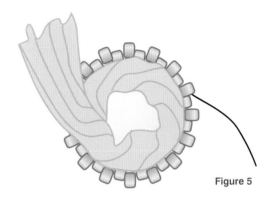

Figure 5

Sew the bezeled pearl to the peyote-stitch strip: Look at the side of the bezel where the remaining thread is exiting; put a needle through a D bead on the second round down from the top of the bezel, as shown in Figure 6. Place another needle through the opposite D bead on Row 1 on the other side of the bezel.

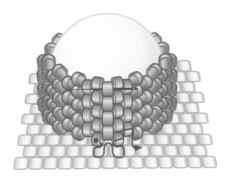

Figure 6

Lay the bezel onto the strip, aligning one of the D beads with the needle in it with the edge of the peyote stitch strip. Make the first connection by sewing into a D bead, with the needle pointing toward the opposite edge on the strip (indented by one on the edge) and out through a D bead with the needle pointing toward the closest edge immediately beside it as shown in Figure 6. Tighten and remove the marking needle on this side. Continue to sew Round 9 of the bezel to the peyote stitch strip, making sure to align the remaining D bead marked with a needle on the other side.

Add the base of the rosette

A combination of stitch-in-the-ditch, a netting-to-peyote stitch technique, and a shapely edge make the base of the rosette.

Round 1: Move the thread through the closest D bead on Round 9 (Figure 7, red dot). With 1D on the needle, sew through the next D on Round 9, working stitch-in-the-ditch (p. 12 and Figure 7, red thread). Continue stitching for a total of 16D added; step up through the first D added in this round.

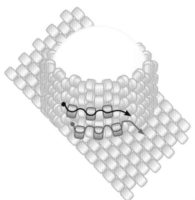

Figure 7

Round 2: Work netting (p. 8) by using 3A on the needle and sewing through the next D added in Round 1; make 16 stitches. Step up through the first 2A of the first net added in this round (Figure 8, red thread).

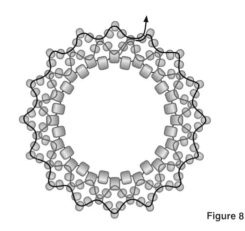

Figure 8

Round 3: *Work netting with 3A on the needle, sewing through the second A bead of the next net (the nets will lie flat, not to worry). Repeat from * 15 more times but on the last net, step up through the first A, not the second, for a total of 16 stitches (Figure 8, blue thread). *Note:* This is not the normal step-up for netting, so make sure that the thread is in the right place before moving on to Round 4.

Round 4: Here you'll work netting-to-peyote stitch. *Work peyote stitch using 1A on the needle, skip the second A on the net the thread is exiting, and sew through the third A on the same net. With 1A on the needle, sew through the first A on the next net (Figure 9, beginning of red thread path). Repeat from * 15 more times for a total of 32 stitches; step up through the first A added in this round (Figure 9, red thread).

Figure 9

Note: If the beadwork begins to ruffle, loosen your tension to give the beads more room.

Round 5: Work flat circular peyote stitch (p. 10) using 1E in each stitch; make 32 stitches. Step up through the first D added in this round (Figure 9, blue thread); roll up the excess thread and place it in a small plastic bag.

Add the next layer of the rosette

A beautiful netting technique adds the faceted glass beads to the rosette.

Round 1: Using 3 feet (91.4 cm) of thread, weave into the bezel, exiting at any D bead on the sixth round down from the top of the bezel (refer back to Figure 7, blue dot). Now prepare the thread. With 1D on the needle, sew through the next D on the same round to stitch-in-the-ditch (Figure 7, blue thread). Continue stitching for a total of 16D added; step up through the first D added in this round.

Round 2: Work netting using 3A for each stitch; make 16 stitches; step up through the first 2A of the first net added in this round (Figure 10, red thread).

Round 3: *String 1A, 1F, 1 faceted rondelle, 1A, 1E, and 1A; pull them down to the beadwork. Skip the 1A, 1E, and 1A; sew back through the rondelle and 1F; and adjust the tension. String 1A and sew through the second A on the next net (Figure 10, blue thread); adjust the tension. Repeat from * 15 more times for a total of 16 rondelles added in this round (Figure 10, blue thread). Weave the thread through the beadwork to exit any D bead on the third round down from the top of the bezel (Figure 10, following the blue thread path).

Set up the thread: Use needles to mark the 2 D beads on the second round from the top of the bezel that are the most centered along each edge of the peyote stitch strip (Figure 11, red dots; for clarity, the lower portion of the rosette has been left out of the illustration). Move the thread to exit a D bead on the third round down from the top of the bezel to place the first stitch-in-the-ditch bead that will align with this bead (Figure 11, beginning of red thread path). Remove the needle markers.

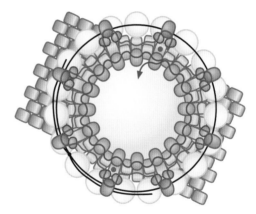

Figure 11

Add the next layer of the rosette: The pearl ring. Using 18 inches (45.7 cm) of prepared thread, string nineteen 3-mm pearls. Center them on the thread and make an overhand knot (p. 17) to tie the pearls into a ring; tighten. Weave off one thread going one direction, making half-hitch knots (p. 16) along the way; weave off the other thread going the opposite direction, making half-hitch knots along the way. Pass the thread attached to the bezel through the ring of pearls and fit the ring around the bezel (Figure 11).

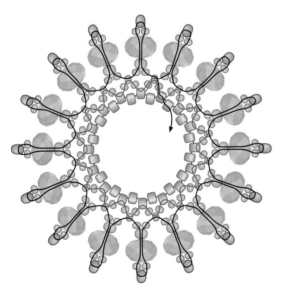

Figure 10

Anchor the pearl ring: *With 1B, 1G, and 1B on the needle, stitch-in-the-ditch by sewing through the next D on the same round that the thread is exiting; adjust the tension. Weave up through the closest D on the second round from the top of the bezel. Sew down through the closest D on the third round of the bezel, skipping a ditch (Figure 11, red thread). Repeat from * 7 more times, but when completing the last repeat, move the thread through the closest D on the second round from the top of the bezel and through the closest D at the top of the bezel (Figure 11, end of red thread path).

Embellish the top of the rosette: Work tubular peyote stitch using 1C in each stitch for 16 stitches (Figure 11, green thread); weave off this thread and trim.

Finish the rosette

Look at the back of the rosette and notice how each rondelle sits between 2E on the last round (Round 5) of the base of the rosette. With the remaining thread attached to the base of the rosette, move the thread into position as in Figure 12, beginning of red thread path.

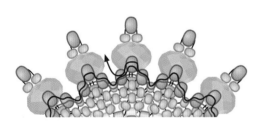

Figure 12

Step 1: *Wrap the thread over the top of the rondelle; then sew through the next E bead on Round 5 of the base (Figure 12, red thread). Tighten, making sure that the thread dropped down between the rondelle and the F bead from Round 3. Weave through the next A bead from Round 4 and the next E bead from Round 5 (Figure 12, red thread path). Repeat from * 15 more times, straightening the picots at the end of the rondelles as you sew.

*Work 1 peyote stitch using 1E; weave the thread forward through the next A on Round 4 and the next E on Round 5 (Figure 12, blue thread). Repeat from * 15 more times then weave off this thread and trim.

Back to the peyote stitch on one side: Continue to work the flat peyote stitch strip on one side until the length is 1 inch (2.5 cm) away from the end of the cuff when the rosette is centered at the top of the cuff; keep the thread.

Back to the peyote stitch on the other side: Continue to work the flat peyote stitch strip on this side until it measures 11¼ inches (28.6 cm) or until the strip goes to the end of the cuff, wraps around it, goes the length of the inside of the cuff, and wraps around the other end of the cuff and comes to within ½ inch (1.3 cm) of touching the other end of the strip (Figure 13).

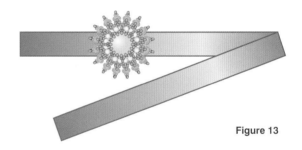

Figure 13

Edge-stitch the sides of the peyote stitch : The edge-stitching (p. 11) has to be started before we put the beadwork onto the cuff, because stitching underneath the rosette wouldn't be possible. However, I prefer to complete the edge-stitching once the strip has been attached to the cuff, as the tension on the edges seems to be tighter. *Note:* You might need to use a size 13 needle when edge stitching under the rosette.

Place a needle onto the thread attached to the short end of the peyote stitch base. *String 1A, tuck the needle under the closest thread on the edge, and pull through; adjust the tension. Repeat from * until the edge-stitching passes the rosette on the same side (Figure 14).

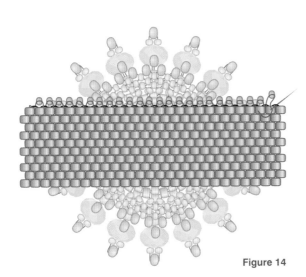

Figure 14

Note: It doesn't matter whether you're working the edge stitching from back to front or front to back, but when you get up next to the back of the rosette, make sure that you work the edge stitching from back to front—it's the only way you'll be able to stitch back there! Keep the thread if it's in good condition; if not, weave it off and trim.

Weave a new thread into the short end of the peyote stitch base to exit the last D bead on the non-edge-stitched edge of the strip. Repeat the edge stitching along this side of the strip until just past the rosette. Keep the thread.

Attach the peyote-stitch base to the prepared cuff blank:
Peel the plastic coating off the double-sided tape without touching the tape. Center the rosette on the marked centerline at the top of the cuff and press the beadwork into the tape. Continue to press the short side of the peyote stitch strip into the tape, keeping it centered on the cuff.

Continue to make sure that the rosette stays centered as you press the long side of the strip to the tape. Stretch the beadwork taut as you press, wrapping the beadwork around the end of the cuff, centering it along the inside of the cuff, and wrapping around the other end of the cuff until you run out of strip. The remaining space should be about ½ inch (1.3 cm) from touching the short side of the strip (Figure 15, light-colored D beads).

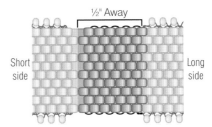

Figure 15

Back to the edge-stitching: Continue edge-stitching on both sides of the peyote-stitch base until you run out of D beads on the strip. Keep the threads.

Finish the base: With the thread that was used for peyote stitch, continue stitching the peyote-stitch base using D beads, until it looks like Figure 15. If the strip ends overlap, tighten or loosen the tension of the peyote-stitch strip on the tape to get the right fit. Stitch the last row, filling in the remaining spaces as in Figure 16, red thread.

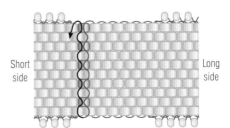

Figure 16

Zip the ends: Sew into the closest D bead on the edge (Row 1 of the base); sew through the closest D on the last row stitched on the strip; repeat across the row. Sew into the closest D on Row 1 (Figure 16, blue thread), and tighten. Weave off this thread and trim.

Finish the edge-stitching: Using the edge-stitching threads, finish up the edge stitching on each side; weave off both threads and trim.

Finish the Sides of the Cuff
Step 1: Using 5 feet (1.5 m) of prepared thread a bit darker than the D beads (to hide the thread path), and leaving a 2-foot (61 cm) tail, sew through an A bead at the end of the cuff on one edge; weave around a bit (Figure 17, red thread), then exit the same A bead that the tail thread is exiting, but from the other side (Figure 17, blue thread).

Figure 17

Step 2: Place a needle onto the tail thread. Using the tail thread, string 6½ inches (16.5 cm)—more if you're using a larger cuff blank than the sample—of E beads. Bring them down to the cuff, then make a stopper bead out of the last E strung (Figure 18, red thread), tightening the beads up against the cuff.

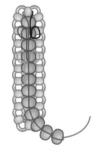

Figure 18

Step 3: Using the longer thread, sew through the first 2E strung (Figure 18, beginning of blue thread path); tighten. *Sew back through the closest A on the right side of the E where the thread is exiting, pointing the needle toward this end of the cuff (Figure 18, blue thread); sew forward through the same E bead just exited (Figure 18, blue thread); sew back through the closest A bead on the left, pointing the needle toward this end of the cuff (Figure 18, beginning of purple thread path). Sew forward through the same E bead plus 2 more E beads (Figure 18, purple thread); tighten and push the E beads into the groove created by the edge-stitching; tighten the stopper bead against the string of E beads.

Note: Don't count the A beads between stitches. Instead, just pick those that align the best with the E beads. The curvature of the cuff won't allow the bead counts to align, so just make sure that the E beads are stitched tightly next to each other without any gaps.

Repeat Step 3 from * to approximately ½ inch (1.3 cm) from the end of the cuff on this side. Disconnect the stopper bead and remove any unwanted beads; if the remaining unstitched E beads don't fit quite right, remove them and pick a different combination, as beads are all a bit different in size.

Push the remaining beads into the groove. Stitch them into place, ending by exiting the last E strung. Sew through the A bead at the end of the cuff. Turn around (Figure 19, red thread) and weave this thread through all the E beads, exiting the other end; weave off this thread and trim.

Figure 19

Using the remaining thread, sew through the A beads at the end of the cuff; weave off this thread and trim.

Repeat Steps 1–3 to finish the remaining edge of the cuff.

HEBE'S FLORAL EARRINGS

CZs IN A HIGHLY FACETED PEAR SHAPE REFLECT THE LIGHT, enhanced by flower and leaf embellishments that add just the right touch to these delicate earrings.

Version #1

{ HISTORICAL PERSPECTIVE }

Pierre Gobert was the son of a famous sculptor and a graduate of the Royal Academy of Painting and Sculpture in Paris. During the reign of Louis XIV, Gobert was the preferred portrait painter of the ladies of the court.

Gobert painted Charlotte-Aglaé d'Orléans, Duchess of Modena and Reggio, many times during her life in France and Italy. In this painting, she's portrayed as Hebe. Referred to as the goddess of youth in Greek mythology, Hebe was the daughter of Zeus and Hera and the cupbearer for the gods and goddesses of Mount Olympus. Zeus is shown here transformed into an eagle and being fed nectar or ambrosia by his daughter.

The allure of Pierre Gobert's many paintings is his subtle reference to mythology, which adds interest and elevates the status of the subject. But it's his skill at painting what look like beaded flowers that has captured my heart. Most of his royal subjects have flowers draped on them in some manner. I've always felt that they looked beaded, and with a beader's eye, the flowers are beautifully rendered.

Portrait of the Duchess of Modena as Hebe by Pierre Gobert

Dimensions

1⅜ x ¾ inches (3.5 x 1.9 cm), including ear wire

Techniques

Peyote stitch, flat, even count
Peyote stitch, tubular, even count

Skill Level

Intermediate

Materials, Version #1

2 salmon sorbet 18 x 13 mm pear-shaped CZs (custom coated)

1 g green metallic iris 15° seed beads (A)

0.5 g matte olive AB 15° seed beads (B)

0.5 g purple-lined blue 15° seed beads (C)

0.5 g fuchsia-lined transparent yellow AB 15° seed beads (D)

0.5 g bronze-lined aqua 15° seed beads (E)

1 g metallic olive green iris 11° cylinder beads (F)

0.5 g purple-lined blue 11° seed beads (G)

1 pair vermeil ear wires with loop

Green nylon beading thread

Materials, Version #2

2 alexandrite 18 x 13 mm pear-shaped CZs (lab-grown)

1.5 g 24-karat gold plated 15° seed beads (A, B, C, E)

0.5 g purple-lined purple 15° seed beads (D)

1 g 24-karat gold plated 11° cylinder beads (F)

0.5 g purple-lined purple 11° seed beads (G)

1 pair vermeil ear wires with loop

Gold/yellow nylon beading thread

Tools

2 size 12 beading needles

1 size 13 beading needle (may be needed when embellishing)

Jewelry chain-nose pliers

Beader's supply kit (p. 5)

Version #2

Instructions

Follow each step twice to make both earrings concurrently, rather than finishing one earring and then making the other.

The CZ Bezel

A straightforward peyote-stitch bezel around a gorgeous CZ sets us up for the flower embellishment for these beautiful earrings.

Rows 1 & 2: Using 3 feet (91.4 cm) of prepared thread (p. 6), string 41F, leaving a 10-inch (25.4 cm) tail.

Row 3: Without a bead on the needle, skip the last 2F added and sew through the third F, making the first stitch (Figure 1, red thread); adjust the tension. Work flat peyote stitch (p. 9) using 1F in each stitch; make 19 more stitches, for a total of 20F added in this row (Figure 1, blue thread).

Figure 1

Zip the ends of the strip: This technique turns flat peyote stitch to tubular (p. 10). Place a needle onto the tail thread. Wrap the strip around your finger or a step gauge. With the longer thread, sew through the closest F on Row 3, the next F on Row 2, and the next F on Row 3 (Figure 2, blue thread). With the tail thread, sew through the closest F on Row 1, the next F on Row 2, and the next F on Row 1 (Figure 2, red thread). Remove the beadwork from the armature and tighten.

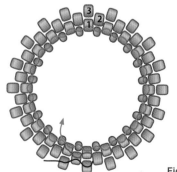

Figure 2

Round 4, for the front of the bezel: Using the tail thread, work tubular peyote stitch, using 1A in each stitch; make 20 stitches. Step up through the first A added in this round (Figure 2, green thread), weave off the tail thread, tightly, in the top 2 rounds, and trim.

Wipe off the CZ. Center it over the bezel with the flat faceted side (the front) touching Round 4 and its point aligned with a Round 4 A bead, as shown with red dot in Figure 3.

Figure 3

Stone front

Round 5, for the back of the bezel: Pick up the CZ and the bezel while keeping the point of the CZ aligned with a Round 4 A bead. Using the remaining thread and working tight, work tubular peyote stitch using 1A in each stitch for 20 stitches. Step up through the first A added (Figure 4, red thread). Adjust the position of the point of the CZ if necessary. Then, without a bead on the needle, sew forward through the next F and the next A and tighten.

Figure 4

Round 6, for the back of the bezel: Look at the front of the bezel. There has to be an A bead from Round 4 at the point on the front. If there isn't, move the beadwork around to align the closest A with the point.

On the back, work tubular peyote stitch using 1A in each stitch for 20 stitches; step up through the first A added (Figure 4, blue thread). Keep the thread.

Add the bead loop for the ear wire: Move the thread to exit an F bead on Row 2 of the bezel as shown in Figure 5, beginning of red thread path (center front top). String 9A and 1 ear wire, making sure that the ear wire faces forward. Skip the next F on Row 2 of the bezel and sew through the next F on Row 2 (Figure 5, red thread). Turn the thread around to exit (Figure 5, blue thread). Reinforce the loop.

Center front top   **Figure 5**

The Flower and Leaves

A delicate flower and 2 leaf shapes add the finishing touches to each beautiful earring. You'll attach these embellishments to each of the bezels as mirror images of each other, as follows. You may need to use a size 13 needle to make them.

The right earring

Move the thread to exit a Row 1 F bead as in Figure 6, beginning of red thread path. String 3B, sew back through the same F bead the thread is exiting, and tighten to form a picot (Figure 6). Weave around to exit the last B bead added on the picot (Figure 6, beginning of red thread path).

Center front top   **Figure 6**

Petal #1

This tiny flower has 3 little petals stitched off the picot just added.

Step 1: String 1B, 9C, and 1B. Sew through the same bead the thread is exiting, in the same direction as before (Figure 7) to make a petal; adjust the tension.

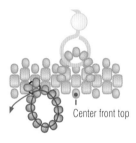

Center front top   **Figure 7**

Step 2: String 2G. Sew through the fifth C bead on the petal. Sew back through the 2G just added and the same B on the picot from which the petal is being made (Figure 8).

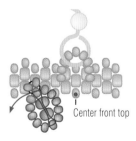

Center front top   **Figure 8**

Step 3: Sew through the closest B and 4C on the petal (Figure 9, red thread). String 3C. Skip the next C added in Step 1 (Figure 9, blue thread) and sew through the next 4C, the next B, and the same B on the picot from which this petal was made (Figure 9, purple thread). Move the thread to exit the next B on the picot (Figure 9, end of purple thread path).

Center front top

Figure 9

Petal #2
Repeat Steps 1 to 3 for the second petal. When complete, move the thread to exit the last B on the picot.

Petal #3
Repeat Steps 1 to 3 for the third petal. When complete, the thread will be exiting the same B on the picot from which the third petal was made (Figure 10).

Center front top

Figure 10

Stamens: String 3A and 1D, and bring them down to the beadwork. Skip the D just added and sew back through the 3A just added and the next B on the picot, forming a stamen; adjust the tension. Repeat 2 more times for a total of 3 stamens (Figure 11).

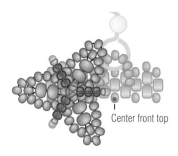

Center front top

Figure 11

Attach the petal to the bezel: Push the needle through the petal to exit the back of the petal. Sew the petal to the closest F bead on Row 1 of the bezel; tighten (Figure 12).

Figure 12

First leaf shape
Weave the thread around a bit in the bezel to exit the F bead on Row 2 that was used to make the bead loop on the other side from the flower, as shown in Figure 13, red dot bead.

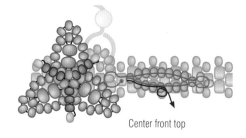

Center front top

Figure 13

Step 1: String 9B and 3D and bring the beads down to the bezel. Skip the 3D just strung, sew back through the last B added to form a picot, and adjust the tension. String 7B and sew through the first B of the 9 strung and through the F bead (red dot bead) on the bezel, forming a leaf; adjust the tension (Figure 13, red thread).

Step 2: Weave around in the bezel to reposition the thread in the leaf, exiting the fifth B added in Step 1. Sew through the closest A on the front of the bezel (the third A down from center top). Sew back through the same B on the leaf (Figure 13, blue thread); tighten.

Step 3: Sew around the leaf to exit the third B up from the end of the leaf. Shape the leaf as desired; then sew this B bead to the bezel. Weave back through the leaf shape to exit the same F from which the loop was made (Figure 13, red dot); then turn the thread around to exit the blue dot F bead as shown in Figure 14, beginning of red thread path.

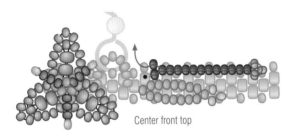

Center front top

Figure 14

Second leaf shape: String 13E and 3C and bring the beads down to the beadwork. Skip the 3C just added and sew back through 12E just added; tighten to form a picot on the end. String 1E and sew through the closest A on Round 6 on the back of the bezel (Figure 14); tighten.

Sew back through the same F from which the leaf was made (Figure 14, blue dot). Sew through 13E (Figure 15, red thread). Shape the leaf in a pleasing manner; then stitch it down in a couple of places (Figure 15, blue thread). Weave off this thread and trim it.

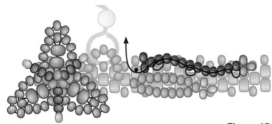

Figure 15

The left earring: Repeat the steps for embellishing the right earring. Make sure to place the flower on the right-hand side and the leaves on the left-hand side so it's a mirror image of the right earring.

TIME IN MOTION RING

A STEM TOPPED WITH A CZ RISES UP from an edge-stitched peyote band. You can't tell from a photograph, but around that stem, a circular piece beaded in peyote stitch, netting, and pearls rotates freely. Representing the moving parts of a pocket watch, this tiny ring revolves on its CZ-embellished stem as the wearer moves. The edge-stitched peyote-stitch band completes the ring.

Version #1

{ HISTORICAL PERSPECTIVE }

Willem van Aelst's *Floral Still Life with a Timepiece* (1663) is one of many paintings he produced showing timepieces, fine glassware, silver goblets, fruit, and cut flowers in luxurious and symbolic compositions. Cut flowers referred to the fleeting nature of life and the pocket watch reminded the viewer of the passing of time.

It wasn't until the sixteenth century that small clocks, known as watches, could be carried around on one's person, and the pocket watch was a technological novelty in van Aelst's time. These watches were quite large, worn on chains around the neck or on a girdle (a sort of belt made of chain) around the waist. Watches were a status symbol signifying wealth and authority, highly prized by their owners.

The earliest watches were poor timekeepers. However, by the seventeenth century, great changes were made in their movements, improving performance. The verge fusee style of watch had magnificent handmade moving parts and was considered among the best. Artisans and watchmakers worked together to hand-make accurate key-wound pocket watches enhanced with beautiful dials, magnificent gold and silver cases, enameled images, and gemstone work, making pocket watches small works of art.

Elizabeth I once said that she would give up all her possessions for a moment of time, and Aristotle stated that time is the measurable unit of movement, concerning a before and an after.

Flower Still Life with a Timepiece by Willem van Aelst

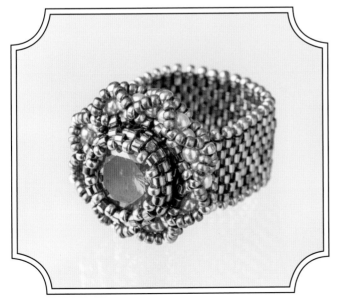

Version #1

Version #2

Dimensions

Top, ⅞ inch (2.2 cm) wide and ⅜ inch (1 cm) tall

Techniques

Edge-stitching

Netting

Peyote stitch, flat, even count

Peyote stitch, flat, odd-count technique called step-up/step-down

Peyote stitch, tubular, even count

Stitch-in-the-ditch

Skill Level

Intermediate

Materials, Version #1

1 rose 10-mm round CZ (custom coated)

1.5 g champagne galvanized 15° seed beads* (A)

0.5 g magenta galvanized 15° seed beads* (B)

2.5 g metallic golden olive iris 11° cylinder beads (C)

0.5 g champagne galvanized metallic 11° seed beads* (D)

26 antique ivory 2-mm Czech glass pearls

Beige nylon beading thread

1 x 1 inch (2.5 x 2.5 cm) piece of plastic kitchen wrap

1 x 1 inch (2.5 x 2.5 cm) piece of template plastic**

Materials, Version #2

1 white 10-mm round CZ

1.5 g platinum electroplate 15° seed beads (A)

0.5 g 24K gold electroplate 15° seed beads (B)

2.5 g platinum electroplate 11° cylinder beads (C)

0.5 g nickel silver electroplate 11° seed beads (D)

26 white 2-mm Czech glass pearls

Beige nylon beading thread

1 x 1 inch (2.5 x 2.5 cm) piece of plastic kitchen wrap

1 x 1 inch (2.5 x 2.5 cm) piece of template plastic**

*I used Duracoat galvanized seed beads

**Available at fabric and stenciling supply stores

Tools

2 size 12 beading needles

Beading awl

Office hole punch (to make a 6-mm hole)

Beader's supply kit (p. 5)

Instructions

Make the Ring Band

Odd-count flat peyote stitch, using a technique I call step-up/step-down peyote stitch, makes this strip a breeze to create. In this step, you merely begin the band; you'll finish making it as long as needed to fit your finger farther down the road.

Rows 1 & 2: Using 6 feet (1.8 m) of prepared thread (p. 6), string 8C, leaving a 6-inch (15.2 cm) tail.

Row 3: Without a bead on the needle, skip the last 2C strung and sew through the third-to-last C strung to make the first stitch (Figure 1); adjust the tension. Work flat peyote stitch (p. 9), using 1C in each stitch for 2 stitches. With 1C on the needle, sew through the first C of the original 8 strung (Figure 2).

Figure 1

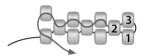

Figure 2

Row 4: Using 1C in each stitch, make 3 stitches (Figure 3).

Figure 3

Row 5: Using 1C in each stitch, make 2 stitches; using 1C, step down through the next 2C (Figure 4). Using 1C, step up through the closest 2C (Figure 5).

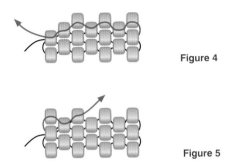

Figure 4

Figure 5

Note: Row 5 is complete, but the thread isn't at the beginning of the row. This is the trick: step-up/step-down odd-count flat peyote stitch begins now!

Rows 6 & 7: You'll alternate between rows.

Row 6: Using 1C in each stitch, make 2 stitches (Figure 6).

Figure 6

Row 7: Using 1C in each stitch, make 1 stitch (Figure 7, red thread).

Figure 7

Using 1C, make 1 stitch and step down (Figure 7, blue thread). *Back to Row 6:* Using 1C, make 1 stitch (Figure 7, green thread). *Back to Row 7:* Using 1C, make 1 stitch (Figure 8, red thread); using 1C, make 1 stitch and step up (Figure 8, blue thread).

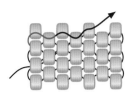

Figure 8

Rows 8 & 9: *Row 8:* Using 1C, make 1 stitch (Figure 9, red thread).

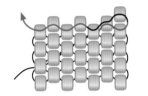

Figure 9

Row 9: Using 1C, make 1 stitch and step down (Figure 9, blue thread). *Back to Row 8:* Using 1C in each stitch, make 2 stitches (Figure 9, green thread). *Back to Row 9:* This is the end of the progression, so pay attention. Using 1C in each stitch, make 2 stitches (Figure 10, red thread); using 1C, make 1 stitch and step down (Figure 10, blue thread). Turn around (Figure 10, green thread).

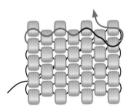

Figure 10

Okay, I know this seems crazy, but I'll explain what has happened! Since the beadwork is odd-count flat peyote, there would normally be a leftover bead at the end of each odd-numbered row, making the thread path a mess. Using the step-up/step-down peyote stitch technique eliminates this thread nightmare. Once you get used to it, you'll never go back.

Rows 10 and beyond: Repeat Rows 4 through 9 (Figures 3–10) until you have about 1 inch (2.5 cm) of beadwork. Weave off the tail thread and trim it, but keep the stitching thread. Set aside.

Bezel Stem

A 10-mm CZ embellishes the top of a stem that will eventually become the focal point of a beautiful beaded ring.

Bezel the CZ

This technique begins with flat peyote stitch strip that gets zipped into a tube. Working tubular peyote stitch on both sides, with a bead size change, creates a beautifully fitted bezel.

Rows 1 & 2: With 2 feet (61 cm) of prepared thread, string 27C, leaving an 8-inch (20.3 cm) tail.

Row 3: Without a bead on the needle, skip the last 2C strung and sew through the third-to-last C (Figure 11, red thread), making the first flat peyote stitch for this row; adjust the tension. Using 1C in each stitch, continue working flat peyote stitch for a total of 13C added in this row (Figure 11, blue thread).

Figure 11

Zip the strip: Put a needle onto the tail thread. Using both threads, zip the strip into a tube (p. 10 and Figure 12, red and blue threads). This needs to be tight and not twisted! The count is now 13 high and 13 low beads. From now on, you'll work in even-count tubular peyote stitch.

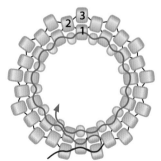

Figure 12

Round 4: This is the front of the bezel. With the tail thread, work tubular peyote stitch, using 1A in each stitch, for a total of 13A added; step up into the first A added in this round (p. 10 and Figure 12, green thread). Stitch this round really tight! Weave off the tail thread in the top 2 rounds, tightly, and trim. Place a 10-mm CZ onto the beadwork, with the flat faceted side of the stone touching this round (Figure 13).

Figure 13

Rounds 5 & 6: This is the back of the bezel. With the working thread, and with the CZ centered on the beadwork, stitch 2 rounds of tubular peyote stitch, using 1A in each stitch, for a total of 13A added in each round; step up at the end of each round through the first A added (Figure 14). Keep this tight!

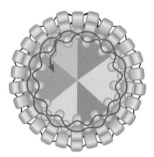

Figure 14

Add the stem

A tubular peyote stitch stem acts as the pivoting point for the revolving component.

Round 7. Two-row decreases—the skips: *Work tubular peyote stitch using 1A in each stitch for 2 stitches; without a bead on the needle, sew through the next A on Round 5 and the next A on Round 6, creating the skip (p. 12 and Figure 15, red thread). Repeat from * 2 more times, ending by making

3 stitches with 1A in each. Skip and step up by sewing through the closest A on Round 5, the next A on Round 6, and the first A added in this round (Figure 15, end of red thread path). There are 4 skips in this round.

Figure 15

Round 8. Completing the decreases—1 over the skips:
*Work tubular peyote stitch using 1C, make 1 stitch; using 1C, sew through the next A added in Round 7, placing 1 over the skips (Figure 15, blue thread). Repeat from * 2 more times, make 2 stitches using 1C in each stitch. Using 1C, sew through the next A added on Round 7 and the first C added on this round, placing one over the skips; step up (Figure 15, end of blue thread path). A total of 9C was added in this round. The beadwork will roll out a bit.

Rounds 9–12: Work 4 rounds of tubular even-count peyote stitch, using 1C in each stitch for a total of 9C added in each round; step up into the first C added in each round. Set aside.

Revolving Component
Using a combination of peyote stitch and netting, this component is created separately, then placed on the stem.

Rows 1 & 2: With 3 feet (91.4 cm) of prepared thread, string 33C, leaving a 6-inch (15.2 cm) tail.

Row 3: Without a bead on the needle, skip the last 2C strung; sew through the third-to-last C added and adjust the tension. Work flat peyote stitch, using 1C in each, for 15 more stitches, for a total of 16C added in this row.

Zip: Put a needle onto the tail thread. Using both threads, zip the strip into a tube. This needs to be tight and not twisted! The count is now 16 high and 16 low beads and even-count tubular peyote stitch. Weave off the tail thread and trim.

Round 4: *String 3A and sew through the next C on Row 3, forming a picot (p. 8). Weave forward through the next C on Row 2 and the next C of Row 3. Repeat from * 7 more times for a total of 8 picots (Figure 16, red thread), but after making the last picot, exit diagonally through a C on Row 1, making sure the C the thread is exiting aligns with a C that was used for making the first picot on Round 3 (Figure 16, beginning of blue thread path). Push the picots up at a right angle to the component base as you work.

Figure 16

Round 5: Repeat Round 4 on this side of the component, pushing the picots up at a right angle to the base as you work. Step up through the second A added in this round. Set the beadwork aside.

Pearls: With 1 foot (30.5 cm) of prepared thread, string 26 pearls and center them on the thread. Wrap the strand around the beaded component, between the picots, and tie an overhand knot (p. 17) to form a tight ring; adjust the pearls so a pearl aligns with each set of picots (Figure 17). Secure the working thread by sewing through the pearls in one direction; secure the tail thread by sewing through the pearls in the opposite direction. Trim both threads.

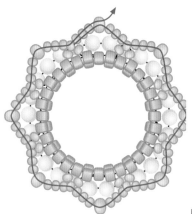

Figure 17

Add the netted edge to the revolving component

Round 6: Using the remaining working thread, work netting (p. 8), string 3B, 1D, and 3B; sew through the middle A of the next Round 5 picot (Figure 17); repeat 7 more times for a total of 8 nets; step up through the first 3A and the D added in this round (Figure 17, end of red thread path).

Round 7: String 3B and pass through the middle A of the nearest picot on the opposite side (Figure 18). String 3B and pass through the middle D of the Round 6 net (Figure 18); repeat 7 more times to connect all the nets and picots. You must work tightly as this connection needs tension to look good. Secure the thread by weaving through the netting rounds to tighten; then trim. Set the ring aside.

Figure 18

Prepare the stem for attachment to the ring band: Using the end of a pen or awl, push a 1-inch (2.5 cm) square of plastic wrap into the opening of the bezel stem (Figure 19).

Figure 19

Using the hole punch, cut 6 circles out of the template plastic. Using the end of an awl, push them into the opening of the bezel stem until they're just shy of the top edge of the stem (Figure 20).

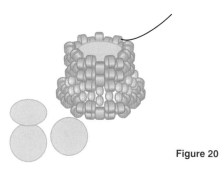

Figure 20

Attach the bezel stem to the ring band: Place a needle onto the remaining thread attached to the bezel stem. Pass the needle through the hole in the rotating component; mount the component on the bezel stem (Figure 21). Place the band over the end of the bezel stem (Figure 22).

Figure 21

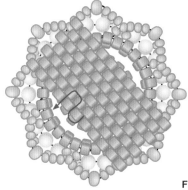

Figure 22

Sew Round 12 (the last round) of the bezel stem to the band, working in and out of the C beads without using any C beads on the edges of the band (Figure 22).

Add support to the base of the bezel stem: Move the thread up 1 round to Round 11 on the bezel stem (Figure 23, beginning of red thread path; this figure is shown without the rotating component for clarity). *Stitch-in-the-ditch using 3A on the needle, sew through the next C on Round 11 of the bezel stem to create a picot (Figure 23). Repeat from * 8 more times for a total of 9 picots. Weave off this thread and trim.

Figure 23

Finish the ring band

Place a needle onto the remaining thread on the ring band. Continue adding rows of peyote stitch to one side until when it is placed on your finger, and with the ends pressed together, the ends meet. If you have to stop working step up/step down in the middle of a progression, just finish a row, then weave the thread over to an end to stitch a regular row or two. The beginning end of the strip and the end being extended have to fit as shown in Figure 24.

Zip the ends: Wrap the ends of the strip around to just touch. Before you zip the band, make sure to try on your ring! If it fits, zip the ends, then move on to the edge-stitching described below; if not, add or subtract rows as needed.

Step 1: Using the thread attached to the extended end of the strip, sew into a C on the beginning end of the strip; sew out through the same C on the extended side of the strip; then sew through the C on the beginning of the strip (p. 11 and Figure 24, beginning of red thread path); adjust the tension.

Step 2: Hold the beadwork together; sew through the next C on the extended side, then through the next C on the beginning side. Continue as shown in Figure 24.

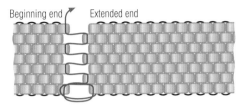

Figure 24

Step 3: Repeat Step 1 on this edge to complete the zip. Try on your ring. If all is well, rework this connection to secure, exiting any C on either edge (Figure 25).

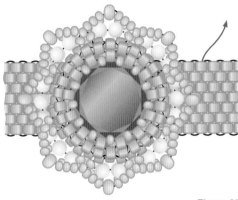

Figure 25

Edge-stitch the ring band: Work edge-stitching using 1A in each stitch, tucking the needle under the closest piece of thread on the outside edge of the ring band; adjust the tension (p. 11 and Figure 26, beginning of red thread path). Continue around one edge of the strip. End with 1A on the needle and sew into the first C exited at the start of this step (Figure 26, red thread arrow). Weave over to the other side and repeat. Weave off the thread and trim.

Figure 26

LABYRINTH BRACELET

A FLAT PEYOTE-STITCHED, MARQUISE-SHAPED CENTRAL COMPONENT is embellished with a crystal-and-pearl right-angle-weave variation for added sparkle. A stiff product called SilverSilk Leather Capture is used to create the bracelet portion of this design, giving the bracelet the feel and structure of a bangle. Beaded components lead to the graceful clasp, making this design not only beautiful but a pleasure to wear.

Version #1

HISTORICAL PERSPECTIVE

In Greek mythology, Ariadne was the fertility goddess of Crete who was transformed into a mortal human. The daughter of King Minos of Crete, she became known in history as the keeper of labyrinths—those complicated networks of passages or paths in which it is easy to get lost—and the bearer of the thread ball that her lover, Theseus, used to find his way out of the Minotaur's labyrinth.

John William Waterhouse (1849–1917) painted the mythological Ariadne, showing his passion for strong and beautiful female figures. In this painting, he portrays her despairing over the loss of her lover, who sails away, leaving her behind. For me, this painting is all about subject matter, beauty, and detail, a typical example of John Waterhouse's gorgeous Pre-Raphaelite style.

My inspiration for this bracelet came from thinking about the labyrinth and what it meant to me in beadwork. Right-angle weave came to mind, as it has the characteristics of circling around and not knowing where to go next! In this case, crystals hold small pearls within their right-angle-weave walls, making this stitch combination feel like being in a labyrinth at times, but with elegant results.

Ariadne by John William Waterhouse

Dimensions

¾ x 7½ inches (1.9 x 19 cm)

Techniques

Edge-stitching

Peyote stitch, flat, even count

Peyote stitch, tubular, even count with decreasing

Peyote stitch, flat, odd count with decreasing

Peyote stitch, flat, odd-count technique called step-up/step-down

Right-angle weave variation

Stitch-in-the-ditch

Skill Level

Intermediate advanced

Materials, Version #1

0.5 g 24-karat white gold metallic 15° seed beads (A)

2 g nickel-plated 11° cylinder beads (B)

4 g 24-karat white gold metallic 11° seed beads (C)

55 crystal AB 2-mm round crystals

9 white 3-mm crystal pearls

30 to 40 inches (76 cm to 1 m) of 2.8-mm SilverSilk Leather Capture in silver wire/black leather*

16 inches (40.6 cm) of 28-gauge nontarnish craft wire in hematite

Gray nylon beading thread

3 feet (91.4 cm) of 4-lb. test crystal polyethylene beading thread**

1 black rhodium clasp with a bar, ¾ inch (1.9 cm) wide***

Materials, Version #2

0.5 g metallic gold iris 15° seed beads (A)

2 g metallic gold iris 11° cylinder beads (B)

4 g metallic gold iris 11° seed beads (C)

55 crystal AB 2-mm round crystals

9 cream 3-mm crystal pearls

30 to 40 inches (76 cm to 1m) of 2.8-mm SilverSilk Leather Capture in gold wire/brown leather*

16 inches (40.6 cm) of 28-gauge nontarnish craft wire in gold

Dark brown nylon beading thread

3 feet (91.4 cm) of 4-lb. test crystal polyethylene beading thread**

1 antique gold clasp with a bar, ¾ inch (1.9 cm) wide ***

*SilverSilk Leather is a knitted wire tube knit around smooth leather cording. It's sold by the yard or packaged in 1-yard (91.4 cm) lengths. The length you'll need is determined by your wrist size.

** I prefer FireLine

*** See Figure 20 for style of clasp.

Tools

2 size 12 beading needles

1 glass-headed straight pin or size 10 beading needle

1 size 24 tapestry needle

Small craft scissors (for cutting fishing line)

Flush wire cutter

Beader's supply kit (p. 5)

Version #1 (right), Version #2 (left)

Version #2

Instructions

Prepare the SilverSilk Leather Capture. This is a really awesome product. A machine-knit tube surrounds a leather cord, making for a structurally sound product that is great fun to play with.

Measure around your wrist without adding any ease. Using flush cutters, measure and cut 5 pieces of SilverSilk exactly as long as your wrist measurement.

Wire one end of the SilverSilk Leather Capture: Using flush cutters, cut 8 inches (20.3 cm) of craft wire; thread it onto a tapestry needle. Align all the ends of the SilverSilk flush with each other, with the curves of the cording going the same way. Leaving a tail 1½ inches (3.8 cm) long, sew under the mesh of all the strands, but not into the leather, ¼ inch (6 mm) away from the ends (Figure 1).

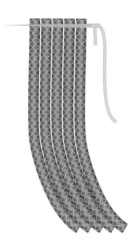

Figure 1

Wrap the wire around to the other side; sew under the mesh, not into the leather, of all 5 strands, ¼ inch (6 mm) away from the ends one more time. Adjust the tension so it's snug but not tight. *Tip:* A great tool for gripping and pulling needles and wire is a little piece of flexible rubber tubing.

The strands should be snug next to each other without overlapping. Repeat the wrapping technique once more; then twist the ends of the wire together to secure; trim ¼ inch (6 mm) away from the wrap (Figure 2). Set aside.

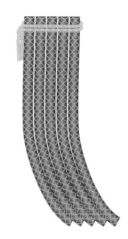

Figure 2

Create the Closure

Peyote stitch is used to create beautiful cones, on each end of the bracelet. Created as a flat strip, the piece is zipped into tubular peyote stitch. The tube is then zipped closed and extended to wrap around the bar of the clasp. Make 2.

Rows 1 & 2: Using 4 feet (1.2 m) of prepared thread (p. 6), string 29C, leaving an 18-inch (45.7 cm) tail.

Row 3: Without a bead on the needle, skip the last 2C strung; sew back through the C to make the first stitch (Figure 3, red thread); adjust the tension. Work flat peyote stitch (p. 9) using 1C for each stitch; make 13 stitches for a total of 14C added in this row (Figure 3, blue thread).

Figure 3

Zip the ends of the strip to create tubular peyote stitch: This technique turns flat peyote stitch to tubular. Place a needle onto the tail thread. Wrap the strip around your finger or a step gauge. With the longer thread, sew through the closest C bead on Row 3, the next C on Row 2, and the next C on Row 3. With the tail thread, sew through the closest C bead on Row 1, the next C on Row 2, and the next C on Row 1 (p. 10 and Figure 4). Remove the needle from the tail thread; tighten the beadwork. The count is now 14 high and 14 low beads.

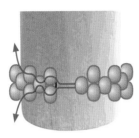

Figure 4

Rounds 4–7: Using the longer thread, work 3 rounds of tubular peyote stitch using 1C in each stitch, making 14 stitches in each round and stepping up into the first C added at the end of each round (p. 10).

Round 8. Four-row decreases—the skip: Work tubular peyote stitch using 1C in each stitch, make 6 stitches. Without a bead on the needle, sew through the next C from Row 6 and the next C from Round 7, creating the skip (Figure 5). Using 1C in each stitch, make 6 stitches, then skip and step up (p. 13 and Figure 6).

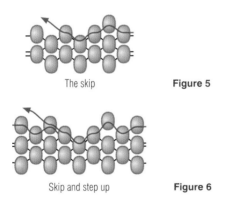

The skip   **Figure 5**

Skip and step up   **Figure 6**

Round 9. Place 2 over the skip: Work tubular peyote stitch using 1C in each stitch; make 5 stitches. With 2C on the needle, sew through the closest C on Round 8, placing 2 over the skip (Figure 7). Using 1C in each stitch, make 5 stitches. With 2C on the needle, place 2 over the skip and step up (Figure 8).

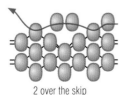

2 over the skip   **Figure 7**

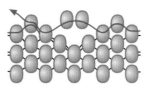

2 over the skip and step up   **Figure 8**

Round 10. Treat 2 as 1: Work tubular peyote stitch using 1C in each stitch; make 4 stitches. Using 1C, sew through the 2C over the skip, treating 2 as 1 (Figure 9). Using 1C in each stitch, make 5 stitches. Using 1C, sew through the 2 over the skip, treating 2 as 1. Using 1C, make 1 stitch and step up into the first C added in this round. *Tip:* The decreases are going to shape the cone on the sides, so squeeze the shape as in Figure 10.

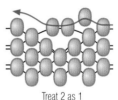

Treat 2 as 1   **Figure 9**

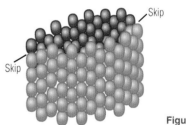

Skip

Skip

Figure 10

Round 11. 1 over 2: Work tubular peyote stitch using 1C in each stitch; make 4 stitches. Using 1C, sew through the next C on Round 10, placing 1 over 2 at the corner (Figure 11). Using 1C in each stitch, make 5 stitches. Using 1C, sew through the next C on Round 10, placing 1 over 2 at the corner. Using 1C, make 1 stitch and step up into the first C added in this round.

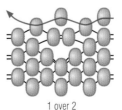

1 over 2   **Figure 11**

Row 12: Move the thread forward to exit the first C bead on Round 11, past a corner (Figure 12, red thread). Work flat peyote stitch using 1C in each stitch; make 4 stitches (Figure 12, blue thread).

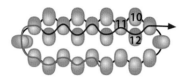

Figure 12

Zip the ends of the cone shape together

Step 1: Sew through the closest C bead on the opposite side (Round 11) of the cone. Sew back through the same C bead just exited (Round 11); then sew back through the opposite C bead (Round 11), as shown in Figure 13, red thread; adjust the tension.

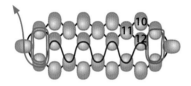

Figure 13

Step 2: Sew through the last C added on Round 12 to begin the zip (p. 11); then sew through the next C on Round 11; keep zipping across the top of the cone, adjusting the tension as you go (Figure 13, blue thread).

Step 3: To secure the last 2 beads, circle the thread around (Figure 13, green thread). Move the thread to exit the C sitting at the top of the decrease on the side of the cone (Figure 13, green thread arrow) to position the thread for the next step.

Add the flat peyote-stitch strip for the clasp

A strip of odd-count step-up/step-down flat peyote stitch wraps around the bar of the beautiful clasp for a fabulous ending. Step-up/step-down peyote stitch gets rid of the thread turnarounds, thread catches, and what I call "homeless" beads, making odd-count peyote stitch a breeze to stitch.

Row 1: Work stitch-in-the-ditch (p. 12). Using 1C, sew through the closest C bead added on Row 12 of the cone, pulling tightly to pull the side bead snug up against the C bead just added (Figure 14, beginning of red thread path). Continue to stitch-in-the-ditch, using 1C in each stitch for 3 more stitches. Using 1C, sew through the closest C bead sitting at the top of the decrease on the side of the cone and back through the last C bead added on the stitch-in-the-ditch row (Figure 14, red thread); tighten.

Figure 14

Row 2: Using 1C in each stitch, make 4 stitches. Sew through the closest C bead at the top of the decrease (Figure 14, blue thread). Turn around with the thread to exit the first C added in the stitch-in-the-ditch row of Row 1, as shown in Figure 14, green thread.

Row 3: Using 1C in each stitch, make 3 stitches (Figure 15, red thread). Using 1C, step down through the next 2C (Figure 15, blue thread). Using 1C, step up through the closest 2C (Figure 15, green thread). *Note:* Row 3 is complete, but the thread isn't at the beginning of the row. Step-up/step-down flat odd-count peyote stitch begins now!

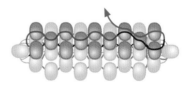

Figure 15

Rows 4 & 5: *Row 4:* Using 1C in each stitch, make 3 stitches (Figure 16, red thread). *Row 5:* Using 1C in each stitch, make 2 stitches. Using 1C, make 1 stitch and step down (Figure 16, blue thread). *Back to Row 4:* Using 1C, make 1 stitch (Figure 16, green thread). *Back to Row 5:* Using 1C in each stitch, make 2 stitches and step up (Figure 16, purple thread).

Figure 16

Rows 6 & 7: *Row 6*: Using 1C in each stitch, make 2 stitches (Figure 17, red thread). *Row 7*: Using 1C in each stitch, make 2 stitches and step down (Figure 17, blue thread). *Back to Row 6*: Using 1C in each stitch, make 2 stitches (Figure 17, green thread). *Back to Row 7*: Using 1C in each stitch, make 3 stitches and step up (Figure 17, purple thread).

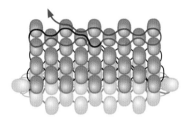

Figure 17

Rows 8 & 9: *Row 8*: Using 1C, make 1 stitch (Figure 18, red thread). *Row 9*: Using 1C, make 1 stitch and step down (Figure 18, blue thread). *Back to Row 8*: Using 1C in each stitch, make 3 stitches (Figure 18, green thread). *Back to Row 8*: This is the end of the progression so pay attention, as the thread path is different. Using 1C in each stitch, make 3 stitches (Figure 19, red thread). Using 1C, make 1 stitch; then step down and turn around (Figure 19, blue thread).

Figure 18

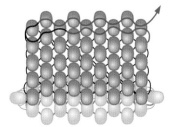

Figure 19

Row 10: Using 1C in each stitch, make 4 stitches (Figure 19, green thread).

Add the clasp: Disconnect the two halves of the clasp. Slip the peyote-stitch strip through the bar on one half of the clasp (Figure 20). Roll the strip around the bar, bringing Row 10 to meet Row 1 on the back.

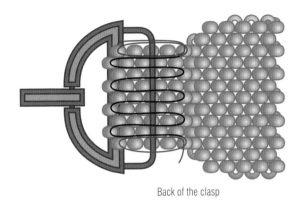

Back of the clasp

Figure 20

Zip the strip closed around the clasp bar

Step 1: Sew through the closest C bead on Row 1 of the strip; then sew back through the same C bead just exited. Sew back through the same Row 1 C bead (Figure 20, red thread); adjust the tension.

Step 2: Sew through the last C added on Row 10 to begin the zip; then sew through the next C on Row 1; keep zipping, adjusting the tension as you go (Figure 20, blue thread).

Step 3: To secure the last 2 Cs on the edge, circle the thread around them as in Step 1 (Figure 20, exiting as in the end of the green thread).

Add edge-stitching (p. 11): Using 1C, tuck the needle underneath the closest edge thread (Figure 21); adjust the tension. Repeat around the end of the strip for a total of 5C added. Weave across the strip to exit any edge C on the other side and repeat the edge stitching. Weave off this thread and trim.

Make 1 more cone clasp (Figure 22).

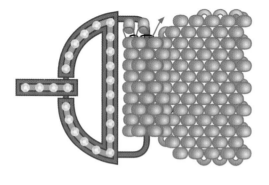

Figure 21

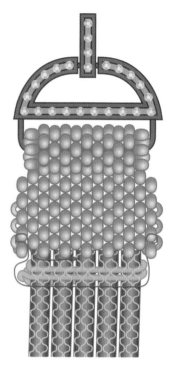

Figure 24

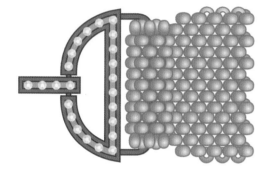

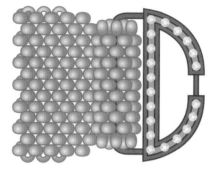

Figure 22

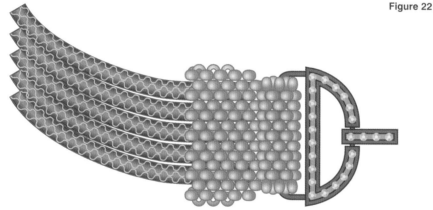

Figure 23

Step 2: Place a needle onto the remaining thread attached to the cone/ clasp. Move the thread around to exit any C bead on Row 3 that is close to the side of the cone. Push the needle to the inside of the cone, right where the thread is exiting. Pull back the SilverSilk and sew through some of the mesh of each cord below the wire wrapping (Figure 24); adjust the tension a bit.

Step 3: From the inside, push the needle through the side of the cone right around Row 3. Sew through a C bead on Row 3 close to the side of the cone. Push the needle to the inside of the cone, right where the thread is exiting (Figure 24).

Attach a Cone

The bracelet needs to be finished before you add the center component; that way, you can center the component properly.

Step 1: Slide 1 cone/clasp component onto the end of the wired SilverSilk, making sure that the front of the clasp is positioned along the outside, not the inside, of the curve of the SilverSilk (Figure 23).

Step 4: On the other side of the SilverSilk, sew through some of the mesh of each cord below the wire-wrapping; push the needle from the inside to the outside of the cone to exit close to a Row 3 bead on the side of the cone. Sew through a C bead on Row 3 close to the side of the cone.

Step 5. Decreasing—the skip: Using your fingers, flatten the cone against the SilverSilk front and back. Move the thread to exit a C bead on Row 1 of the cone just past the corner (Figure 25, bead marked 1). Work tubular peyote stitch, snugly, using 1A in each stitch, for 6 stitches. Without a bead on the needle, sew through the next C on Row 2 and the next C on Row 1, making a skip at the corner (Figure 25, red thread).

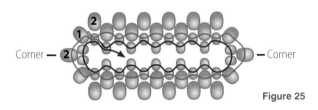

Figure 25

Using 1A in each stitch, make 6 stitches; without a bead on the needle, sew through the next C on Row 2, the next C on Row 1, and the first A added in this round, making a skip, and step up at the corner (Figure 25, end of red thread path).

Step 6. Decreasing—Place 2 over the skip: Work tubular peyote stitch, snugly, using 1A in each stitch, make 5 stitches; using 2A, place 2 over the skip by sewing through the closest A bead from Step 5 (Figure 25, blue thread). Using 1A in each stitch, make 5 stitches. With 2A, place 2 over the skip and step up by sewing through the closest A from Step 5 and the first A added in this round (Figure 25, end of blue thread path). Keep the thread.

Attach the SilverSilk to the base of the cone: Using the remaining thread attached to the cone, and exiting any A bead from Step 6, sew the opposite direction from the thread exiting this bead to catch a tiny bit of wire on a cord. Sew back through the same bead from behind; adjust the tension. Weave forward through the next A from Step 5 and

the next A from Step 6. Repeat the attachment 11 more times around the base of the cone (Figure 26). Weave off the thread and trim.

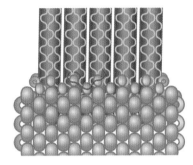

Figure 26

Prepare the SilverSilk for the other cone/clasp: The completed cone/clasp connection is 2¼ inches (5.7 cm) long. Due to the length of the cone/clasp, the amount of SilverSilk being sewn into the ends of the cones, and the fact that there needs to be a bit of ease in the bracelet, I've found that very little of the SilverSilk needs to be trimmed off this end. The bracelet looks more like a bangle when clasped, which looks great.

Wrap the bracelet around something round with a bigger circumference than your bracelet (a tub of hand cream, for example). Shape the beadwork around the circumference of your form, straighten the cords, and then place a needle through all 5 cords, catching the mesh, ½ inch (1.3 cm) up from the end (Figure 27). Also place another needle in the back.

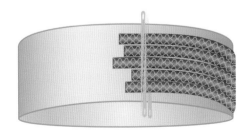

Figure 27

Test the fit by attaching the clasp ends together and wrapping the bracelet around your wrist, overlapping the clasp to match up to the needle markers and approximately where the SilverSilk would be connected to the clasp. The central component will not affect the size of your bracelet, so you need to decide now whether you want more ease or not. If you want more ease, move your needles out a bit, if less, move the needles in.

Wire the other end of the SilverSilk Leather Capture: Thread the remaining 8 inches (20.3 cm) of craft wire onto a tapestry needle. Right behind the needle, sew under the mesh, not the leather, of all 5 strands, leaving a tail 1½ inches (3.8 cm) long. Remove the needle on this side. Wrap the wire around to the other side close to the needle and sew under the mesh, not the leather, of all 5 strands. Adjust the tension to be snug but not too tight; remove the needles.

The strands should be snug beside each other without overlapping. Repeat the wrapping technique again; then wrap the 2 ends of the wire together to secure. Trim wire ends ¼ inch (6 mm) away from the wrap. Trim the SilverSilk ⅛ inch (3 mm) away from the wire-wrapping.

Attach the other cone/clasp: The attachment of this cone/clasp is done exactly like the first side. Repeat "Attach one cone/clasp component" and "Attach the SilverSilk to the base of the cone."

The base of the center component

Flat peyote stitch, with decreasing on the edges, creates a lovely marquise shape. An added strap makes the connection to the bracelet.

Rows 1 & 2: Using 4 feet (1.2 m) of prepared thread, string 22B, leaving an 18-inch (45.7 cm) tail.

Row 3: Without a bead on the needle, skip the last 2B strung. Sew back through the third B (Figure 28, red thread); adjust the tension. Work flat peyote stitch using 1B for each stitch to make 9 more stitches (Figure 28, blue thread). Using 1B, sew through the remaining B bead on the tail thread, as shown in Figure 28, end of blue thread,

adjust the tension and your hold on the beadwork. The thread is now exiting the same B bead as the tail thread. A total of 11B were added in this row.

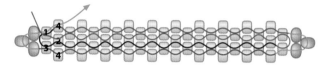

Figure 28

Row 4, for one side: With the longer thread, work flat peyote stitch, using 1B in each stitch, making 10 stitches (Figure 28, green thread). With 3C on the needle, sew through the closest B bead on the edge (Row 3), as shown in Figure 28, orange thread, making a picot.

Row 4, for the other side: With the longer thread, work flat peyote stitch, using 1B in each stitch, making 10 stitches (Figure 28, purple thread). With 3C on the needle, sew through the closest B bead on the edge (Row 1) and through the first B bead added in Row 4 on the first side, as shown in Figure 28, lime green thread, making a picot.

Okay, back to working on only one side.

Row 5: With the longer thread, work flat peyote stitch, using 1B in each stitch, making 9 stitches (Figure 29, red thread). Decrease on the edge by tucking the needle under the thread between the bead that the thread is exiting and the next bead on the edge; adjust the tension; then step up through the closest 2B to exit the last B added in this row (Figure 29, blue thread). I call this technique of decreasing on the edge tuck and turn (p. 18).

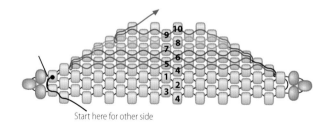

Start here for other side

Figure 29

Row 6: Work flat peyote stitch, using 1B in each stitch, making 8 stitches; tuck and turn (Figure 29, green thread).

Row 7: Work flat peyote stitch, using 1B in each stitch, making 7 stitches; tuck andturn (Figure 29, purple thread).

Row 8: Work flat peyote stitch using 1B in each stitch, making 6 stitches; tuck and turn (Figure 29, orange thread).

Row 9: Work flat peyote stitch, using 1B in each stitch, making 5 stitches; tuck and turn (Figure 29, turquoise thread).

Row 10: Work flat peyote stitch, using 1B in each stitch, making 4 stitches; tuck and turn (Figure 29, magenta thread).

Row 11: Work flat peyote stitch, using 1B in each stitch, making 3 stitches; tuck and turn (Figure 30, red thread).

Figure 30

Row 12: Work flat peyote stitch, using 1B in each stitch, making 2 stitches; tuck and turn (Figure 30, blue thread). Secure this area by weaving around to stabilize, exiting as in Figure 30, green thread. String 3C and sew through the other Row 12 B bead, forming a picot (Figure 31, blue thread).

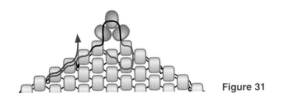

Figure 31

Set up the thread: Sew through the next 3B on the edge (Figure 31, green thread), turn around the thread by tucking the needle under the thread right where the thread is exiting the beadwork; then sew back through last 2B bead just exited (Figure 31, purple thread).

Rows 5 through 12 for the other side: Place a needle onto the tail thread; step up through the closest B bead (Row 3) and the closest B bead (Row 4), as shown in Figure 29, marked as the starting point. Repeat Rows 5 through 12. Weave off the tail thread around the outside edge of the shape and trim.

Add the step up/step down strip to the central component
A stitch-in-the-ditch (p. 12) start sets us up for step-up/step-down peyote stitch for a small strip that will zip to itself around the bracelet.

Row 1: Work stitch-in-the-ditch using 1B in each stitch, making 3 stitches (Figure 32, red thread).

Row 2: Work step up/step down using 1B in each stitch, making 3 stitches, and step down (Figure 32, blue thread). Using 1B, make 1 stitch and step up (Figure 32, green thread).

Rows 3 & 4: *Row 3*: Using 1B in each stitch, make 2 stitches

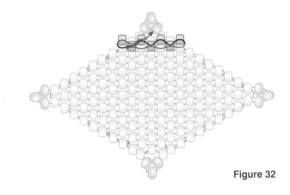

Figure 32

(Figure 33, red thread). *Row 4*: Using 1B in each stitch, make 2 stitches and step down (Figure 33, blue thread). *Back to Row 3*: Using 1B, make 1 stitch (Figure 33, purple thread). *Back to Row 4*: Using 1B in each stitch, make 2 stitches and step up (Figure 33, green thread).

Figure 33

Rows 5 & 6: *Row 5:* Using 1B, make 1 stitch (Figure 34, red thread). *Row 6:* Using 1B, make 1 stitch and step down (Figure 34, blue thread). *Back to Row 5:* Using 1B in each stitch, make 2 stitches (Figure 34, orange thread). *Back to Row 6:* This is the end of progression, so pay attention, as the thread path is different. Using 1B in each stitch, make 3 stitches and step down and turn around (Figure 34, green thread).

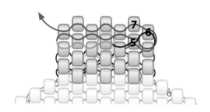

Figure 34

Row 7: Using 1B in each stitch, make 3 stitches (Figure 34, purple thread).

Repeat Rows 2 through 7 until you have 22 rows. The last pattern repeat won't be complete. Keep the thread. Set aside.

The pearl and crystal embellishment

A beautiful right-angle-weave (p. 14) variation adds a pearl to the center of each cell, creating a pavé-style component. *Note: Pavé* is a jewelry term for a setting filled with stones placed so closely together that the metal hardly shows.

As you probably already know, because of the sharp edges in their holes, crystals can be treacherous to your thread. Tighten the stitches gently and always in the direction that the thread is exiting the crystal.

Row 1

Cell 1: Using 4 feet (1.2 m) of prepared polyethylene fishing line, string 8 crystals, leaving a 6-inch (15.2 cm) tail. Rethread through the first 5 crystals (Figure 35, red thread); adjust the tension gently. String 1 pearl, skip the next 3 crystals, and sew through the fourth crystal (Figure 35, blue thread); nestle the pearl gently into the center of the cell. Sew back through the pearl and the same crystal used to add the pearl, as shown in Figure 35 (green thread); adjust the tension gently.

Figure 35

Cell 2: String 7 crystals. Sew through the same crystal the thread is exiting; adjust the tension gently. Add 1 pearl to the center of this cell, as in Cell 1. Sew through the next 4 crystals (Figure 36, red thread).

Figure 36

Cell 3: String 7 crystals. Sew through the same crystal the thread is exiting; adjust the tension gently. Add 1 pearl to the center of this cell as in Cell 2; adjust the tension gently. Sew through 2 crystals (Figure 36, blue thread).

Row 2

Cell 1: String 7 crystals. Sew through the same crystal the thread is exiting; adjust the tension gently. Sew forward through 2 crystals. Add 1 pearl to the center of this cell. Sew through 4 crystals (Figure 37, red thread).

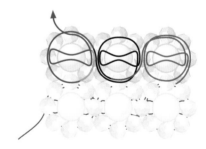

Figure 37

Cell 2: String 1 crystal. Sew through the top crystal of Row 1, Cell 2 (Figure 37, purple thread); adjust the tension. String 5 crystals; sew through the Row 2, cell 1 crystal from which this cell was started and adjust the tension. Add 1 pearl to the center of this cell. Sew through 4 crystals (Figure 37, blue thread).

Cell 3: String 5 crystals. Sew through the top crystal of Row 1, Cell 1; adjust the tension (Figure 37, green thread). String 1 crystal; sew through the Row 2, Cell 2 crystal from which this cell was started (Figure 37, orange thread) and adjust the tension. Add 1 pearl to the center of this cell. Sew through 2 crystals (Figure 37, green thread).

Row 3

Cell 1: String 7 crystals; sew through the same crystal the thread is exiting. Adjust the tension gently. Sew forward through 2 crystals. Add 1 pearl to the center of this cell. Sew through 4 crystals (Figure 38, red thread).

Figure 38

Cell 2: String 1 crystal; sew through the top crystal of Row 2, Cell 2. Adjust the tension gently. String 5 crystals; sew through the Row 3, Cell 1 crystal from which this cell was started and adjust the tension. Add 1 pearl to the center of this cell. Sew through 4 crystals (Figure 38, blue thread).

Cell 3: String 5 crystals. Sew through the top crystal of Row 2, Cell 1. Adjust the tension gently. String 1 crystal; sew through the Row 3, Cell 2 crystal from which this cell was started and adjust the tension. Add 1 pearl to the center of this cell. Sew through 2 crystals (Figure 38, green thread). Weave off the tail thread and trim.

Add the pavé embellishment to the surface of the central component: Center the pavé embellishment on the front of the central component (Figure 39). Gently sew 1 to 2 crystals of each cell, along the outside edge, to the central component, plus make a couple of attachments through the interior of the crystal shape (Figure 40). Weave off this thread and trim.

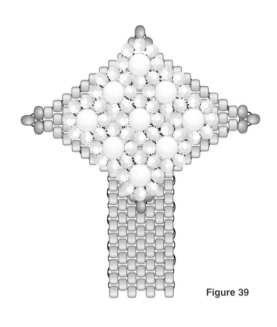

Figure 39

Figure 40

Zip the strip on the central component around the bracelet: Before we get started, the thread has to be moved. Place a needle onto the thread attached to the central component and move the thread into position, as shown in Figure 41, red thread path. Wrap the component around the bracelet at about the middle, with the embellishment at the top.

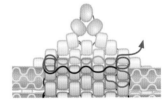

Figure 41

Step 1: Bring the end of the strip on the component around to touch the back edge of the marquise-shaped base as in Figure 41. Off the end of the strip, work flat peyote stitch, using 1B in each stitch, to make 3 stitches (Figure 41, blue thread).

Step 2: Looking at the back of the marquise-shaped central component, count down one edge of the component by 3B. This is the stitch-in-the-ditch row onto which the strip will be zipped. Keep your eye on the prize as here we go!

Step 3: Sew through the third B down from the picot. Sew back through the same B bead just exited. Sew back through the same B on the component (p. 11 and Figure 41, green thread).

Step 4: Sew through the closest B on the last row of the strip, then through the next B on the base. Continue to zip the beadwork together across the row (Figure 41, orange thread), ending by sewing the edge beads together as in Step 3 (Figure 41, purple thread).

Getting the right placement: Before we edge-stitch the strip and sew it to the SilverSilk bracelet, we need to get the right placement. Open the hinge on the clasp; put on the bracelet with the working portion of the clasp in your hand, and the portion of the clasp on the side of your wrist in line with your thumb. You're probably wondering why I'm being so particular. Well, one of my pet peeves on commercial bracelets with a stationary central embellishment is that the component is centered, so that during wear either the component is centered and the clasp isn't, or vice versa. I prefer both to be centered. This is how I do it.

With your bracelet on your wrist, as explained above, center the component on the top of your wrist. Take off the bracelet and reinforce the zipper, exiting the third B bead down from the picot (Figure 42, beginning of red thread path).

Edge-Stitch and Attach the Strip to the SilverSilk

Before we begin, make sure that the component is straight and the SilverSilk is smooth and even.

String 1A and tuck the needle under the closest piece of thread on the edge of the strip; adjust the tension. String 1A, tuck the needle under the next piece of thread on the edge of the strip, and adjust the tension (p. 11 and Figure 42).

Tuck the needle under a tiny bit of SilverSilk mesh and back under the same edge thread that the thread is currently exiting (Figure 42, red thread); adjust the tension. Repeat the edge stitching along the edge of the strip, hooking into SilverSilk when it can be done; end by stringing 1A and sewing through the third B bead down from the picot on the base.

Weave over to the other edge and repeat the edge stitching and attaching the SilverSilk down this side. Weave off the thread and trim.

Figure 42

AMALIE'S PEARL NECKLACE

A PEYOTE-STITCHED THREE-DIMENSIONAL SQUARE holds a string of crystals in the channel and is the basis of a unique approach for a bezel that frames a beautiful cushion-cut CZ. The CZ sparkles on a necklace of pearls stitched in a hexagonal weave variation. The pear-shaped CZ that hangs below the square stone is bezeled simply and adds a delicate balance to the necklace. Beaded pearl buttons and a connector add the finishing touches.

Version #1

{ HISTORICAL PERSPECTIVE }

Joseph Karl Stieler was appointed court painter by various Bavarian sovereigns, including King Ludwig I, from 1820 to 1855. Among his most notable works are his neoclassical portraits of the most beautiful young women, both noble and middle class, of mid-nineteenth-century Munich. These paintings constitute most of the 36 portraits known as the Gallery of Beauties at Nymphenburg Palace in Munich, Germany.

Among the Gallery of Beauties is the portrait of Amalie von Schintling (c. 1831). Typical of Stieler's style, the lack of a dramatic background forces you to view the details of the sitter. There are no distracting decorative additions, causing the focus to fall solely on Amalie. Stieler's use of high contrasts of light and dark highlights her further, adding to her radiance.

I have loved this painting for a long time, and it remains among my favorites. Her beauty and the detail of her costume and jewelry continue to draw my attention and admiration. My inspiration for Amalie's Pearl Necklace was drawn from the necklace that is attached to Amalie's hairstyle in the style of a diadem. Here, pearls are stitched in a variation of right-angle weave, connecting to a jeweled focal component, drawing your eyes directly to hers.

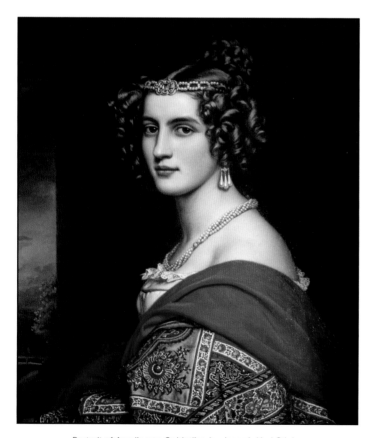

Portrait of Amalie von Schintling by Joseph Karl Stieler

Dimensions

Necklace, 17½ inches (44.5 cm) long

Central component, 1 inch (2.5 cm) in diameter

Techniques

Hexagonal weave, a variation of right-angle weave

Netting

Peyote stitch, flat, even count

Peyote stitch, tubular, even count

Peyote stitch, tubular, even count with increasing

Stitch-in-the-ditch

Skill Level

Advanced

Materials, Version #1

1 ruby 18-mm square antique briolette cushion-cut CZ (lab grown)

1 ruby 15 x 10 mm faceted pear-shaped CZ (lab grown)

1.5 g galvanized champagne 15° seed beads (A)*

0.5 g platinum electroplate 15° seed beads (B)*

1.5 g galvanized champagne 11° cylinder beads (C)*

1 g galvanized champagne 11° seed beads (D)*

0.5 g platinum electroplate 11° seed beads (E)

51–53 crystal AB 2-mm round crystals**

900 platinum 2-mm Czech glass pearls***

34 light gray 3-mm crystal pearls

10 light gray 6-mm crystal pearls

5 light gray 8-mm crystal pearls

Gold nylon beading thread

White nylon beading thread

Gray/blue nylon beading thread

Materials, Version #2

1 lunar lavender 18-mm square antique briolette cushion-cut CZ (custom coated)

1 alexandrite 15 x 10 mm faceted pear-shaped (lab grown)

1.5 g galvanized yellow gold 15° seed beads (A)*

0.5 g silvery green matte metallic iris 15° seed beads (B)

1.5 g galvanized yellow gold 11° cylinder beads (C)*

1 g galvanized yellow gold 11° seed beads (D)*

0.5 g silvery green matte metallic iris 11° seed beads (E)

51–53 crystal AB 2-mm round crystals**

900 ivory 2-mm Czech glass pearls***

34 light gold 3-mm crystal pearls

10 light gold 6-mm crystal pearls

5 light gold 8-mm crystal pearls

Gold nylon beading thread

White nylon beading thread

Beige nylon beading thread

*I prefer Duracoat galvanized seed beads

**Amount depends on the fit within the channel of the bezel.

***The amount depends on the desired length. My sample uses 822 pearls; beyond the sample length, plan on 60 pearls per inch (2.5 cm) of strap.

Tools, both versions

2 size 12 beading needles

1 size 13 beading needle (may be needed when embellishing)

Measuring tape

Beader's supply kit (p. 5)

Version #2

Instructions

Square Bezel

A beautiful cushion-cut CZ with antique-style faceting on both sides is used as the dramatic focal point of this stunning necklace. A combination of flat peyote stitch, tubular peyote stitch with increasing, and a lovely lacing technique captures a string of crystals and the beautiful stone.

Rows 1 & 2: With 6 feet (1.8 m) of prepared thread (p. 6), string 41C, leaving a 30-inch (76.2 cm) tail.

Row 3: Without a bead on the needle, skip the last 2C strung and sew through the third C (Figure 1, red thread); adjust the tension. Using 1C in each stitch, continue working flat peyote stitch, making 19 more stitches, for a total of 20C added in this row (p. 9 and Figure 1, blue thread).

Figure 1

Zip: Put a needle onto the tail thread. Wrap the beadwork around a step gauge or your finger. Using both threads, zip the strip into a tube (p. 10 and Figure 2, red and blue threads). The count is now 20 high and 20 low beads and even-count tubular peyote stitch (p. 10).

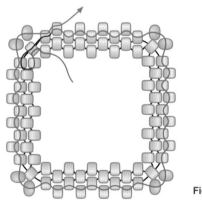

Figure 2

Note: The following increase rounds will create a channel, around which the crystals will be tied.

Round 4. Increase: With the working thread, *work tubular peyote stitch, using 1C in each stitch, to make 4 stitches. Using 2D, make 1 stitch for the corner. Repeat from * 3 more times, stepping up (p. 10) into the first C added in this round as in Figure 2, green thread. There are 4 increases in this round.

Round 5. Complete the increase: On the same side, work tubular peyote stitch, using 1C in each stitch, to make 3 stitches (Figure 3, red thread). Using 1C, make 1 stitch, sewing through the closest D bead from Round 4; using 1C, sew through the next D from Round 4, completing the increase for the corner (Figure 3, blue thread).

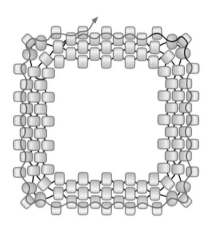

Figure 3

*Work tubular peyote stitch, using 1C in each stitch, to make 5 stitches; using 1C sew through the next D on Round 4, completing the increase for the corner. Repeat from * 2 more times. Using 1C, make 1 stitch and step up through the first C added in this round (Figure 3, green thread).

Rounds 6 & 7 on the other side: Using the tail thread, repeat Rounds 4 and 5 on this side, making sure that the increases align with the ones on the other side. Roll the increased edges toward each other, forming a square shape with a channel in the middle (Figure 4). Keep both threads.

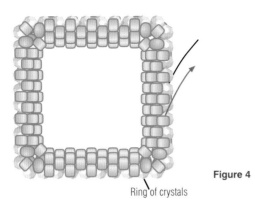

Figure 4

Ring of crystals

Add the crystals: Crystals can really mess up your thread, so take this next step with care. String 40 crystals on 18 inches (45.7 cm) of prepared thread, centering them on the thread. Wrap the crystals tightly around the square, nestling the crystals into the channel of the square. Do you have too many crystals or not enough? Add or remove crystals to get the right amount, then tie an overhand knot (p. 17) to secure the crystals tightly around the square (Figure 4). Weave off threads within the crystals and trim.

Net lacing for the bottom of the bezel

A beautiful lacing technique captures the crystals and begins the CZ bezel technique.

Step 1: Move the tail thread forward by 1 stitch (Figure 5, beginning of red thread path). String 3A, 1E, and 3A, skip the next C bead on Round 7, and sew through the one after that, forming a net (p. 8 and Figure 5, red thread). Move the thread forward by 1 stitch through the closest D from Round 6 and the corner C from Round 7, as shown in Figure 5, blue thread.

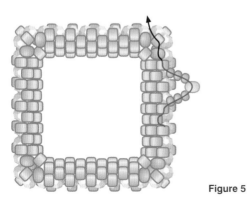

Figure 5

Step 2: String 1A, 1E, and 1A; then sew through the opposite C bead at the corner, as shown in Figure 6, red thread; tighten. String 1A and sew back through the E bead just added; string 1A and sew back through the same C bead, as in Figure 6, blue thread; tighten.

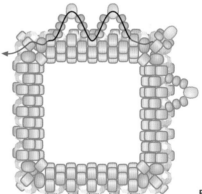

Figure 6

Step 3: Move the thread forward by 1 stitch through the D on Round 6 and the next C on Round 7 (Figure 7, red thread). String 3A, 1E, and 3A, skip the next C bead on Round 7, and sew through the one after that, forming a net. Repeat 1 more time (Figure 7, blue thread). Move the thread forward by 1 stitch (Figure 7, green thread).

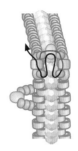

Figure 7

Step 4: Repeat Steps 2 and 3 two more times and end by stringing 3A, 1E, and 3A. Skip the next C on Round 7 and sew through the one after that, forming a net; step up through the first net added, exiting the E bead (Figure 8, end of green thread path).

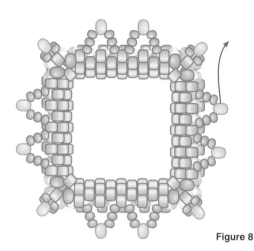

Figure 8

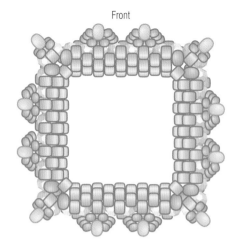

Front

Figure 10

Back

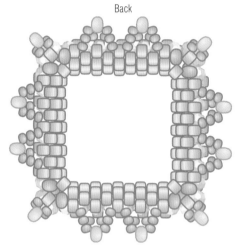

Figure 11

Step 5: *String 1A; sew through the closest aligning C bead on the opposite side (Round 5) by pointing the needle in the opposite direction from how it exits the E bead of the net. String 1A, sew back through the closest E bead, with the thread exiting in the same direction as at the beginning of this technique (Figure 9); tighten. This rolls the lacing toward the front. Weave forward through the bezel to the next E bead at the top of the net past the corner. Repeat this step from * for a total of 8 laced nets (Figure 10 shows the front, Figure 11 shows the back). Weave off this thread and trim.

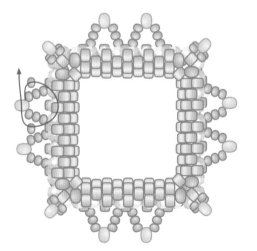

Figure 9

The CZ bezel

These rounds are the setup for attaching the CZ and are on the front.

Step 1: Move the remaining thread forward by 1 stitch through 1C from Round 4 and 1C from Round 5 (Figure 12, red thread). String 2A, 1D, and 2A; skip the next C bead on Round 5 and sew through the C after that, forming a net. Weave forward 1 stitch through the D bead from Round 4 and exit the C bead on Round 5 (Figure 12, blue thread).

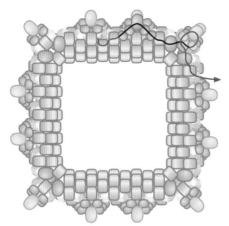

Figure 12

Add the CZ: Wipe off the CZ and place it into the cup of the square bezel (Figure 14).

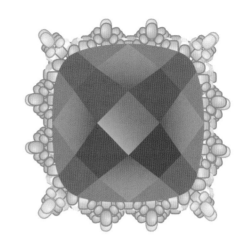

Figure 14

Step 2: String 1B, 1E, and 1B; sew through the same C bead the thread is exiting as in Figure 12, green thread. Move the thread forward 1 stitch (Figure 12, purple thread).

Step 3: *String 2A, 1D, and 2A; skip the next C bead on Round 5 and sew through the one after that, forming a net. Repeat from * 1 more time (Figure 13, red thread). Weave forward 1 stitch to exit the C bead at a corner (Figure 13, blue thread).

Complete the bezel

A beautiful ending to a fabulous bezel!

Step 1: *String 3A, 1D, and 3A; skip the corner picot and sew through the D bead of the next net (Figure 15, red thread). String 3A; sew through the D bead of the next net (Figure 15, blue thread). Repeat from * 3 more times (Figure 15, green thread).

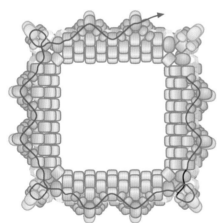

Figure 13

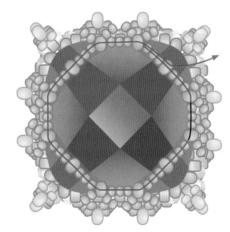

Figure 15

Step 4: Repeat Steps 2 and 3 two more times. Repeat Step 2 one more time. End by stringing 2A, 1D, and 2A; skip the next C bead on Round 5 and sew through the one after that, forming a net. Weave the thread through the first net added to exit the D bead (Figure 13, green thread); keep the thread.

This will not be tight yet! Okay, now pick up the bezel and CZ and start to rework this round, pulling tight! I go around 2 more times. When the bezel wants to hold together without any gaps, stop by exiting any D bead added on this round, which aligns to a corner (Figure 15, end of green thread path).

Step 2: *String 1B, sew through the E bead at the top of the corner picot, and string 1B; sew back through the same D bead on the bezel as shown in Figure 16, beginning of red thread path. Weave to the next corner, pulling tight. Repeat from * 3 more times. Weave off this thread and trim. Set aside.

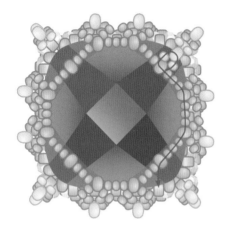

Figure 16

Bezel the Pear-Shaped CZ
A simple peyote-stitch bezel with a crystal edging completes the focal point of this design.

Rows 1 & 2: With 3 feet (91.4 cm) of prepared thread, string on 33C, leaving a 10-inch (25 cm) tail.

Row 3: Without a bead on the needle, skip the last 2C strung and sew through the 3rd C, making the first stitch (Figure 17, red thread). Work flat peyote stitch, using 1C in each stitch; make 15 more stitches for a total of 16C added in this row (Figure 17, blue thread).

Figure 17

Zip: Put a needle onto the tail thread. Wrap the beadwork around a step gauge or your finger. Using both threads, zip the strip into a tube (Figure 18, red and blue threads), as was done with the 18-mm CZ. The count is now 16 high and 16 low beads and even-count tubular peyote stitch.

Figure 18

Round 4 for the front of the bezel: Using the tail thread, work tubular peyote stitch, using 1B in each stitch, for a total of 16B added; step up through the first B added in this round (Figure 18, green thread). Weave off this thread and trim.

Wipe off the CZ. Place it into the beadwork with the flat faceted side (the front) touching Round 4. Position the point to nestle into the space between 2C beads from Row 1 and aligned to a Round 4 B bead (Figure 19, left illustration, red dot bead). This is important. If you can keep the point there, when it comes time to embellish and to add the bead loop, everything will be centered with the point of the CZ.

Center front

Figure 19

Rounds 5 & 6 for the back of the bezel: Using the remaining thread, work 2 rounds of tubular peyote stitch (on the back), using 1A in each stitch, for a total of 16A added in each round; step up at the end of each round (Figure 19, right illustration, red and blue thread). Massage the beadwork so that when you look at the front of the bezel, an A bead from Round 4 is centered over the point of the pear-shaped CZ (Figure 19, left illustration).

Round 7: Move the thread into an A bead from Round 5 (Figure 19, right illustration, green thread). Work stitch-in-the-ditch; with 1C on the needle sew through the next A on Round 5. Using 1C in each stitch, continue stitching-in-the-ditch for a total of 16C added in this round; step up into the first C added (Figure 20, red thread).

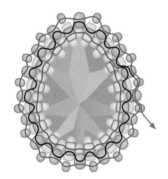

Figure 20

Round 8: Work tubular peyote stitch, using 1D in each stitch, for a total of 16D added; step up through the first D added in this round (Figure 20, blue thread).

Round 9: Work tubular peyote stitch, using 1A in each stitch, for a total of 16A added; step up through the first A added in this round (Figure 20, green thread). Pull the beadwork tight so that this round rolls in toward the back of the CZ. Weave around to secure Rounds 8 and 9.

Using the marked center front B bead as a guide, move the thread to exit a Round 7 (stitch-in-the-ditch round) C bead, as shown in Figure 21, beginning of red thread path. Keep the thread.

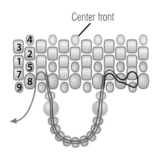

Center front

Figure 21

Add the bead loop: String 1B, one 2-mm pearl, 9A, one 2-mm pearl, and 1B; skip the next 2C on Round 7 and sew through the one after that (Figure 21, red thread). Turn the thread around (Figure 21, blue thread) and reinforce the loop to secure (Figure 21, green thread), exiting as in Figure 21, end of green thread path.

Embellish
Crystals add the finishing touch.

Round 1: Work stitch-in-the-ditch (p. 12). String 1D and sew into the next C bead on Round 7 (Figure 22, beginning of red thread path). Repeat for a total of 13C added in this round. Weave the thread forward through Rounds 8 and 9; exit the first D added in this round (Figure 22, end of red thread).

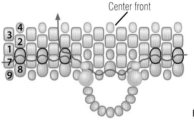

Center front

Figure 22

Round 2: String 1 crystal; sew through the next D bead from Round 1 (Figure 23, beginning of red thread path). Be careful, they're sharp! Continue adding crystals for a total of 12 crystals added in this round. Weave the thread forward through Rounds 8 and 9, then reinforce the crystal round to secure (Figure 24). Weave off the thread and trim. Set aside.

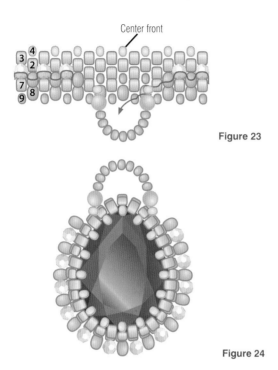

Center front

Figure 23

Figure 24

Necklace Straps

This hexagonal weave variation of right-angle weave (p. 14) is lovely, as the cells are round and are created on the diagonal, and the thread path is hidden.

Row 1

Cell 1: Using 6 feet (1.8 m) of prepared thread, string six 2-mm Czech glass pearls, leaving a 24-inch (61 cm) tail. Sew again through the first 3 pearls strung, forming a cell (Figure 25).

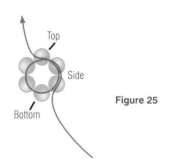

Top

Side

Bottom

Figure 25

Cell 2: String five 2-mm pearls; sew through the pearl from which the thread is exiting on the previous cell, forming a new cell. Pass through the next 3 pearls on this cell (Figure 26).

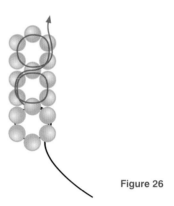

Figure 26

Cell 3: String five 2-mm pearls; sew through the pearl from which the thread is exiting on the previous cell, forming a new cell. Pass through the next 2 pearls, exiting a top pearl on this cell (Figure 26).

Row 2

Cell 1: String five 2-mm pearls; sew through the same pearl from which the thread is exiting, forming a new cell. Pass through the next 5 pearls on this cell, through the closest pearl of the closest cell from the previous row, and the closest pearl on the middle cell in the previous row (Figure 27).

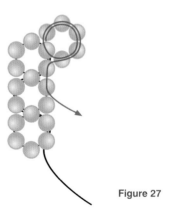

Figure 27

Cell 2: String three 2-mm pearls; sew through the closest pearl on the previous cell added in this row, forming a new cell. Pass through the next 3 pearls on this cell (Figure 28, red thread).

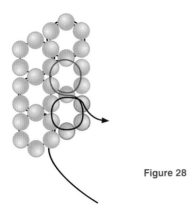

Figure 28

Cell 3: String three 2-mm pearls; sew through the closest pearl on the next cell in the previous row, forming a new cell. Pass through the next 3 pearls on this cell (Figure 28, blue thread).

Row 3
Cell 1: String four 2-mm pearls; sew through the closest pearl on the middle cell of the previous row, forming a new cell. Pass through the next 5 pearls on this cell, the closest pearl on the middle cell from the previous row, and the closest pearl on the next cell from the previous row (Figure 29, red thread).

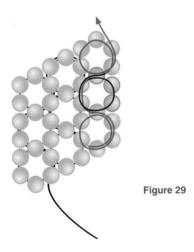

Figure 29

Cell 2: String three 2-mm pearls; sew through the closest pearl on the last cell added, forming a new cell. Pass through the next 3 pearls on this cell (Figure 29, blue thread).

Cell 3: String four 2-mm pearls; sew through the closest pearl on the closest cell from the previous row, forming a new cell. Pass through the next 3 pearls on this cell (Figure 29, green thread).

Note: This variation is a bit of a brain tease, as there is a top and bottom pearl but no centered side pearl to each cell, as in right-angle weave. This technique utilizes all 6 pearls, as needed, depending on the desired direction of the thread path. For the straps, this technique creates a diagonal stitching path, which is lovely.

Repeat Rows 2 and 3 for a total of 36 rows (Figure 30). You'll have an opportunity to add to the straps once the necklace is ready to connect in the front. You'll have to add new thread about halfway, so check out how I do it using a bookbinder's knot (p. 14).

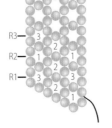

Figure 30

Setup for the clasp

A simple ending to the hexagonal weave sets up the end of the strap for the beaded loop that connects to the buttons. Make sure that the working thread is in position as shown in Figure 31, red dot, beginning of red thread path.

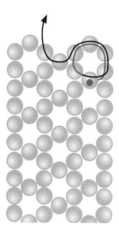

Figure 31

Cell 1: String four 2-mm pearls; sew through the closest pearl on the middle cell of the previous row, forming a new cell (Figure 31, red thread). Pass through the next 5 pearls on this cell, the closest pearl on the middle cell from the previous row, and the closest pearl on the next cell from the previous row (Figure 31, blue thread).

Cell 2: String three 2-mm pearls; sew through the closest pearl on the last cell added, forming a new cell (Figure 32, red thread). Weave the thread around to exit as in Figure 32, blue thread.

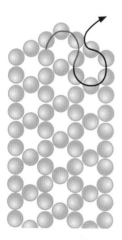

Figure 32

Set aside this strap, keeping both threads attached, and make a second, identical strap.

The Buttons

I like the center back of my necklaces to look beautiful. I also prefer to have a double closure for necklaces with stationary focal points, as the necklace is more balanced on the neck. Two pretty buttons and a connector add the finishing touches to the necklace straps. Make 2 buttons.

Step 1: With 1 foot (30.5 cm) of prepared thread, *string 1D and one 6-mm pearl; repeat from * 4 more times, for a total of 5D and 5 pearls added; center on the thread. Overhand knot (p. 17) the beads into a circle. Place a needle onto the tail thread; rework the threads, making half-hitch knots (p. 16 and Figure 33) at intervals, and trim.

Figure 33

Step 2: With 18 inches (45.7 cm) of prepared thread and leaving a 6-inch (15.2 cm) tail, string 11A, 1E (for version #1), or 1D (for version #2), one 8-mm pearl, the pearl ring made in Step 1, one 8-mm pearl, 1A, 1E (version #1) or 1D (version #2), and 1A, as in Figure 34.

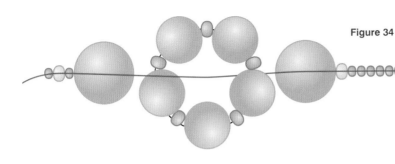

Figure 34

Skip the last 3 beads strung and sew back through the two 8-mm pearls and the first E or D bead strung (Figure 35, beginning of red thread path); adjust the tension.

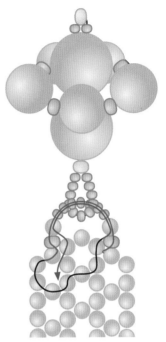

Figure 36

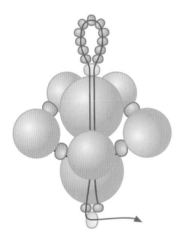

Figure 35

Step 3: Sew through the 11A, 1D or 1E, and both pearls, exiting through the picot as in Figure 35; adjust the tension to form a loop out of the 11A. Reinforce the loop to secure, making half-hitches in the loop. Trim.

Add the Buttons to the Necklace Straps
Using the working thread, string 1D, one 2-mm pearl, 7A, the loop on a button, one 2-mm pearl, and 1D; skip the next cell on the strap and sew through the closest pearl of the cell after that (Figure 36, red thread).

Weave the thread through the strap to exit a pearl on the middle cell (Figure 36, blue thread). Sew through the closest pearl on the loop, the next 7A, and the last pearl on the loop. Sew through the closest pearl on the middle cell (Figure 36, green thread); tighten. Weave around to reinforce this attachment; then weave off and trim this thread. Repeat the attachment of the button to the other strap.

Button Connector
This figure-8 shape connects to the buttons for a centered closure that can be opened and closed with either hand.

With 2 feet (61 cm) of prepared thread and leaving a 6-inch (15.2 cm) tail, string seventeen 3-mm pearls, one 8-mm pearl, and seventeen 3-mm pearls. Sew back through the 8-mm pearl; adjust the tension to form a loop. Place a needle onto the tail thread. Sew back through the 8-mm pearl; adjust the tension to form the other loop (Figure 37, red thread).

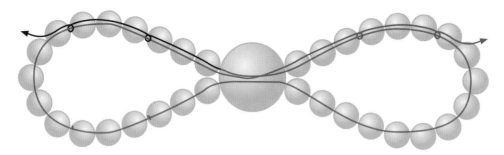

Figure 37

With each thread, make half-hitch knots between every third or fourth pearl on both loops to secure (Figure 37, blue and green threads); then trim.

Test the length: With the ends of the straps buttoned together, try on the necklace. The unfinished ends of the necklace will be where the 18-mm bezeled CZ will be attached momentarily, so if the strap needs to be extended on each side, do it now. When you're ready, move one of the remaining tail threads into position as shown in Figure 38, red dot.

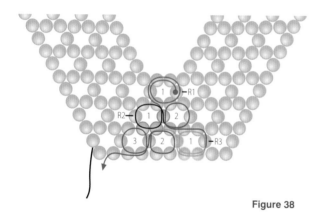

Figure 38

Lace the Necklace Straps

The ends of the straps get zippered together using the right-angle weave variation, working from the top of the straps to the bottom.

Row 1: Place the straps in front of you as shown in Figure 38. tring two 2-mm pearls and sew through the closest pearl at the top of the other strap shown in Figure 38 (R1 circle). String two 2-mm pearls and sew back through the same pearl on the first strap, forming a new cell. Pass through the next 4 pearls on this cell (Figure 38, red thread).

Row 2

Cell 1: String three 2-mm pearls; sew through the closest pearl of the middle cell on the strap on the left, forming a new cell. Pass through the next 3 pearls on this cell (Figure 38, blue thread).

Cell 2: String two 2-mm pearls; sew through the closest pearl of the middle cell on the right strap, forming a new cell. Pass through the next 5 pearls on this cell, the closest pearl of the middle cell on the right strap, and the closest pearl on the bottom cell of the same strap (Figure 38, green thread).

Row 3

Cell 1: String three 2-mm pearls; sew through the closest pearl on Row 2/Cell 2, forming a new cell. Pass through the next 5 pearls on this cell, the closest pearl on the previous Row 2/Cell 2, plus the closest pearl on Row 2/Cell 1 (Figure 38, orange thread).

Cell 2: String three 2-mm pearls; sew through the closest pearl of the cell just completed, forming a new cell. Pass through the next 3 pearls on this cell (Figure 38, purple thread).

Cell 3: String three 2-mm pearls; sew through the closest pearl on the bottom of the left strap, forming a new cell. Pass through the next 5 pearls on this cell and the closest pearl on lowest cell on the left strap (Figure 38, turquoise thread).

Row 4

Cell 1: String four 2-mm pearls; sew through the closest pearl of Row 3/Cell 3, forming a new cell. Pass through the next 5 pearls on this cell, the closest pearl of Row 3/Cell 3, and the closest pearl on Row 3/Cell 2 (Figure 39, red thread).

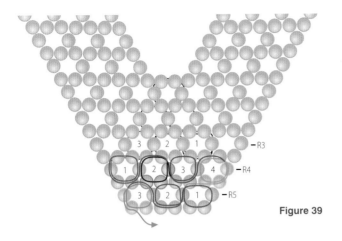

Figure 39

Cell 2: String three 2-mm pearls; sew through the closest pearl on the previous cell, forming a new cell. Pass through the next 3 pearls on this cell (Figure 39, blue thread).

Cell 3: String three 2-mm pearls; sew through the closest pearl on Row 3/Cell 1, forming a new cell. Pass through the next 5 pearls on this cell, the next pearl on Row 3/Cell 1, and the closest pearl on the lowest cell on the right strap (Figure 39, green thread).

Cell 4: String three 2-mm pearls; sew through the closest pearl of the previous cell, forming a new cell. Pass through the next 5 pearls on this cell and the closest pearl from the previous cell (Figure 39, orange thread).

Row 5

Cell 1: String four 2-mm pearls; sew through the closest pearl on Row 4/Cell 4, forming a new cell. Pass through the next 2 pearls on this cell (Figure 39, purple thread).

Cell 2: String three 2-mm pearls; sew through the closest pearl on Row 4/Cell 2, forming a new cell. Pass through the next 5 pearls on this cell, and the closest pearl on Row 4/Cell 2 and Row 4/Cell 1 (Figure 39, turquoise thread).

Cell 3: String three 2-mm pearls; sew through the closest pearl of the previous cell. Pass through the next 4 pearls on this cell (Figure 39, lime green thread).

Add the bead loop: String 1D, one 2-mm pearl, 7A, one 2-mm pearl, and 1D; sew through a pearl on Row 5/Cell 1 as

shown in Figure 40, red thread. Weave around, and weave back through the loop to reinforce (Figure 40, blue thread); then weave off this thread and trim it.

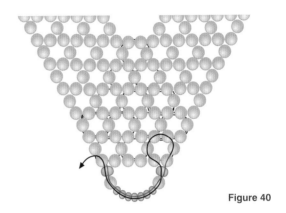

Figure 40

Attach the 18-mm CZ

You'll probably need a smaller size needle for this technique. Wipe off the back of the CZ, then place it face down on your work surface, as shown in Figure 41, with the front of the necklace over the back of the CZ. Move the remaining thread on the necklace into the position shown in Figure 41, blue dot beads and red thread.

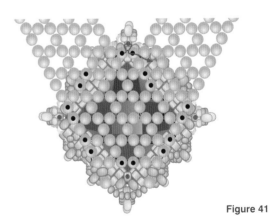

Figure 41

Sew through a corner C bead (Figure 41, red dot bead) on the back of the bezel. Sew through the next blue dot pearl on this cell (Figure 41, red thread). Weave in the pearls to line up to another C bead on the bottom edge of the bezel. Continue to sew as many of the C beads to the pearls as possible, making sure to center the bottom of the CZ with the center bottom of the necklace. Align the sides as well so that the CZ is centered and straight. Use the lacings and nets on the bezel and the blue dot pearls and red dot beads as guides for centering (Figure 41). Once complete, weave off this thread and trim.

Attach the Pear-Shaped CZ Drop

Using 24 inches (61 cm) of prepared thread and leaving a 6-inch (15.2 cm) tail, string 13B (for version #1) or 13A (for version #2). Tuck the needle through the loop at the bottom of the necklace and the loop at the top of the pear-shaped CZ (Figure 42, red thread). Overhand-knot the beads into a tight ring, making sure that the pear-shaped CZ faces the front. Weave off each thread in opposite directions, then trim. Using the remaining thread, make one more beaded jump ring (Figure 42, blue thread).

Figure 43. Shows the completed assembly.

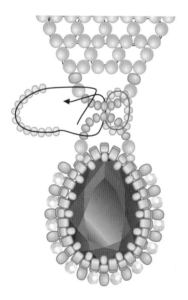

Figure 42

VICTORIAN GARLAND NECKLACE

A VARIATION OF ST. PETERSBURG CHAIN has a dramatic effect in this lovely necklace. A crystal pearl cabochon, with a beautiful but simple bezel, links to a crystal pearl drop, topped with a beaded cap. Two crystal pearl cabochons are miniature versions of the focal point, leading the eye to the details of the closure. A beaded connector secures the necklace while it is worn.

Version #1

⟨ HISTORICAL PERSPECTIVE ⟩

Frederick Sandys, an English pre-Raphaelite artist of the Victorian era, was inspired by classical stories with romantic elements. He drafted primarily in black-and-white, creating drawings that could be translated by wood carvers into wood engravings, a means of early graphic reproduction.

It's surprising that, although he was one of the foremost artists of his time, very few of his works were paintings. His sensuous lines and beautiful color palettes are a glorious combination, especially in this painting, *Grace Rose* (c. 1866). As a bead artist, of course, I'm attracted to her jewelry. But beyond that, the embellishment of her gown, her casual approach to flower arranging, and the background of the painting are a pleasure to view.

Inspired by the sophisticated color palette and decorative details shown in Grace Rose, my Victorian Garland Necklace plays with color, pearls, and a romantic design for a delicate necklace worthy of this lovely lady.

Grace Rose by Frederick Sandys

Dimensions

16¾ inches (42.5 cm) long

Techniques

Netting

Peyote stitch, flat circular, even count with increasing

Single St. Petersburg chain

Skill Level

Intermediate

Materials, Version #1

1 g crimson copper galvanized 15° seed beads* (A)

1 g matte olivine AB 15° seed beads (B)

1 g bronze metallic 15° seed beads (C)

6 g crimson copper galvanized 11° seed beads* (D)

4 g chartreuse lined olivine AB 11° seed beads (E)

1 g bronze metallic 11° seed beads (F)

132 round 3-mm antique gold granulated spacers*

47 cream rose 6-mm crystal pearls**

2 peach 10-mm flat-backed round crystal pearl cabochons

1 peach 16-mm flat-backed round crystal pearl cabochon

1 cream rose 11 x 8 mm crystal pearl drop

Apricot nylon beading thread

Dark beige nylon beading thread for the pearl drop

Materials, Version #2

1 g olivine bronze matte metallic iris 15° seed beads (A)

1 g aqua bronze lined luster 15° seed beads (B)

1 g 24-karat gold electroplate 15° seed beads (C)

6 g olivine bronze matte metallic iris 11° seed beads (D)

4 g aqua bronze-lined luster 11° seed beads (E)

1 g 24-karat gold electroplate 11° seed beads (F)

132 round 3-mm bright gold granulated spacers**

47 cream 6-mm crystal pearls***

2 gold 10-mm flat-backed round crystal pearl cabochons

1 gold 16-mm flat-backed round crystal pearl cabochon

1 cream 11 x 8 mm crystal pearl drop

Dark beige nylon beading thread

Gold nylon beading thread for the pearl drop

I prefer Duracoat galvanized seed beads.

** This is the quantity used in the version shown. To make yours longer, plan on 8 more spacers for every additional inch (2.5 cm).

*** This is the quantity used for the length shown. To make your necklace longer, plan on 4 more pearls for every additional inch (2.5 cm).

Tools

2 size 12 beading needles

Beading awl (optional, but helpful)

Permanent marker in a color that blends with the C and F beads

Beader's supply kit (p. 5)

Details from Version #1

Version #2

Instructions

St. Petersburg Chain Necklace Straps

This lovely stitch becomes even more elegant with the addition of 6-mm pearls and little metal spacers on the tips of every other row. Make 2 straps.

Step 1: Using 7 feet (2.1 m) of prepared thread (p. 6) in a color that blends with the D beads, string 1E, leaving a 12-inch (30.5 cm) tail. Sew through this bead again to form a stopper bead (p. 18 and Figure 1, red thread).

Figure 1

Step 2: String 6D; pull the beads down to the stopper bead. Skip the first 2D strung; sew up through the third and fourth D as in Figure 1 (blue thread); adjust the tension. The 2D that stick out create the beginning of the next row.

Step 3: String 1E and sew back through 3D (Figure 1, green thread); adjust the tension. String 1E; sew up through the 2D on the new row (Figure 1, green thread); adjust the tension.

Step 4: String 4D; pull the beads down to the beadwork. Sew up through the first 2D strung, creating the beginning of the next row (Figure 2, red thread); adjust the tension.

Figure 2

Step 5: String 1 spacer, one 6-mm pearl, 1 spacer, and 1E; pull the beads down to the beadwork. Skip the E bead just strung and sew back through the spacer, pearl, and first spacer just added, plus 3D (Figure 2, blue thread); adjust the tension.

Step 6: String 1E; step up through the 2D on the new row (Figure 2, green thread); adjust the tension.

Step 7: String 4D; pull the beads down to the beadwork. Sew up through the first 2D strung, creating the beginning of the next row (Figure 3, red thread); adjust the tension.

Figure 3

Step 8: String 1E, then sew back through 3D; adjust the tension (Figure 3, blue thread). String 1E; step up through the 2D on the new row (Figure 3, green thread); adjust the tension.

Repeat Steps 4 through 8 twenty-two more times for a total of 23 pearls added. There will be an opportunity to add to the necklace a bit later. Set this strap aside; keep both threads. Make another strap.

Bezel the 16-mm Pearl Cabochon

A flat circular peyote stitch disc covers the back of the crystal pearl cabochon, while spikes lace together atop of the pearl to create a beautiful bezel that is embellished with small spacers for a granulated look.

Round 1: Using 5 feet (1.5 m) of prepared thread, string 3D, leaving a 12-inch (30.5 cm) tail. Make an overhand knot (p. 17) to tie the beads into a circle. Sew through the closest D bead (Figure 4, red thread).

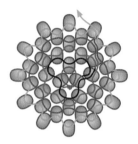

Figure 4

Round 2: Increase: Using the working thread, work flat circular peyote stitch using 2D in each stitch (p. 12); make 3 stitches. Step up through the first D added in this round (Figure 4, blue thread).

Round 3: Complete the increases: *Work flat circular peyote stitch using 1D in each stitch; sew through the next D added on Round 2, completing an increase. Using 1D, sew through the next D added on Round 2. Repeat from * 2 more times, then step up as shown in Figure 4, green thread; 6D were added in this round.

Round 4: Increase: Work flat circular peyote stitch using 2D in each stitch; make 6 stitches. Step up through the first D added in this round (Figure 4, purple thread).

Round 5: Completing the increases: *Work flat circular peyote stitch using 1D in each stitch; sew through the next D added on Round 4, completing an increase. Using 1D, sew through the next D added on Round 4. Repeat from * 5 more times, then step up through the first D added in this round; 12D were added in this round (Figure 4, orange thread).

Round 6: Work flat circular peyote stitch using 1E in each stitch; make 12 stitches (Figure 5, red thread). Step up through the first E added in this round..

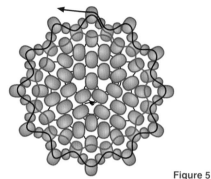

Figure 5

Round 7: *Work netting stitch (p. 8) using 1A, 1D, and 1A; sew through the next E added on Round 6 (Figure 5, blue thread). Repeat from * 11 more times; then step up through the first A and D added in this round.

Add the spikes: *String 1A, 2D, 1A, 1E, and 1A (Figure 6, red thread); skip the last A, E, and A strung and sew back through 2D (Figure 6, blue thread); adjust the tension. String 1A; sew through the same D bead on Round 7 in the same direction as before (Figure 6, blue thread); adjust the tension. Weave through the next A, E, A, and exit the D bead at the tip of the next net (Figure 6, green thread). Repeat from * 11 more times for a total of 12 spikes. Step up through the A, 2D, A, and E on the first spike added (Figure 7, beginning of red thread path).

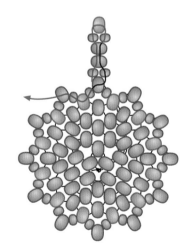

Figure 6

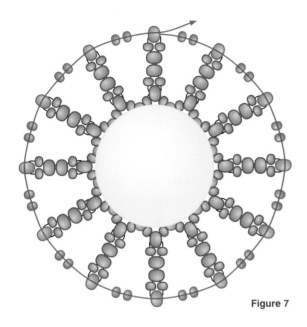

Figure 7

Add the lacing: Place the 16-mm crystal pearl cabochon on top of the peyote stitch disc. *String 2B; sew through the next E bead at the top of the next spike. Repeat from * 11 more times (Figure 7); adjust the tension; reinforce the bezel until the tension holds.

Add the embellishment: Weave the thread to exit the closest A bead on the closest spike as in Figure 8, red thread. *String 1 spacer and 1C; bring these beads down to the beadwork, skip the C just added, and sew back through the spacer and up through the opposite A bead on the same spike, as shown in Figure 8, blue thread. Weave the thread through the closest E, 2B, and E on the lacing; then sew down through the closest A bead on the next spike (Figure 8, blue thread). Repeat from * 11 more times for a total of 12 spacers added in this round. Weave off this thread and trim.

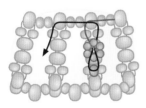

Figure 8

Add the bead loop: Place a needle onto the tail thread. Weave the thread to exit an A bead at the base of a spike as in Figure 9, beginning of red thread path. String 1A, 1E, 7C, 1E, and 1A; skip the next spike and sew down through the closest A bead on the spike after that; adjust the tension.

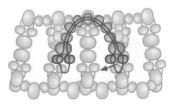

Figure 9

String 1A; sew through the last E, 7C, and E on the loop; adjust the tension. String 1A; sew through the same A bead on the spike from bottom to top (Figure 9); adjust the tension. Reinforce the loop to secure, then weave off this thread and trim.

The Pearl Drop

A beaded cap tidies up the pearl drop, adding an elegant touch.

Round 1: Using 3 feet (91.4 cm) of prepared thread in a color that blends with the C and F beads, string 3C, leaving an 8-inch (20 cm) tail; rethread through the 3C to form a circle (Figure 10, red thread).

Figure 10

Round 2. Increase: Using the working thread, work flat circular peyote stitch, using 2C in each stitch; make 3 stitches. Step up into the first C added in this round (Figure 10, blue thread).

Round 3. Complete the increases: *Work flat circular peyote stitch using 1C in each stitch; sew through the next C added on Round 2, completing an increase. Using 1C, sew through the next C added on Round 2. Repeat from * 2 more times, then step up into the first C added in this round (Figure 10, green thread); 6C were added in this round.

Round 4: Work flat circular peyote stitch using 1F in each stitch; make 6 stitches. Step up through the first F added in this round (Figure 10, purple thread); pull tight. Weave through Rounds 3 and 4 to form a cup out of the beadwork, exiting the closest F bead on this round.

Add the pearl: Place a needle on the tail thread; sew through the closest C bead on Round 1 (Figure 11, red dot). Push the thread through the center top to exit the inside of the cap. String 1 pearl drop, 1C, 1E, and 1C; skip the C, E, and C just added; sew back through the pearl, exiting center top on the cap (Figure 11). Sew through a C bead that was added on Round 1. Reinforce this connection; weave off this thread and trim.

Figure 11

Tip: The tightness of this cap has a lot to do with the size of the 15° seed beads. Some are small and round and others are square. I cull my beads if I'm using the more square-shaped 15° seed beads, picking the smallest ones for Rounds 5 to 7.

Round 5: Using the remaining thread, *work netting stitch using 1C, 1E, and 1C; sew through the next F bead added on Round 4. Repeat from * 5 more times, then step up through the first C and E added in this round (Figure 12, red thread). *Note:* Figures 12 through 14 are shown flat for clarity.

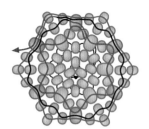

Figure 12

Round 6: *Work netting stitch using 3C; sew through the next E bead added on Round 5. Repeat from * 5 more times, then step up through the first C added in this round (Figure 12, blue thread). Note: This is not the normal step up for netting as the next rounds head for peyote stitch.

Round 7: *Work tubular peyote stitch (p. 10) using 1C, skip the next C added on Round 6, and sew through the next C, E, and C. Make the stitch sit tightly below the C bead that was skipped. Repeat from * 5 more times, working tight (Figure 12, green thread). End by exiting the closest E bead (Figure 12, purple thread).

Round 8: *String 1 spacer and 1C and bring them down to the beadwork. Skip the C bead just added, and then sew back through the spacer and the next E bead on the cap (Figure 13). Center the embellishment between the E beads. Repeat from * 5 more times; then weave the thread to exit a C bead on Round 3 as in Figure 14 (lower blue dot bead).

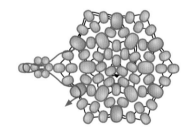

Figure 13

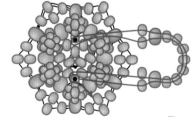

Figure 14

Tip: Depending on bead size, the thread may show on either side of the little spacer. I color the thread with a fine-point permanent marker that blends with the beadwork so it's less noticeable.

Add the bead loop: String 1C, 1E, 7C, 1E, and 1C; sew through the opposite C on Round 3 as shown in Figure 14, upper blue dot bead. String 1C; sew back through the E, 7C, and E on the loop; adjust the tension. String 1C; sew through the same lower C bead (Figure 14, red thread); adjust the tension. Reinforce the loop to secure, then weave off this thread and trim.

Attach the pearl drop to the crystal pearl cabochon bezel: Using 12 inches (30.5 cm) of prepared thread in a color that blends with the C beads, string 13C and center them on the thread; tuck the needle through the bead loops on the cabochon bezel and the pearl drop; make an overhand knot to form a beaded jump ring (Figure 15, red and blue threads); weave off each thread in opposite directions, then trim. Repeat for another beaded jump ring (Figure 15, blue thread.

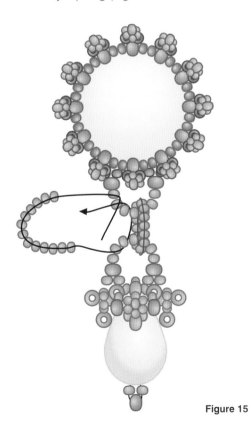

Figure 15

The Buttons for the Neck Closure

These little beauties are made the same way as the pearl cabochon bezel, just smaller. Make 2.

Round 1: Using 3 feet (91.4 cm) of prepared thread, string 3D, leaving a 6-inch (15.2 cm) tail. Make an overhand knot to tie the beads into a circle; sew through the closest D (Figure 16, red thread).

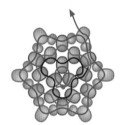

Figure 16

Round 2: Increase: Work flat circular peyote stitch, using 2D in each stitch; make 3 stitches (Figure 16, blue thread). Step up through the first D added in this round..

Round 3: Complete the increases: *Work flat circular peyote stitch using 1D in each stitch; sew through the next D added on Round 2, completing an increase. Using 1D, sew through the next D added on Round 2 (Figure 16, green thread). Repeat from * 2 more times. Step up through the first D added in this round. 6D were added in this round.

Round 4: *Work netting stitch using 1B, 1E, and 1B; sew through the next D added on Round 3 (Figure 16, purple thread). Repeat from * 5 more times, then step up through the first B and E added in this round.

Add the spikes: *String 3A, 1B, and 1A; bring the beads down to the beadwork. Skip the last A, B, and A strung and sew back through the next A; adjust the tension. String 1A; sew through the same E bead on Round 4 in the same direction as before; adjust the tension. Weave through the next B, D, B, and E to exit the E bead at the tip of next net (Figure 17, red thread).

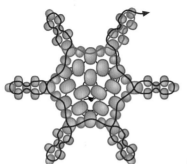

Figure 17

Figure 19

Repeat from * 5 more times for a total of 6 spikes added (Figure 17, blue thread); sew through the 3A and 1B on the first spike added in this round (Figure 17, end of blue thread path).

Add the lacing: Place a 10-mm crystal pearl cabochon on top of the peyote stitch disc (Figure 18). *String 3B; sew through the next B bead at the top of the next spike. Repeat from * 5 more times (Figure 18). Adjust the tension; reinforce the bezel until the tension holds.

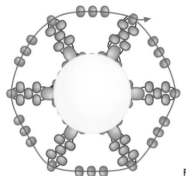

Figure 18

Add the embellishment: Weave the thread off the lacing round to exit the closest A bead on the closest spike. *String 1 spacer and 1C; bring them down against the beadwork. Skip the C just added, sew back through the spacer and up through the opposite A bead on the same spike, as shown in Figure 19. Weave the thread through the closest 5B on the lacing; then sew down through the closest A bead on the next spike, as shown in Figure 19. Repeat from * 5 more times for a total of 6 spacers added in this round. Weave off the tail thread and trim.

Add the bead loop: Weave the remaining thread to exit a D bead on Round 3 (Figure 20, beginning of red thread path). String 1A, 1E, 7A, 1E, and 1A; sew through the opposite D bead on Round 3; adjust the tension. String 1A; sew through the last E, 7A, and E on the loop; adjust the tension. String 1A; sew through the same D bead on Round 3 in the same direction as before (Figure 20); adjust the tension. Reinforce the loop to secure; then weave off this thread and trim. Set aside and make the other button.

Figure 20. Only bezel bottom shown for clarity.

Tip: I like to round out all bead loops with an awl or other armature (Figure 21).

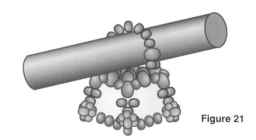

Figure 21

Attach the Buttons to the Ends of the Necklace Straps

Step 1: Disconnect the stopper bead on the beginning end of one necklace strap. Place a needle onto the tail thread. Restring the E bead, skip the E bead just strung, and sew back through the 4D on the last row of the strap (Figure 22, red thread).

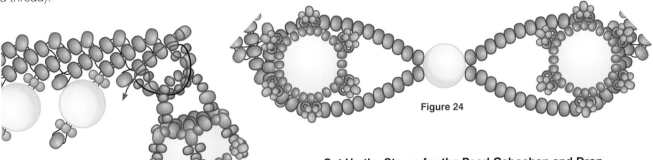

Figure 22

Step 2: String 1A, 1E, 5A, 1E, 1A, and one button; sew through the first D bead strung on this row as in Figure 22, blue thread. String 1A; sew back through 1E, 5A, and 1E on the loop; adjust the tension. String 1A; sew through the fourth D bead on the last row of the necklace strap as in Figure 22, green thread. Reinforce the loop; weave off the thread and trim.

Repeat the attachment of the button on the other strap.

The Closure Connector

Using 18 inches (45.7 cm) of prepared thread, string 33D, one 6-mm pearl, and 33D beads. Center the beads on the thread. Place a needle onto the tail thread. With one thread, sew back through the pearl, forming a loop. Repeat for the other thread (Figure 23, red thread). Weave off each thread to reinforce, half-hitching (p. 16) between every third or fourth D bead (Figure 23, blue and green threads); then trim.

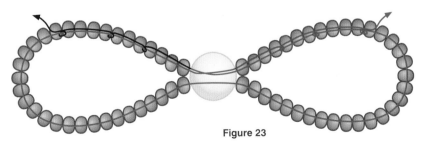

Figure 23

Test the length: Attach the closure connector (Figure 24). Try on the necklace with the buttons in the back. The ends of the straps are within 2 rows of the connection to the pearl cabochon. If needed, extend the straps now, ending as done in Figure 3.

Figure 24

Set Up the Straps for the Pearl Cabochon and Drop

Step 1: String 4D; pull the beads down to the beadwork. Sew up through the first 2D strung, creating the beginning of the next row; adjust the tension (Figure 25, red thread).

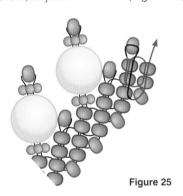

Figure 25

Step 2: String 1E, then sew back through 3D (Figure 25, blue thread); adjust the tension. String 1E; step up through the 2D on the new row; adjust the tension (Figure 25, green thread).

Add the pearl cabochon and the drop: Place the necklace and pearl cabochon component on your work surface, face down, as shown in Figure 26. Place a needle onto the thread attached to the left-hand strap. Find the center top on the cabochon bezel. Each connection is made off a D bead from Round 7, one on either side of center (Figure 26).

Sew through the D bead (Round 7) on the bezel; sew through the E bead on the strap; sew through the 3D on the second row on the strap (Figure 26, red thread). Sew through the E bead on the strap, 2D on the last row on the strap, and back through the D bead on the bezel to secure (Figure 26, blue thread). Reinforce again, then weave off this thread within the strap, following the thread path on the strap. Trim.

Repeat the attachment for the other strap.

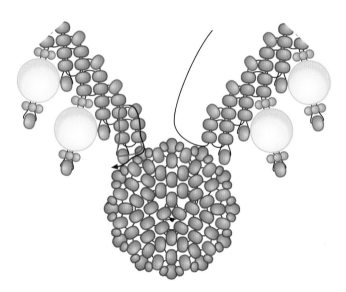

Figure 26. Only back of cabochon shown for clarity.

THE QUEEN'S LACE BRACELET

A RIGHT-ANGLE WEAVE VARIATION that I call *lattice weave* shows off what it can do in this beautiful bracelet. Bands of lattice weave are alternated with another variation using pearls, fire-polished beads, and seed beads. Delicate beaded buttons add the finishing touches to this lacy design. The combination is striking and lends itself to many color options.

Version #1

{ HISTORICAL PERSPECTIVE }

Franz Xaver Winterhalter (1805–1873) was best known for his fashionable court portraits of royalty in the mid-nineteenth century. Trained at an early age in drawing and engraving, he was granted a stipend by Ludwig I, Grand Duke of Baden, to study at the Academy of Arts in Munich, where he met the artist who was to be his mentor, Joseph Karl Stieler.

Winterhalter's abilities grew under Stieler's guidance, garnering him positions as court painter for some of the largest royal houses in Europe. Among his many royal portraits is the full-length portrait of the beautiful Queen Louise Marie Thérèse Charlotte Isabelle of Orleans (c. 1841), the first Queen of the Belgians.

As with all royals of the time, arranged marriages were part and parcel of doing one's duty to family and country. The union of King Leopold I and Queen Louise was one of respect and duty. Queen Victoria of England wrote in her journal that Louise was "so kind & so good; the more one sees her the more one must love her; she is so thoroughly unselfish, indeed she never thinks of herself" and "the dearest friend, after my beloved Albert, I have."

Queen Louise is portrayed here in an outdoor setting. The elegant background only seems to accent the queen as she is shown in a red velvet gown with lace trim. Beyond being impressed by her grace, her confidence yet reserve, I was most attracted to the incredible lace shawl that is casually draped over her arms, which became the inspiration for The Queen's Lace Bracelet.

Portrait of Marie-Louise, the first Queen of the Belgians by Franz Xaver Winterhalter

Dimensions
7½ x 1¼ inches (19 x 3.2 cm)

Techniques
Lattice weave, a variation of right-angle weave

Skill Level
Intermediate

Materials, Version #1
2 g champagne galvanized 15° seed beads* (A)

6 g champagne galvanized 11° seed beads* (B)

56 crystal champagne 2-mm metallic Czech fire-polished beads (FP)**

2 cream 2-mm Czech glass pearls

20 cream 6-mm crystal pearls***

Dark beige nylon beading thread

Materials, Version #2
2 g yellow gold galvanized 15° seed beads* (A)

6 g yellow gold galvanized 11° seed beads* (B)

56 green turquoise luster 2-mm Czech fire-polished beads (FP)**

2 pale pink/peach 2-mm Czech glass pearls

20 peach 6-mm crystal pearls***

Gold nylon beading thread

* I prefer Duracoat galvanized seed beads.

**The amount depends on the desired length. Plan on 16 beads for every added row. Also, 2-mm fire-polished beads are not all the same! There are 2-mm fire-polished beads that are truly 2 mm and 2-mm fire-polished beads that are actually around 2.25 to 2.5 mm. The most common size is the 2.25 to 2.5 mm, and that is what you want to use here.

*** The amount depends on the desired length. Plan on 3 pearls for every added row.

Tools
2 size 12 beading needles
Beading awl (optional, but helpful)
Beader's supply kit (p. 5)

Detail from Version #1

Details from Version #2

Instructions

The Bracelet Band

A beautiful combination of seed beads, fire-polished beads, and 6-mm pearls in a right-angle weave variation (p. 14) come together in a lacelike pattern.

Row 1

Cell 1: Using 6 feet (1.8 m) of prepared thread (p. 6), string 1B, 1FP, 1B, 1FP, 1B, 1FP, 1B, 1FP, 1B, 1FP, 1B, and 1FP; pull the beads down to within 18 inches (45.7 cm) of the tail. Make an overhand knot to tie the beads into a ring (p. 17). Move the working thread forward through 1FP and 1B (which will be one of the 2 axis beads), as shown in Figure 1.

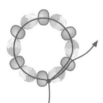

Figure 1

String one 6-mm pearl; sew through the opposite B bead (axis bead) on the ring; sew back through the pearl and back through the opposite axis B bead in the same direction as before (Figure 2, red thread); tighten. *Note:* The pearl will not sit centered within the ring. The front of the bracelet has the pearls sticking up; on the back, the pearls are flush against the beadwork.

Figure 2

Sew forward through the next FP, 1B, FP, 1B, and FP (Figure 2, blue thread). String 1A, 1B, and 1A; skip the next B on the ring, sewing through the next FP and 1B (Figure 2, green thread).

String 2A, 1B, and 2A; skip the next FP, then sew through the next B and FP (Figure 3, red thread).

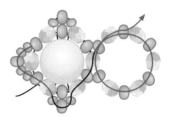

Figure 3

String 1A, 1B, and 1A; skip the next B bead on the ring and sew through the following FP, B, and FP (Figure 3, blue thread).

Cell 2: String 1B, 1FP, 1B, 1FP, 1B, 1FP, 1B, 1FP, 1B, 1FP, and 1B; sew back through the side FP of the previous cell, forming the next ring for Cell 2. Sew forward through the next B, FP, and B (Figure 3, green thread).

String one 6-mm pearl; sew through the opposite B bead (axis bead) on the ring; sew back through the pearl and back through the axis B bead in the same direction as before (Figure 4, red thread); tighten.

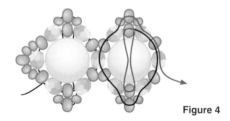

Figure 4

Sew forward through the next FP, B, FP, B, and FP; string 1A, 1B, and 1A; skip the next B on the ring and sew through the next FP, B, FP, B, and FP (Figure 4, blue thread).

String 1A, 1B, and 1A; skip the next B on the ring and sew through the next FP, B, and FP (Figure 4, green thread).

Cell 3: String 1B, 1FP, 1B, 1FP, 1B, 1FP, 1B, 1FP, 1B, 1FP, and 1B; sew back through the side FP from the previous cell, forming the next ring; sew forward through the next B, FP, and B (Figure 5, red thread).

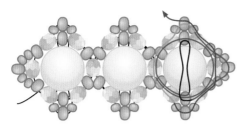

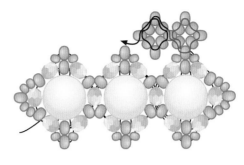

Figure 5

Figure 6

String one 6-mm pearl; sew through the opposite B bead (axis bead) on the ring; sew back through the pearl and back through the axis B bead in the same direction as before (Figure 5, blue thread); tighten.

Sew forward through the next FP and B; string 2A, 1B, and 2A; skip the next FP; then sew through the following B and FP (Figure 5, green thread).

String 1A, 1B, and 1A; skip the next B bead on the ring and sew through the following FP, B, FP, B, and FP (Figure 5, orange thread).

String 1A, 1B, and 1A; skip the next B bead on the ring and sew through the following FP, B, FP, B, FP, A, and B (Figure 5, purple thread).

Row 2

A plain row of lattice-weave breaks up the pearl and fire-polished bead rows. This variation of right-angle weave creates a square cell. I find that when I move the thread to each location, sewing through only 2 B beads at a time helps to shape the cell. Notice that the thread direction changes here, as is typical of right-angle weave and its variations.

Cell 1: String 7B; sew through the same B the thread is exiting in the same direction as before. Sew through 2B, shape the cell into a square, exiting the side bead (Figure 6, red thread).

Cell 2: String 7B; sew through the side B bead of the previous cell in the same direction as before. Sewing through 2B at a time, shape the cell into a square, exiting the side bead of the cell just added (Figure 6, blue thread).

Cell 3: String 1B; sew through the B bead at the top of the center cell from the previous row (Figure 7, red thread). String 5B; sew through the side B on Cell 2 in the same direction as before. Sewing through 2B at a time, shape the cell into a square, exiting the side bead of the cell just added (Figure 7, blue thread).

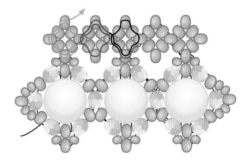

Figure 7

Cell 4: String 7B; sew through the same side B bead the thread is exiting on Cell 3 in the same direction as before. Sewing through 2B at a time, shape the cell into a square, exiting the side bead of the cell just added (Figure 7, green thread).

Cell 5: String 1B; sew through the B bead at the top of the closest cell from the previous row (Figure 7, beginning of orange thread path). String 5B; sew through the side B bead on Cell 4 in the same direction as before. Sewing through 2B at a time, shape the cell into a square, exiting the top bead of the cell just added (Figure 7, end of orange thread path).

Set-up stitch: To begin each row of the fire-polished bead and pearl lattice weave, you need to make a set-up stitch at the top of the last lattice-weave cell added.

String 1A, 1B, and 1A; sew back through the same B bead that the thread is exiting in the same direction as before. Reinforce this stitch to secure, exiting the B just added (Figure 8, red thread).

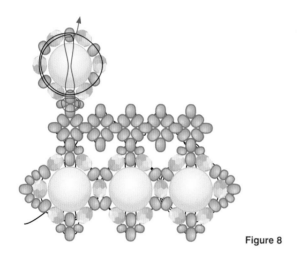

Figure 8

Row 3

Cell 1: String 1FP, 1B, 1FP, 1B, 1FP, 1B, 1FP, 1B, 1FP, 1B, and 1FP; sew through the B bead on the set-up stitch in the same direction as before; sew forward through the next FP, B, FP, B, FP, and B of the cell (Figure 8, blue thread).

String one 6-mm pearl; sew through the opposite axis B bead on the ring; sew back through the pearl and back through the starting axis B bead in the same direction as before (Figure 8, green thread); tighten.

Sew forward through the next FP, B, FP, B, and FP; sew through the closest A of the set-up stitch, the B at the top of the cell on the previous row, the A added in the set-up stitch, and the next FP and B bead (Figure 9, red thread).

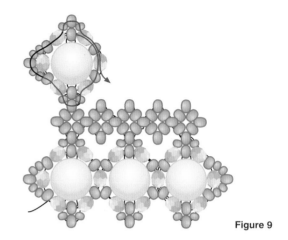

Figure 9

String 2A, 1B, and 2A; skip the next FP on the ring and sew through the next B and FP (Figure 9, blue thread). String 1A, 1B, and 1A; skip the next B on the ring and sew through the next FP, B, and FP (Figure 9, green thread).

Cell 2: String 1B, 1FP, 1B, 1FP, 1B, 1FP, 1B, 1FP, 1B, 1FP, and 1B; sew back through the side FP on the previous cell in the same direction as before, forming the next ring. Sew forward through the next B, FP, and B (Figure 10, red thread).

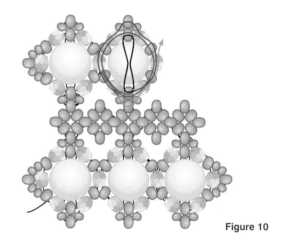

Figure 10

String one 6-mm pearl; sew through the opposite axis B bead on the ring; sew back through the pearl and back through the starting axis B bead in the same direction as before (Figure 10, blue thread); tighten.

Sew forward through the next FP, B, FP, B, and FP. String 1A, 1B, and 1A; skip the next B on the ring and sew through the next FP, B, FP, B, and FP (Figure 10, green thread).

String 1A; sew through the top B bead on the middle cell from the previous row; string 1A; sew through the next FP, B, and FP (Figure 10, orange thread).

Cell 3: String 1B, 1FP, 1B, 1FP, 1B, 1FP, 1B, 1FP, 1B, 1FP, and 1B; sew back through the side FP on Cell 2 in the same direction as before, forming the next ring. Sew forward through the next B, FP, and B (Figure 11, red thread).

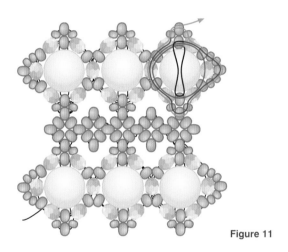

Figure 11

String one 6-mm pearl; sew through the opposite axis B bead on the ring; sew back through the pearl and back through the starting axis B bead in the same direction as before; tighten (Figure 11, blue thread).

Sew forward through the next FP and B; string 2A, 1B, and 2A; skip the next FP, then sew through the next B and FP. String 1A; sew through the top B bead of the closest cell from the previous row. String 1A; sew through the next FP, B, FP, B, and FP (Figure 11, green thread).

String 1A, 1B, and 1A; skip the next B on the ring and sew through the next FP; sew around the cell to exit the last B added (Figure 11, orange thread).

Row 4
The thread direction has changed again.

Cell 1: String 7B; sew through the same B the thread is exiting, in the same direction as before. Sewing through 2B at a time, shape the cell into a square, exiting the side bead (Figure 12, red thread).

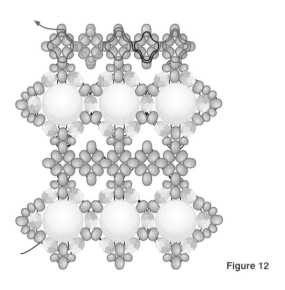

Figure 12

Cell 2: String 7B; sew through the same side B bead the thread is exiting on Cell 1 in the same direction as before. Sewing through 2B at a time, shape the cell into a square, exiting the side bead of the cell just added (Figure 12, blue thread).

Cell 3: String 5B; sew through the top B bead on the middle cell from the previous row. String 1B; sew through the side B bead from the previous cell. Sewing through 2B at a time, shape the cell into a square, exiting the side bead of the cell just added (Figure 12, green thread).

Cell 4: String 7B; sew through the same side B bead the thread is exiting on Cell 3, in the same direction as before. Sewing through 2B at a time, shape the cell into a square, exiting the side bead of the cell just added (Figure 12, orange thread).

Cell 5: String 5B; sew through the top B bead on the closest cell from the previous row. String 1B; sew through the side B bead from the previous cell. Sew through 2B and shape the cell into a square, exiting the top bead of the cell just added (Figure 12, purple thread).

Set-up row: String 1A, 1B, and 1A; sew back through the same B bead that the thread is exiting from, in the same direction as before. Rethread through this stitch again to secure, exiting the B bead just added (Figure 13, red thread).

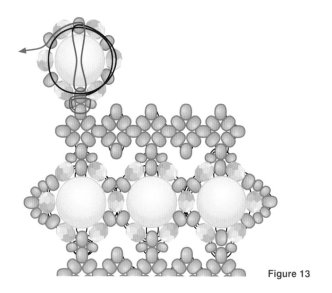

Figure 13

Row 5

Cell 1: String 1FP, 1B, 1FP, 1B, 1FP, 1B, 1FP, 1B, 1FP, 1B, and 1FP; sew through the set-up stitch B bead just added, in the same direction as before. Sew forward through the next FP, B, FP, B, FP, and B (Figure 13, blue thread).

String one 6-mm pearl; sew through the opposite axis B bead on the ring; sew back through the pearl and back through the starting axis B bead in the same direction as before; tighten. Sew forward through the next FP and B (Figure 13, green thread).

String 2A, 1B, and 2A; skip the next FP on the ring and sew through the next B, FP, and A bead on the set-up stitch, the B bead at the top of the last cell from the previous row, the next A bead on the set-up stitch, and the next FP, B, FP, B, and FP (Figure 14, red thread).

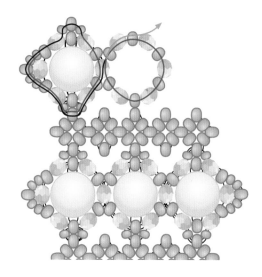

Figure 14

String 1A, 1B, and 1A; skip the next B on the ring and sew through the next FP; weave around the cell to exit the side FP (Figure 14, blue thread).

Cell 2: String 1B, 1FP, 1B, 1FP, 1B, 1FP, 1B, 1FP, 1B, 1FP, and 1B; sew back through the side FP on the previous cell in the same direction as before, forming the next ring (Figure 14, green thread). Sew forward through the next B, FP, and B (Figure 14, orange thread).

String one 6-mm pearl; sew through the opposite axis B bead on the ring; sew back through the pearl and back through the starting axis B bead in the same direction as before (Figure 15, red thread); tighten.

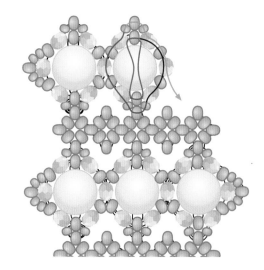

Figure 15

Sew forward through the next FP, B, FP, B, and FP (Figure 15, blue thread). String 1A; sew through the top B bead of the closest cell from the previous row; string 1A; sew through the next FP, B, FP, B, and FP (Figure 15, green thread).

String 1A, 1B, and 1A; skip the next B on the ring and sew through the next FP, B, and FP (Figure 15, orange thread).

Cell 3: String 1B, 1FP, 1B, 1FP, 1B, 1FP, 1B, 1FP, 1B, 1FP, and 1B; sew back through the side FP on Cell 2 in the same direction as before, forming the next ring. Sew forward through the next B, FP, and B (Figure 16, red thread).

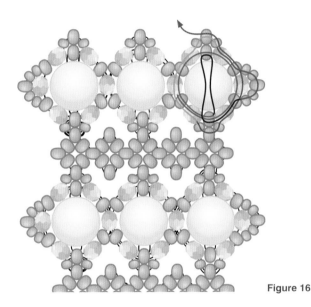

Figure 16

String one 6-mm pearl; sew through the opposite axis B bead on the ring; sew back through the pearl and back through the starting axis B bead in the same direction as before; tighten. Sew forward through the next FP and B (Figure 16, blue thread).

String 2A, 1B, and 2A; skip the next FP, and then sew through the next B and FP (Figure 16, green thread).

String 1A, 1B, and 1A; skip the next B on the ring and sew through the next FP, B, FP, B, and FP (Figure 16, orange thread).

String 1A; sew through the top B bead on the closest cell from the previous row; string 1A; sew through the next FP, then weave around the cell to exit the B bead at the top of the cell just added (Figure 16, purple thread).

Adding New Thread

You'll have to add thread at some point. When that happens, move the thread into a fire-polished bead that doesn't need to be used for the next cell. Use the bookbinder's knot (p. 14). Once the knot is secure, move the new working thread into position to continue, weave off the 2 tail threads, and trim tail ends.

The pattern repeat has been established. From here on out, repeat Row 2 (the set-up row), Row 3, Row 4 (the set-up row), and Row 5 three more times to achieve the bracelet length.

If you need a different length, bead until your piece is about ⅝ inch (1.6 cm) away from the ends touching when it's wrapped around the wrist. The bracelet ends with a pearl and fire-polished row, so plan your needs.

Add the loops for the buttons on one end: Move the thread on one end to exit a B bead, as in Figure 17. The direction of the thread isn't critical. String 1B, 9A, and 1B; sew through the same B bead the thread is exiting in the same direction as before (Figure 17, red thread). Adjust the tension; reinforce the loop, then weave the thread to exit the last cell in the row, as in Figure 17. Add the other loop (Figure 17, blue thread); reinforce the loop, then weave off this thread and trim.

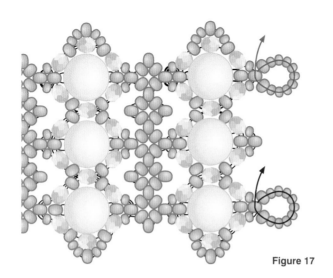

Figure 17

The Buttons

A series of little bands wrap around a 6-mm pearl, lacing together on the outer edge to form a beautiful little button. Make 2.

Bands 1 & 2: With 3 feet (91.4 cm) of prepared thread, string 1B, 1FP, 1B, 1FP, 1B, 1FP, 1B, 1FP, 1B, 1FP, 1B, and 1FP; pull the beads down to within 6 inches (15.2 cm) of the tail. Rethread through the first 9 beads to form a ring (Figure 18, red thread).

Figure 18

String one 6-mm pearl; sew through the opposite B bead (axis bead) on the ring; sew back through the pearl and back through the starting B bead (axis bead) in the same direction as before (Figure 18, blue thread); tighten.

Bands 3–6: String 1FP, 1B, 1FP, 1B, and 1FP; sew through the opposite B axis bead on the ring you just made. Repeat once more, placing this band next to the one just added (Figure 19). Turn the button over; repeat two more times on this side, for a total of 6 bands. Exit a B on the axis of the button (Figure 19, red thread).

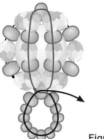

Figure 19

Add the button loop: String 1B, 9A, and 1B; sew through the same B bead the thread is exiting in the same direction as before, forming a loop (Figure 19, blue thread). Reinforce the loop.

Move the thread through the closest FP and B on the band that has the tail thread (Figure 20, beginning of red thread path). For clarity, I'll call this Band 1. We'll be working to the right, using the loop as a reference point.

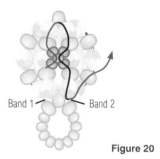

Band 1 — — Band 2

Figure 20

Lacing the bands on the button

A side lacing hooks the bands together and adds more detail to this great component.

Bands 1 & 2: String 3A, skip the next FP on Band 1, and sew up through the next B and FP. Push the 3A to the right (Figure 21, red thread); adjust the tension.

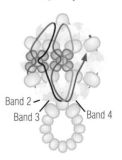

Band 2 — —
Band 3 — — Band 4

Figure 21

Sew down through the FP and B bead on Band 2. String 1A; sew through the middle A just added on Band 1; string 1A; sew through the next B and FP on Band 2 (Figure 21, blue thread); adjust the tension.

Bands 2 & 3: Sew up through the next FP and B on Band 3 (Figure 20, green thread). String 3A, then skip the next FP on Band 3; sew through the next B and FP, pushing the 3A to the left (Figure 21, orange thread); adjust the tension.

Sew down through the next FP and B bead on Band 2. String 1A; sew through the middle A just added on Band 3; string 1A; sew through the next B and FP on Band 2 (Figure 21, green thread); adjust the tension.

Bands 3 & 4: Sew up through the next FP and B bead on Band 3 (Figure 21, purple thread). Repeat the instruction for Bands 1 and 2 to attach Band 3 to Band 4.

Bands 4 & 5: Sew up through the next FP and B on Band 5. Repeat the instruction for Bands 2 and 3 to attach Band 4 to Band 5.

Bands 5 & 6: Sew up through the next FP and B bead on Band 5. Repeat the instruction for Bands 1 and 2 to attach Band 5 to Band 6.

Bands 6 & 1: Sew up through the next FP and B on Band 1. Repeat the instructions for Bands 2 and 3 to attach Band 6 to Band 1.

To add the picot at the top of the button, sew up through all beads of Band 1, exiting the last FP; string 1B, one 2-mm pearl, and 1B; skip the B bead at the axis and sew through the opposite FP, forming a picot (Figure 22). Make sure that the picot lines up with the button loop. Weave off both threads and trim.

Figure 22

Add the Buttons

With 18 inches (45.7 cm) of prepared thread, string 11A; tuck the needle through a loop on the bracelet and the loop on one button (Figure 23, blue thread). Center the beads on the thread; then make an overhand knot to tie the beads into a jump ring (Figure 23, red thread). Weave off both threads in opposite directions, then trim. Repeat for the other button (Figure 23, blue thread).

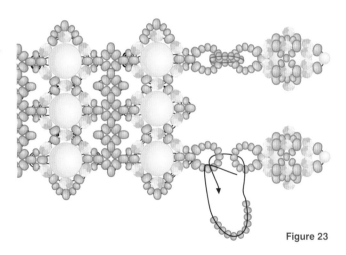

Figure 23

Add the Bead Loops

Move the remaining thread into position as in Figure 24, red dot. The direction isn't important.

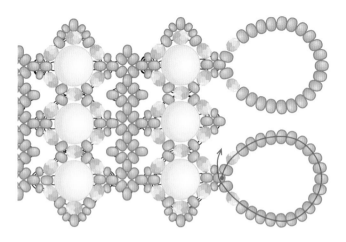

Figure 24

String 1B, 1FP, 21B, 1FP, and 1B; sew through the same B bead on the bracelet in the same direction as before, forming a loop (Figure 24, red thread). Before this loop is reinforced, hold onto the thread tightly and test the fit over the button. If the loop is too small, disconnect the loop and add B beads, 2 at a time, to the 21B count. If the loop is too large, disconnect the loop and remove B beads, 2 at a time, from the 21B count. When the size is right, reinforce the loop.

Weave through the bracelet to exit the B bead at the end of the last cell on the bracelet. Repeat the instructions for adding the second bead loop (Figure 24). Weave off this thread and trim.

A TOKEN OF LOVE & AFFECTION

TWO THREE-DIMENSIONAL BEADED RINGS, lined with little crystals, are joined together to form the band of this glamorous ring. The addition of a CZ with a simple bezel and two crystal pearls creates finishing touches that are classical and full of romantic history.

Version #1

{ HISTORICAL PERSPECTIVE }

Jacques-Louis David's painting, *The Farewell of Telemachus and Eucharis* (c. 1818) shows, in great detail, the obvious love and affection of the two lovers. The dreamy gaze of Telemachus draws the eye of the viewer, allowing an intimate glance into their relationship. Sadly, he must break off his relationship with Eucharis, as he is preparing to part, as is his duty, in pursuit of his father. Based on a seventeenth-century French novel detailing the conflict between duty and love, the story reminds one of the famous star-crossed lovers Romeo and Juliet.

My ring design is inspired by the history of the engagement ring and wedding ring. Today, we assume that the engagement gift would be a portion of the wedding band set, but that tradition is relatively new. Historically, a gift was given to prove the groom's love, but it could be anything of value that was worthy enough to seal the promise of marriage. His gesture symbolized undying love that was stronger and more enduring than any other emotion, a love so precious that its worth is priceless.

The Farewell of Telemachus and Eucharis by Jacques-Louis David

Dimensions

Versions #1 & #3: 1⅜ inches (3.5 cm) in diameter, including stone, and ½ inch (3.5 cm) wide (size 7)

Version #2: 1 ⅜ inches (3.5 cm) in diameter, including stone, and ½ inch (3.5 cm) wide (size 6½)

Techniques

Netting

Peyote stitch, flat, even count

Peyote stitch, tubular, even count

Stitch-in-the-ditch

Skill Level

Intermediate

Materials, Version #1

1 Swiss blue 10-mm round CZ (lab grown)

2 g metallic gold iris 15° seed beads (A)

1 g sea foam galvanized 15° seed beads* (B)

1 g dark metallic gold iris 11° cylinder beads (C)

1.5 g metallic gold iris 11° seed beads (D)

0.5 g sea foam galvanized 11° seed beads* (E)

80 to 100 crystal AB 2-mm round crystals**

4 ivory 2-mm Czech glass pearls

2 light gold 6-mm crystal pearls

Dark brown nylon beading thread

Materials, Version #2:

1 alexandrite 10-mm round CZ (lab grown)

2 g light pewter galvanized 15° seed beads* (A)

1 g yellow gold galvanized 15° seed beads* (B)

1 g silver gold iris (palladium electroplated AB) 11° cylinder beads (C)

1.5 g light pewter galvanized 11° seed beads* (D)

0.5 g yellow gold galvanized 11° seed beads* (E)

80 to 100 crystal AB 2-mm round crystals**

4 white 2-mm Czech glass pearls

2 white 6-mm crystal pearls

Gray/blue nylon beading thread

Materials, Version #3:

1 tanzanite 10-mm round CZ (lab grown)

2 g champagne galvanized 15° seed beads* (A)

1 g platinum electroplate 15° seed beads (B)

1 g champagne galvanized 11° cylinder beads (C)

1.5 g champagne galvanized 11° seed beads* (D)

0.5 g platinum electroplate 11° seed beads (E)

80 to 100 crystal AB 2-mm round crystals**

4 light beige 2-mm Czech glass pearls

2 cream 6-mm crystal pearls

Dark beige nylon beading thread

I prefer Duracoat galvanized seed beads.

**The number depends on the size of the ring and the varying sizes of the crystals.*

Tools

2 size 12 beading needles

1 size 13 beading needle (may be needed when embellishing)

Step gauge

Beader's supply kit (p. 5)

Version #2

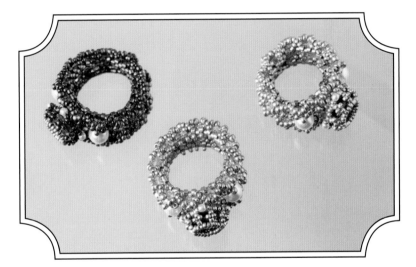

Version #3

Instructions

The rings: A strip of flat peyote stitch is joined in the round. Netting is used to add a lacing embellishment, holding into place a string of crystals that form a beautiful ring.

Rows 1 & 2: Using 5 feet (1.5 m) of prepared thread (p. 6), string enough C beads to wrap around your index finger plus a few extras, leaving an 18-inch (45.7 cm) tail.

Row 3: Without a bead on the needle, skip the last 2C strung; sew back through the third C, creating the first stitch (Figure 1, red thread). Using 1C in each stitch, work flat peyote stitch to the end of the row (p. 9 and Figure 1, blue thread). Don't worry if there is a bead left over on the tail thread. Tighten the strip.

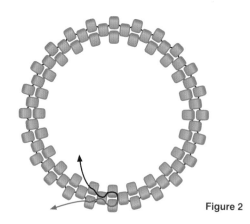

Figure 2

Figure 1

Test the fit around your index finger. Count the number of C beads on Row 1 or Row 3 (Figure 1). Two of my rings have 24 beads, and one has 22 beads. You need an even number. Add or subtract to get the right number and fit. If your ring ends up being a tiny bit too large, you will have an opportunity to add a ring-sizing addition to make the ring a bit smaller. The beadwork needs to end as in Figure 1.

Zip: Using the working thread, wrap the strip around a step gauge or your finger; sew forward through the first 3C beads on one side of the strip. Repeat on the other side of the strip, using the tail thread (p. 10 and Figure 2, red and blue threads); adjust the tension. The beadwork is now even-count tubular peyote stitch (p. 10). Test the fit on your index finger. It should fit, not too tight and not to loose.

Round 4: Using the working thread, *work netting; using 3A on the needle, sew through the next C bead on Row 3, creating a net. Without beads, weave forward through the next C on Row 2 and the next C on Row 3. Repeat from * to the end of the round (Figure 3, red thread). Step up through the first 2A added in this round (p. 8 and Figure 3, red thread).

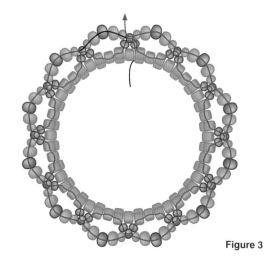

Figure 3

Round 5: Using the working thread, *work netting; string 1A, 1D, 1E, 1D, and 1A; sew through the next A at the point of the next net (Figure 3, blue thread). Repeat from * until you finish the round; do not step up (Figure 3, green thread).

Turn the beadwork over. Weave the thread through the next A on the net, diagonally through the next 3C to exit a C bead on Row 1, so that when a net is added on this side, it aligns to a net added on Round 4 on the other side (Figure 4).

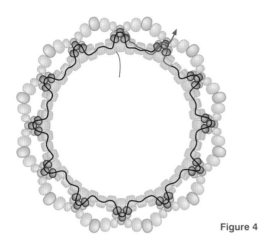

Figure 4

Round 6: Repeat Round 4 on this side, making sure that the nets align (Figure 4, blue thread); step up through the first 2A added in this round (Figure 4, green thread). Keep the thread.

Add the crystals: Place a needle onto the tail thread. Weave the thread forward 1C to exit a C bead on Row 2 of the (Figure 5, beginning of red thread). String enough 2-mm crystals that, when pushed into the channel between the netting rounds, the last crystal added meets the first crystal added (Figure 5). This needs to be a tight fit. Reinforce the ring of crystals to tighten; keep the thread.

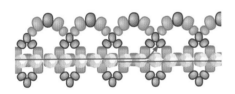

Figure 5

Note: The number of 2-mm crystals will vary. My versions used 41, 44, and 45 crystals.

Stitch-in-the-ditch to add the ring-sizing beads

A simple addition of 4 beads changes the size of the ring. Two versions of my ring have 12 nets and the third has 11. The number will depend on the size of your ring. Having an even or an odd number of nets will change things a bit, so there are instructions below for both approaches.

For rings with an even number of nets: Try on the ring. If it's a good fit, weave off the tail thread and trim, and then move onto the next technique. If the ring is a bit too loose, move the tail thread to exit a Row 2 C bead on the underside of the ring that is centered on a net from Round 4 (Figure 6, beginning of red thread).

Even number of picots

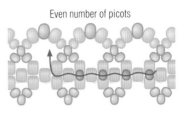

Figure 6

String 1A, stitch-in-the-ditch (p. 12) by sewing through the next C on Row 2 of the strip. Repeat for a total of 4A added (Figure 6). Check the fit. If the ring is still too big, remove the 4A and replace them with 4C to take up a bit more room. When complete, weave off this thread within the peyote stitch and trim.

For rings with an odd number of nets: Try on the ring. If it's a good fit, weave off the tail thread and trim. If the ring is a bit too loose, move the tail thread to exit a C bead on Row 2 of the strip, on the inside of the ring, to align with an E bead on a net (Figure 7, beginning of red thread).

Odd number of picots

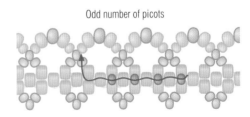

Figure 7

String 1A, stitch-in-the-ditch (p.12) by sewing through the next C on Row 2 of the strip. Repeat for a total of 4A added (Figure 7). Check the fit. If the ring is still too big, remove the 4A and replace them with 4C to take up a bit more room. When complete, weave off this thread within the peyote stitch and trim.

Round 7, lacing: Using the remaining thread, which is exiting a middle A bead of a net from Round 4, *string 1A and 1D; sew through the E bead on Round 5 on the opposite side; string 1D and 1A; sew through the center A bead on the next net from Round 6 (Figure 8). Tighten. Repeat from * until all nets have been laced; weave forward through some of the nets until the tension holds; keep the thread.

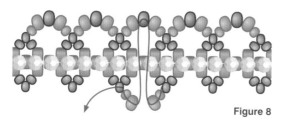

Figure 8

Positioning the thread: Having an even or an odd number of lacing nets will affect how many lacing nets are at center bottom. Even numbers will have 2 nets and odd numbers will have a single net.

For an even number of nets: If you didn't add ring-sizing beads, pick two lacings that are right next to each other and close to your thread. If you did add ring-sizing beads, these beads mark center bottom.

Weave the thread forward to exit an E bead that is on the left-hand side of center bottom, as Figure 9, red dot bead. If you have to turn around the thread, use a half-hitch knot (p. 16). Set this component aside.

Even number of picots

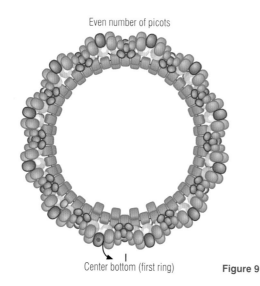

Center bottom (first ring)   **Figure 9**

Make another ring, using 4 feet (1.2 m) of prepared thread, leaving an 18-inch (45.7 cm) tail; adding the resizing beads, if they were added to the first component. When the second is complete, weave off this thread and trim.

For an odd number of nets: If you didn't add ring-sizing beads, pick one lacing that is close to your thread, exiting an E bead (Figure 10).

Odd number of picots

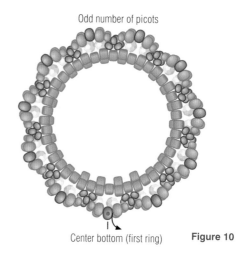

Center bottom (first ring)   **Figure 10**

If you did add ring-sizing beads, these beads mark center bottom. Weave the thread forward, to exit the E bead that is at center bottom, as in Figure 10, red dot bead. If you have to turn around the thread, use a half-hitch knot (p. 16). Set this component aside.

Make another ring, using 4 feet (1.2 m) of prepared thread, adding the ring-sizing beads, if they were added to the first component. When the second is complete, weave off this thread and trim.

Attach the Ring Components together at Center Bottom

For rings with an even number of nets: Place a needle onto the remaining thread, which is exiting an E bead on the left-hand side of center bottom. Place the component without thread on top of the first component, aligning center bottom and the lacing (Figure 11).

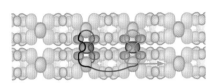

Figure 11

String 1A, 1E, and 1A; sew through the opposite E bead on the top component as in Figure 11, red thread. String 1A; sew back through the E bead just added; string 1A; sew back through the E bead on the bottom ring (Figure 11, blue thread); tighten. Reinforce this connection.

Weave forward through the lacing to exit the E bead on the right-hand side of center bottom (Figure 11, green thread). Repeat the attachment here as well (Figure 11, orange thread); keep the thread.

For odd-numbered nets: The connection for this component is the same as above except there is only one attachment at center bottom. Place the component without thread on top of the first component, aligning center bottom and the lacings (Figure 12).

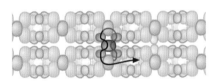

Figure 12

String 1A, 1E, and 1A; sew through the opposite E bead on the top component as in Figure 12, red thread. String 1A; sew back through the E bead just added; string 1A; sew back through the E bead on the bottom ring (Figure 12, blue thread); tighten. Reinforce this connection; keep the thread.

Add the 6-mm Pearl Embellishment

Find the center top on the ring components, which is between two lacings and opposite the center bottom attachment (Figure 13). We will be using the lacings on the left and right of center top. Weave the thread to exit the inside D bead on the second lacing back from center top (Figure 13, red dot bead and beginning of red thread).

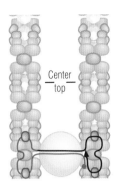

Figure 13

Turn the components to the side, with center bottom down, center top up, and the component with the thread on your right. I use the terms "up" and "down" to explain the direction of the thread path. The thread is now in the up position on the right-hand ring (Figure 13, beginning of red thread) and is exiting at the red dot bead.

Step 1: String one 6-mm pearl and sew down through the opposite D bead on the left-hand ring; string 1A; sew up through the closest outside D bead on the lacing; sew through the middle E bead and the upper outside D bead; string 1A; sew down through the upper D bead on the inside of the left-hand ring (Figure 13, red thread).

Step 2: Sew back through the pearl; up through the inside upper D bead; string 1A; sew down through the closest outside D bead on the lacing; sew through the middle E bead, down through the outside D bead; string 1A; sew up through the lower D bead on the inside of the right-hand ring (Figure 13, blue thread).

Step 3: String 1D; sew through the upper inside D bead; weave through the A, D, E, D, A, and D, and back through the pearl (Figure 14, red thread); weave through the D, A, D, E, D, A, D; string 1D (Figure 14, blue thread). Sew through the lower inside D bead, completing the connection (Figure 14, green thread).

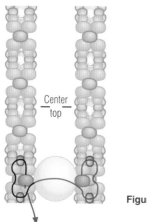

Center
top

Figure 14

Repeat Steps 1 through 3 on the other side of center top (Figures 13 and 14); weave off the thread and trim.

Bezel the CZ
A quick and easy bezel is the crowning glory of this fabulous ring.

Round 1: Using 3 feet (91.4 cm) of prepared thread, string 16D, leaving a 6-inch (15 cm) tail; overhand-knot the beads into a circle (p. 17). Using the working thread, sew through 1D to get away from the knot (Figure 15, red thread).

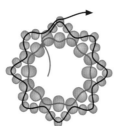

Figure 15

Round 2: *Work netting using 3A; skip the next bead on Round 1, and sew through the one after that. Repeat from * 7 more times for a total of 8 nets; step up through the first 2A of the first net added (Figure 15, blue thread).

Note: Before we begin Rounds 3 and 4, and because color is really important to me, when I did versions #2 and #3, I switched the bead color around a bit. I have put version #1's stringing pattern first, then versions #2 and #3 in parentheses next to it. Feel free to change it to your liking.

Round 3: *Work spikes: using 3A and 1B (2A, 1B, 1A), bring the beads down to the beadwork; skip the last bead added, sew back through the next bead; adjust the tension (Figure 16, red thread).

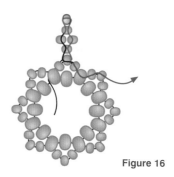

Figure 16

String 1A, skip the next bead on the spike; sew through the one after that, making 1 peyote stitch; sew through the top bead of the net in the same direction as before (Figure 16, blue thread).

Weave through the beadwork to exit the top bead of the next net (Figure 16, green thread). Repeat from * 7 more times for a total of 8 spikes, but after completing the last spike, end by stepping up through the first spike added, exiting the topmost bead (Figure 17, beginning of red thread path).

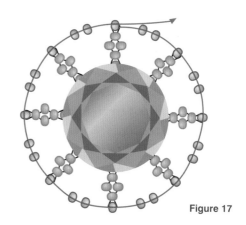

Figure 17

Round 4: Work lacing using 2B (2A for versions #2 and #3); sew through the top bead of the next spike (Figure 17, red thread). Repeat around, not pulling tight, for 8 stitches, exiting the top bead of the first spike (figure 17).

Wipe off the CZ and place it on the bezel, point down. Pull the lacing tight; reinforce the lacing to hold the CZ in place (Figure 18). Weave off the tail thread and trim. Weave the remaining thread down through a spike to exit the top bead of a net on Round 2 (Figure 19).

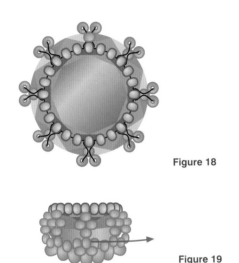

Figure 18

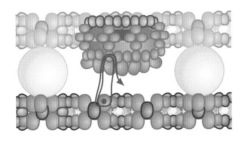

Figure 19

Add CZ Bezel to the Ring

Lay the bezel on top of the ring between the two pearl embellishments, centering the net that the thread is exiting and the one to the right of the thread with the 2 centered E beads on the lacing (Figure 20).

Figure 20

Step 1, left side: Sew through the D bead, on the inside, to the right of the E bead on the lacing that is left of center as in Figure 20, red dot bead. Sew back through the middle A bead on the bezel in the same direction as before; reinforce once more, ending by exiting the middle A bead on the bezel (Figure 20).

Step 2: String 1A, one 2-mm pearl, and 1A; sew through the middle A bead on the net to the right of the center top (Figure 21).

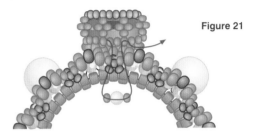

Figure 21

Step 3, right side: Sew through the inside D bead that is to the left of the right-hand E bead on the lacing. Sew back through the middle A bead on the bezel in the same direction as before. Reinforce once more, ending by exiting the middle A bead of a net on the bezel.

Step 4: Weave the thread in the bezel to exit the middle bead of the next net. String 1A, one 3-mm pearl, and 1A; sew through the middle A bead on the next net (Figure 22).

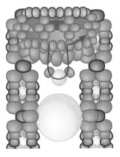

Figure 22

Step 5: Weave the thread in the bezel to exit the middle bead of the next net.

Repeat Steps 1, 2, 3, and 4; weave off the thread and trim.

BYZANTINE PEARL CUFF

TWO PEARL- AND FIRE-POLISH–EMBELLISHED END CAPS terminate at the opening of a peyote stitch band cuff. A laced picot embellishment holds fire polish beads in place on the band, adding extra texture. Built around a brass cuff blank and worn with the opening at the top of the wrist, this cuff design evokes the antique Byzantine style of jewelry, worn throughout the centuries since 334 AD.

Version #1

140

{ HISTORICAL PERSPECTIVE }

Byzantine-style jewelry appears in the spectacular portrait painting, *Princesse de Broglie* (c. 1851–1853) by the French painter Jean-Auguste-Dominique Ingres (1780–1867). Ingres captured the great beauty and reserve of his sitter and the true essence of her style, making this painting one of his most famous. His brilliant skill is evident in the quality of the material objects seen, as in the rich satin and lace of her gown, the upholstery of the chair, the evening scarf, and her exquisite antique jewelry.

My inspiration for Byzantine Pearl Cuff came to me while standing in front of this painting in New York City in 2014. Ingres' beautiful painting reminded me of the course that Byzantine-inspired jewelry has taken since its inception. The designs have remained elegant, stylish, and timeless.

Version #2

Princesse de Broglie by Jean-Auguste-Dominique Ingres

Detail from Version #1

Dimensions

6¼ inches (15.9 cm) long x ⅜ inch (9.5 mm) wide [focal end caps are approximately ½ inch (12.7 mm) wide]

Techniques

Edge-stitching

Peyote stitch, flat, odd-count technique called step up/step down

Peyote stitch, tubular, even count with decreasing

Stitch-in-the-ditch

Skill level

Intermediate

Materials, Version #1

5–7 g pewter galvanized 15° seed beads (A)*, **

0.5 g metallic dark bronze 15° seed beads (B)

5–7 g pewter galvanized 11° cylinder beads (C)*, **

2 g pewter galvanized 11° seed beads (D)**

0.5 g metallic dark bronze 11° seed beads (E)

76–94 garnet 3-mm Czech fire-polished beads (FP)*

2 light gold 12-mm crystal pearls

13–16 inches (33–40.6 cm) of ¼ inch (6-mm) wide double-sided craft tape

1 brass cuff blank, ¼ inch (6 mm) wide ***

Dark beige nylon beading thread

Card stock

Small piece of clear tape

Materials, Version #2

5–7 g yellow gold galvanized 15° seed beads (A)*, **

0.5 g palladium electroplate 15° seed beads (B)

5–7 g yellow gold galvanized 11° cylinder beads (C)*, **

2 g yellow gold galvanized 11° seed beads (D)**

0.5 g palladium electroplate 11° seed beads (E)

76–94 amethyst glow 3-mm Czech fire-polished beads (FP)*

2 cream 12-mm crystal pearls

13–16 inches (33–40.6 cm) of ¼ inch (6-mm) wide double-sided craft tape

1 brass cuff blank, ¼ inch (6 mm) wide***

Gold nylon beading thread

Card stock

Small piece of clear tape

*Amounts needed depend on the size of the bracelet.

**I prefer Duracoat galvanized seed beads.

***Cuff blanks come in different lengths: 5¾ inches (14.6 cm), 6 inches (15.2 cm), 6½ inches (16.5 cm), and 7 inches (17.8 cm). The best fit is a cuff that can be shaped around your wrist for a comfortable fit with a 1-inch (2.5 cm) opening.

Tools

2 size 12 beading needles

1 size 13 beading needle (may be needed when embellishing)

Small Teflon-coated craft scissors

Beader's supply kit (p. 5)

Instructions

Make a pattern to determine cuff blank size: Cut a ¼-inch (6-mm) wide strip of card stock that is 3 inches (7.6 cm) longer than your wrist measurement. Stick a piece of clear tape onto one end. Wrap the strip around your wrist; tape one end of the strip to the other end of strip, forming a bangle shape that is comfortable, but not too tight. Test the feel of the bangle. Adjust to your desired size.

Cut the paper bangle off your wrist on the opposite side of the join and place it onto your work surface. With a pen or pencil make a mark 1 inch (2.5 cm) from the end of the strip. Measure the strip up to the mark that you have made. Mine measured 5⅞ inches (14.9 cm). If your measurement is between cuff blank sizes, always pick the one that is shorter, as you can widen the cuff blank a bit.

Shaping the brass cuff blank: In most cases the cuff blank will need to be shaped a bit. For this design, the blank is used with the opening at the top of your wrist, versus the standard approach. I like the blank to be round, so shape it with your fingers to fit with a 1-inch (2.5 cm) opening.

Prepare the cuff blank: Using Teflon-coated scissors, cut two 7-inch (17.8-cm) long pieces of double-sided tape, leaving the plastic coating attached. Starting at the center top of the outside of the cuff blank, press one piece of tape to the cuff blank, smoothing the tape along the blank and keeping the tape centered. Fold the tape smoothly around the end of the blank and continue to stick the tape to the underside until you run out of tape. Repeat for the other side, using the remaining strip of double-sided tape. Cut off what is not needed. Don't overlap the tape and don't remove the plastic top coating. Using the Teflon-coated scissors, trim away any tape that is sticking out beyond the long edges of the cuff (Figure 1).

Figure 1

Peyote-Stitch Strip

Flat odd-count peyote stitch completely covers the brass cuff blank. I use a technique I call step-up/step-down peyote stitch, as the thread path removes the need to add a homeless bead at the end of every odd-numbered row. The thread path leaves the edges of the beadwork neat and tidy.

Rows 1 & 2: Using 6 feet (1.8 m) of prepared thread (p. 6), string 6C, leaving a 6-inch (15.2 cm) tail (Figure 2, red thread).

Figure 2

Row 3: Without a bead on the needle, skip the last 2C added; sew through the third-to-last added C, making the first stitch; adjust the tension (Figure 2, red thread). Work flat peyote stitch (p. 9) using 1C in each stitch; make 1 stitch. Using 1C, sew back through the remaining C bead on the tail thread, from the tail-end side, as in Figure 2, blue thread. Adjust the tension and your hold on the beadwork.

Row 4: Using 1C in each stitch, make 2 stitches (Figure 3, red thread).

Figure 3

Row 5: Using 1C, make 1 stitch; using 1C, make 1 stitch and step-down (Figure 3, blue thread). Using 1C, step up (Figure 3, green thread). The thread is now exiting the middle C bead on Row 5. Step-up/step-down peyote stitch begins now.

Rows 6 & 7: *Row 6:* Using 1C, make 1 stitch (Figure 4, red thread). *Row 7:* Using 1C, make 1 stitch and step down (Figure 4, beginning of blue thread). *Back to Row 6:* Using 1C, make 1 stitch (Figure 4, blue thread). *Back to Row 7:* Using 1C, make 1 stitch; using 1C, make 1 stitch and step down and turn around (Figure 5).

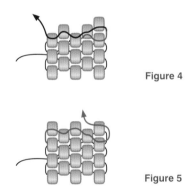

Figure 4

Figure 5

Note: The step-down and turnaround technique denotes the end of the progression and will alternate sides as you make the strip.

Rows 8 & beyond: Repeat Rows 4 through 7 until the strip is twice as long as the cuff blank length. For example, my bracelets use a 5¾-inch (14.6 cm) cuff blank, so I stitched 11½ inches (29.2 cm) of strip. Add new thread when needed. When you reach the desired length, weave off all threads except the working one.

Add the peyote-stitch base to the prepared cuff blank: Peel the plastic coating off the double-sided tape attached to the cuff blank without touching the tape too much. Begin pressing one end of the peyote-stitch strip to the blank, about 1 inch (2.5 cm) up from one end, on the outside of the curve. Continue pressing the strip onto the tape along the outside, stretching the beadwork taut as you press. Wrap the strip around one end, keeping the strip centered as you continue to press the strip along the inside. Wrap around the other end and finish pressing down the last little bit of strip. The remaining space should be about ¼ to ½ inch (6 to 13 mm) from touching the other end of the strip.

Take a look at the edge of the strip that is rolling around each end of the cuff blank. It would be best if the strip were positioned as in Figure 6, red dot bead, on both ends. Placement for the focal pearls will be more even and easier to count. Adjust strip if needed.

Figure 6

Finish the peyote-stitch strip: Continue stitching the peyote-stitch strip until the ends meet. My thread ended up exiting a middle C bead as in Figure 7, beginning of red thread. Your ending thread position may be different because of the length of the strip, so move your thread to match mine. If needed, tighten or loosen the tension of the peyote-stitch strip on the tape to get the right fit.

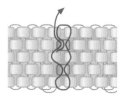

Figure 7

Zip the ends of the peyote-stitch base: Work peyote stitch using 1C; make 1 stitch. Sew back through the outside C bead at the end of the opposite strip, the C bead just added and the middle bead on the next C bead. Using 1C, make 1 stitch. Tighten the beadwork to pull the edges together. Reinforce the connection; weave off the thread and trim.

Set Up for the Center Embellishment

A series of picots build a track that will later hold a string of fire-polish beads.

Tip: Don't wax your thread while working Steps 1 through 8. The wax will come off onto the beadwork and can be difficult to remove.

Step 1: Push a needle as a marker through the 3 C beads on the row that is centered with the end of the blank (Figure 6, red dot bead and Figure 8, marked beads at far right). Counting from the marked row, count the C beads along the outer edge, finding the eighth and ninth C beads away from the marked row. It is the indented row between these 2 edge beads that we want (Figure 8, red dot bead).

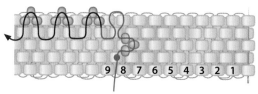

Figure 8

Using 6 feet (1.8 m) of thread, sew through the C bead on this indented row (Figure 8, red dot bead), leaving an 18-inch (45.7 cm) tail.

Step 2: String 3A; sew through the other C bead in this row, stitching-in-the-ditch, to form a picot (Figure 8, beginning of red thread path). This is one of 2 picots that will be used to string the fire-polished beads.

Step 3: For clarity, I am going to use the words "in" and "out" to denote whether the tip of the needle is pointing in toward the center of the strip or out toward the edge of the strip. Move the thread to exit out of the marked C bead as in Figure 8, end of red thread path.

Step 4: *String 3A; sew in through the next C bead, working away from the end of the cuff, forming a picot; sew out through the next C bead on the same ridge of beads (Figure 8, blue thread). Repeat from * until the picots are within 1 inch (2.5 cm) of the other end of the cuff blank.

Step 5: Push a needle through the 3C beads on the row that is centered on the other end of the blank (Figure 9). Count the C beads along the outer edge, finding the ninth C bead away from the marked row. Continue adding picots until the last picot added is right next to the ninth C bead (Figure 9, end of red thread).

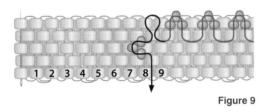

Figure 9

Step 6: Move the thread to exit a C bead (indented from the edge) that is between the eighth and ninth C beads along the edge (Figure 9, blue thread). String 3A; sew through the other C bead in this row, stitching-in-the-ditch, to form a picot (Figure 9, end of blue thread path). This is the second picot that will be used to string the fire-polished beads.

Step 7: Move the thread to exit out of a C bead as in Figure 10, beginning of red thread path. Repeat Step 4, aligning these picots to the other side, until the picots meet up with the stitch-in-the-ditch picots on the other end.

Figure 10

Step 8: Place a needle onto the tail thread and move the tail thread to exit the center A bead of the stitch-in-the-ditch picot (Figure 11, red thread); move the working thread to exit the center A bead of the side of the last picot added, as in Figure 11, green thread.

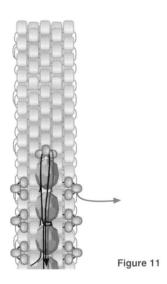

Figure 11

Add the fire-polished beads: Place a needle onto the tail thread that is exiting the stitch-in-the-ditch picot (Figure 11, red thread); string enough fire-polished beads to stretch tightly to the opposite stitch-in-the-ditch picot. Sew through the center A bead of the stitch-in-the-ditch picot on the opposite end. Weave back through the fire-polished beads and back through the opposite picot. Weave back through the fire-polished beads again, making half-hitch knots (p. 16) between every fifth or sixth bead (Figure 11, blue thread). Trim the thread.

Lace down the fire-polished beads
A simple lacing technique is an effective way to anchor the fire-polished beads beautifully.

Step 1: Using the remaining thread, string 2A, 1B, and 2A; stitch through the center A bead of the opposite picot (Figure 12, red thread). String 2A, and sew through the center A bead of the stitch-in-the-ditch picot; string 2A, and sew through the center A bead of the next picot around the corner (Figure 12, blue thread).

Figure 12

Step 2: String 1A; skip the next A bead on the lacing, sew through the next A, B, A, and tighten. String 1A; sew through the center A bead of the opposite picot (Figure 13, red thread); sew back through 2A, B, 2A, of the lacing and the A bead at the top of the opposite picot and tighten (Figure 13, blue thread).

Step 3: Sew down through the next A bead on the picot, letting the needle go underneath the fire-polished beads for ease in moving the thread forward. Tuck the needle back under the fire-polished beads while sewing up through the first A bead of the next picot (Figure 13, beginning of green thread path).

Sew through the center A bead and the next A of the same picot, letting the needle tuck under the fire-polished beads. Tuck back under the fire-polished beads while sewing up through the next A bead of the next picot. Sew through the center A of the picot (Figure 13, green thread).

Step 4: Repeat Steps 2 and 3, lacing every other set of picots (Figure 13, purple thread, Figure 14, and Figure 15) until close to center bottom. Since the lacing is done using every other set of picots, we need to know if your bracelet has an even or an odd number of picot sets. Count forward to see how many picot sets remain. If it is an odd number, continue lacing to the end. If your bracelet has an even number, 2 lacings have to be next to each other at center bottom (Figure 16). Once the center bottom has been taken care of, continue working Steps 2 and 3 to the end.

Figure 13

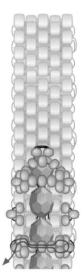

Figure 14

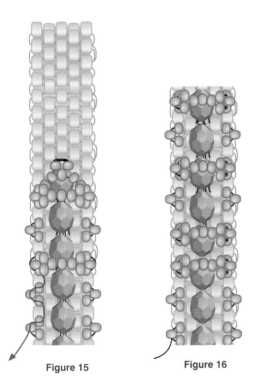

Figure 15　　　　**Figure 16**

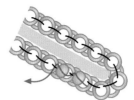

Figure 18

For the other edge: Using the remaining thread, edge-stitch the other edge in the same way. Weave off this thread and trim.

Finish the sides of the cuff

A neat and tidy edging hides the rest of the cuff blank. Using 5 feet (1.5 m) of unwaxed thread, sew through an A bead on the edging at the end of the cuff on one edge, leaving a 2-foot (61 cm) tail (Figure 19, beginning of red thread path).

Step 5: Repeat Step 1; weave off this thread and trim.

Edge-stitch the sides of the peyote-stitch base

With 6 feet (1.8 m) of unwaxed thread, sew through any edge C bead close to one end; even up the thread ends, and then weave across the strip to exit any C bead on the opposite edge (Figure 17).

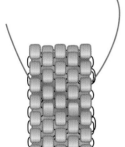

Figure 17

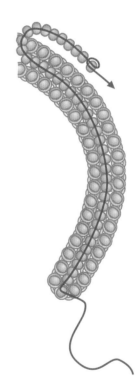

Figure 19

For one edge: *To edge-stitch (p. 11), string 1A, tuck the needle under the closest thread on the edge, pull through; adjust the tension (Figure 18). Repeat from * until the last stitch meets the first; weave off this thread and trim.

Step 1: Place a needle on the tail thread. Using the tail thread, string enough A beads that when the string of beads is laid along the channel of the bracelet, the beads stretch from one end to the other. Make a stopper bead (p. 18) of the last A strung (Figure 19).

Step 2: Using the longer thread, tighten the thread so that the first A strung is touching the A bead that the thread is exiting on the edge-stitching. Sew through the first 2A strung; tighten (Figure 20, red thread).

Figure 20

Lacing: *Sew through the closest A bead on the edge stitching on the right side, pointing the needle towards this end of the cuff; sew forward through the same A bead on the string of beads (Figure 20, blue thread).

Sew through the closest A bead on the edge-stitching on the left side, pointing the needle toward this end of the cuff; sew forward through the same A bead on the string plus 2 to 3 more (Figure 20, green thread); tighten. Push the beads into the groove created by the edge-stitching; tighten the stopper bead against the string of A beads.

Note: Pick beads that align the best to the edge-stitching beads, about 2 to 3 beads between each lacing. The curvature of the cuff will not allow the bead counts to align, so just make sure that the A beads are stitched tightly next to each other without any gaps.

Repeat the lacing technique from * to the opposite end of the cuff. Disconnect the stopper bead and remove any unwanted beads. If the remaining unstitched beads don't fit quite right, remove them and pick a different combination, as beads are all a bit different in size.

Push the remaining beads into the groove; stitch them into place and end by exiting the last A strung. Sew through the A bead at the end of the cuff. Weave this thread back through all of the strung A beads, half-hitching (p. 16) every once in a while. Anchor the thread and trim.

Using the remaining thread, sew through the A bead at the end of the cuff; weave off this thread within the peyote strip and trim.

Pearl End Caps

Two big crystal pearls with peyote-stitch bezels are the focal points for the ends of this cuff-style bracelet. Bezel 2 pearls.

Rounds 1 & 2: Using 5 feet (1.5 m) of prepared thread, string 1 pearl, leaving an 18-inch (45.7 cm) tail. String 15D; sew through the pearl again, from the tail thread side, laying the D beads along one side of the pearl. String 15D; sew through the pearl again, from the tail thread side, laying the beads along the opposite side of the pearl (Figure 21, red thread). Adjust the tension.

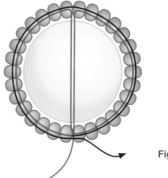

Figure 21

Sew around the ring, closing the gap at each end of the pearl's hole, ending as in Figure 21, blue thread.

Round 3: Work tubular even-count peyote stitch (p. 10) using 1D in each stitch and pushing all new beads to one side; make 15 stitches. Step up through the first D added in this round (Figure 22, red thread).

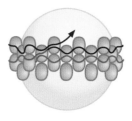

Figure 22

Round 4: On the same side that Round 3 was added, work tubular even-count peyote stitch using 1D in each stitch; make 15 stitches. Step up through the first D added in this round (Figure 22, blue thread).

Rounds 5–7: On the same side Round 4 was added, work 3 rounds of tubular even-count peyote stitch, using 1A in each stitch; make 15 stitches in each round. Step up through the first A added in each round (Figure 23, red thread).

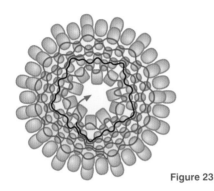

Figure 23

Round 8. Two-row decreases—the skip: Starting where you left off in Round 7, *work tubular peyote stitch using 1A in each stitch; make 2 stitches. Without a bead on the needle, sew through the next A bead on Round 6 and the next A on Round 7, creating a skip (p. 12). Repeat from * 4 more times, ending with a skip and step up (Figure 23, blue thread).

Round 9. Complete the decrease—1 over the skip: *Work tubular peyote stitch using 1C; make 1 stitch. Using 1C, jump over the skip and sew through the closest A bead from Round 8, placing 1 over the skip (Figure 23, green thread). Repeat from * 4 more times, ending with 1 over the skip, and step up.). This side of the bezel is now the back.

Setting up for the fire-polished bead ring: Move the thread forward through the next A from Round 8 and the next A from Round 7 (Figure 24, red thread). *String 1E; sew through the next A bead on Round 7, stitching-in-the-ditch. Repeat from * 14 more times; step up. Weave the thread forward to exit any C bead on Round 9 (Figure 24, blue thread). Set aside, keeping both threads.

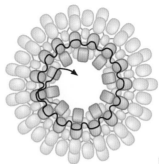

Figure 24

Attach the pearl bezels: There is a space between the end of the cuff and the beginning of the fire-polished lacing, and that space is a perfect fit for a pearl bezel. The C beads from Round 9 have to be stitched to the peyote stitch strip, and when needed, to the edge-stitching beads.

I start by butting the pearl bezel up against the lacing; spin it around so that the thread is exiting toward the end of the cuff (Figure 25), as it will be easier to work from here.

Count back from the edge to enter a C bead on the strip as in Figure 25, red dot bead (shown with the pearl component lifted up for a better view of the stitching area). Lift the bezel up so you can see where you are stitching. We will tighten this later.

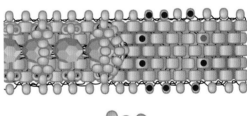

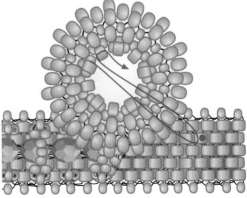

Figure 25

Sew forward through the next C bead on Round 9 on the bezel. Sew out through the closest edge bead on the strip. Sew through the next C bead on the bezel (Figure 25, red thread). Sew through the next edge bead on the strip. Continue in this manner about halfway aroundusing the blue dot beads on the band as a guide for stitching; tighten. Lift up the bezel a bit to finish the stitching; tighten.

When complete (Figure 26), weave the thread up to exit any E bead on the set-up round (Figure 26, blue thread).

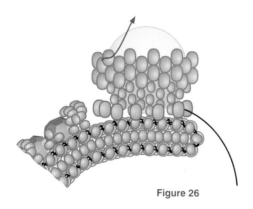

Figure 26

Add the fire-polished beads: String 15 FP; wrap them around the bezel, keeping the FP beads on top of the set-up round of E beads; sew through the first 3FP strung (Figure 27); tighten. Continue to weave in the FP ring, tightening and half-hitching as you weave off this thread; trim.

Figure 27

Add the picots at the top of the fire-polished ring: Place a needle onto the tail thread that is still exiting the pearl. Sew through the closest D bead at the top of the bezel (Figure 26, red thread), plus 2 more at a diagonal (Figure 27, beginning of red thread).

*String 3A; stitch-in-the-ditch to the next D bead on the same row as the thread is exiting, forming a picot (Figure 27). Repeat from * 14 more times for a total of 15 picots added in this round (Figure 28). Weave the thread back up to any E bead at the top of the bezel.

Work tubular peyote stitch using 1B for each stitch; make 15 stitches (Figure 28). Weave off this thread in the top 2 rounds; trim.

Figure 28

Repeat the instruction for attaching the remaining pearl bezel, adding the fire-polished ring, the picots, and the last peyote-stitch round at the top of the bezel.

NECKLACE OF DANCING CIRCLES

VARYING SIZES OF FLAT CIRCULAR PEYOTE STITCH DISCS are linked together and attached to a herringbone-stitch necklace. Each disc is edged in black to accent the playful use of color. The necklace ends in a herringbone loop and a beaded button. Light and airy, simple yet dramatic, with color taking center stage!

Version #1

{ HISTORICAL PERSPECTIVE }

Barbara Campanini (1721–1799), known as La Barbarina, was the most famous Italian ballerina of the eighteenth century. Many famous artists painted her, although the paintings that I like the most are the ones that show Campanini in motion, joyfully dancing her way to stardom.

Antoine Pesne (1683–1757), a French portrait painter, painted *La Barbarina* (c. 1745), showing her as she does a playful dance step while playing a tambourine. The gown is quite unique, as the petticoat appears to be embellished with a form of animal print, or fur, with an elaborate ruched (pleated) edging. The petticoat has colorful rosettes on a field of shimmering silk, which dances in the light.

Necklace of Dancing Circles follows the theme of the colorful rosettes found on Campanini's gown, resulting in a very contemporary design.

The Dancer Barbara Campanini, La Barbarina by Antoine Pesne

Dimensions, both versions
16 inches (40.6 cm) long

Techniques
Herringbone stitch, tubular
Ladder stitch
Peyote stitch, flat circular, even count with increasing
Right-angle weave

Skill level
Intermediate

Materials, Version #1
3 g teal/turquoise lined 15° seed beads (A)
4 g blue/ purple lined 15° seed beads (B)
2 g olive/bronze lined 15° seed beads (C)
2 g citrine/celery lined 15° seed beads (D)
2 g blue/blue-green lined 15° seed beads (E)
1 g black 15° seed beads (F)
16 g black 11° seed beads (G)
Black nylon beading thread

Materials, Version #2
3 g peach gold galvanized 15° seed beads* (A)
4 g dark orange galvanized 15° seed beads* (B)
2 g sea green galvanized 15° seed beads* (C)
2 g sea foam galvanized 15° seed beads* (D)
2 g magenta galvanized 15° seed beads* (E)
1 g black 15° seed beads (F)
16 g black 11° seed beads (G)
Black nylon beading thread

*I prefer Duracoat galvanized seed beads.

Tools
2 size 12 beading needles
1 glass-headed straight pin
Some small plastic bags, 1½ x 2 inches (3.8 x 5 cm) or other method to hold threads
Macramé board (optional, but handy, as it has a marked grid on it, which makes it easier to align all of the circles on the necklace)
Beader's supply kit (p. 5)

Detail from Version #1

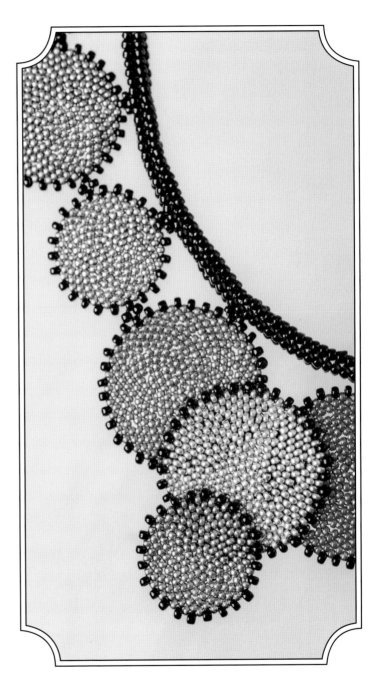

Detail from Version #2

Instructions

Getting started: The herringbone necklace is created separately, ending with a herringbone loop and a flat circular peyote-stitch button. The varying sizes of colored circles are created separately, then sewn to each other and attached to the herringbone necklace in an attractive pattern.

Creating the Herringbone Necklace

Herringbone stitch makes a great square tube, which works well for attaching the colorful circles to it later. The herringbone tube begins with a ladder. I use the words "up" and "down" to denote whether the needle is pointing up and away from the tail thread or down and toward the tail thread.

Round 1, Beads 1 & 2: With 8 feet (20.3 cm) of prepared thread (p. 6), string 2G; sew up through the first G strung to begin a ladder, leaving an 18-inch (45.7 cm) tail; sew down through the second G; adjust the tension (p. 7 and Figure 1, red thread).

Figure 1

Bead 3: String 1G; sew down through the second G bead; adjust the tension; sew up through the G bead just added; adjust the tension (Figure 1, blue thread).

Bead 4: String 1G; sew up through the third G bead; adjust the tension; sew down through the G bead just added; adjust the tension (Figure 1, green thread).

Form tubular herringbone: Sew up through G bead #1, sew down through G bead #4, sew up through G bead #1; adjust the tension to form a tight 4G square with all holes up (p. 7 and Figure 2 top and side views).

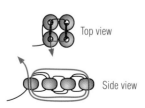

Top view

Side view

Figure 2

This tube has 2 stitches: one on one side and one on the other side, creating a square-shaped tube.

Round 2: String 2G, sew down through the closest G bead on Round 1 in the direction you wish to stitch; sew up through the next G on Round 1. String 2G, sew down through the next G on Round 1 (Figure 3, red thread); step up through 1G from Round 1 and 1G from Round 2, as in Figure 3, blue thread.

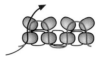

Figure 3

Rounds 3 & beyond: String 2G, sew down through the next G bead of the previous round; sew up through the top G of the next stitch. String 2G, sew down through the next G of this stitch (Figure 4, red thread); step up through 2G (1G from the previous round and 1G from this round; Figure 4, blue thread).

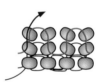

Figure 4

Continue in this manner for 15 inches (38.1 cm) or the desired length. Set aside. *Tip:* The closure adds 1 inch (2.5 cm) to the necklace length, so plan accordingly. Also, when you have to add thread, use the bookbinder's knot (p. 14); then weave the ends within the beadwork. Keep the tail thread and the working thread. Set aside.

Creating the Flat Circular Peyote-Stitch Circles

There are 16 flat circular peyote-stitch circles in varying sizes that make up the playful and colorful embellishments for this design. Each color of seed bead will be used in specific places, so to make it easier to see what is going on, check out the numbered circle guide on page p. 166 (Figure 33).

We are going to work from the largest circles, which are in the front of the necklace, down to the smallest circles. All circles are numbered so that you know what colors to use and what the placement will be on the necklace.

Tip: Beads are not all the same size, so if you create any circles that take on a domelike shape, make sure to stitch them to the necklace concave-side down, dome up.

Circle #1

Make 1 circle with color A.

Round 1: With 3 feet (91.4 cm) of prepared thread, string 3A, leaving a 6-inch (15.2 cm) tail; rethread through 2A to form a circle (Figure 5, red thread).

Rounds 1 & 2   **Figure 5**

Round 2. Increase: Work flat circular peyote stitch; using 2A in each stitch, make 3 stitches; step up through the first A added in this round (p. 12 and Figure 5, blue thread).

Round 3. Complete the increases: Work flat circular peyote stitch; *using 1A, sew through the next A added on Round 2, completing the increase; using 1A, sew through the next A added on Round 2. Repeat from * 2 more times for a total of 6A added; step up through the first A added in this round (Figure 6, red thread).

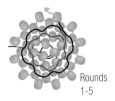

Rounds 1-5   **Figure 6**

Round 4. Increase: Work flat circular peyote stitch; using 2A in each stitch, make 6 stitches; step up through the first A added in this round (Figure 6, blue thread).

Round 5. Complete the increases: Work flat circular peyote stitch; *using 1A, sew through the next A added on Round 4, completing the increase; using 1A, sew through the next A added on Round 4. Repeat from * 5 more times for a total of 12A added; step up through the first A added in this round (Figure 6, green thread).

Round 6: Work flat circular peyote stitch; using 1A in each stitch, make 12 stitches; step up through the first A added in this round (Figure 7, red thread).

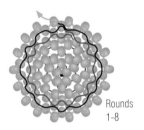

Rounds 1-8   **Figure 7**

Round 7. Increase: Work flat circular peyote stitch; *using 1A, make 1 stitch; using 2A, make 1 stitch. Repeat from * 5 more times; step up through the first A added in this round (Figure 7, blue thread).

Round 8. Complete the increases: Work flat circular peyote stitch; *using 1A, sew through the next A on Round 7; using 1A, sew through the next A added on Round 7, completing the increase; using 1A, make 1 stitch. Repeat from * 5 more times for a total of 18A added; step up through the first A added in this round (Figure 7, green thread).

Round 9. Increase: Work flat circular peyote stitch; *using 1A in each stitch, make 2 stitches; using 2A, make 1 stitch. Repeat from * 5 more times; step up through the first A added in this round (Figure 8, red thread).

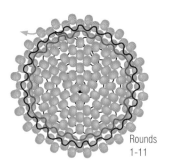

Rounds
1-11   **Figure 8**

total of 30A added; step up through the first A added in this round (Figure 9, blue thread).

Round 14. Increase: Work flat circular peyote stitch; *using 1A in each stitch, make 4 stitches; using 2A, make 1 stitch. Repeat from * 5 more times; step up through the first A added in this round (Figure 9, green thread).

Round 10. Complete the increases: Work flat circular peyote stitch; *using 1A, make 1 stitch; using 1A, sew through the next A on Round 9; using 1A, sew through the next A added on Round 9, completing the increase; using 1A, make 1 stitch. Repeat from * 5 more times for a total of 24A added; step up through the first A added in this round (Figure 8, blue thread).

Round 15. Complete the increases: Work flat circular peyote stitch; *using 1A in each stitch, make 3 stitches; using 1A, sew through the next A on Round 14; using 1A, sew through the next A added on Round 14, completing the increase; using 1A, make 1 stitch. Repeat from * 5 more times for a total of 36A added; step up through the first A added in this round (Figure 9, orange thread).

Round 11: Work flat circular peyote stitch; using 1A in each stitch, make 24 stitches; step up through the first A added in this round (Figure 8, green thread).

Round 16: Work flat circular peyote stitch; using 1A in each stitch, make 36 stitches; step up into the first A bead added in this round (Figure 9, purple thread).

Round 12. Increase: Work flat circular peyote stitch; *using 1A in each stitch, make 3 stitches; using 2A, make 1 stitch. Repeat from * 5 more times; step up through the first A added in this round (Figure 9, red thread).

Round 17: Work flat circular peyote stitch; using 1G in each stitch, make 36 stitches; step up into the first G bead added in this round (Figure 10). Weave off the tail thread and trim. Reserve the stitching thread for later use. Set aside.

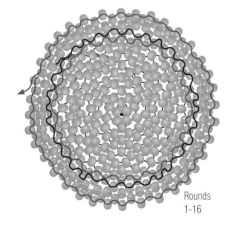

Rounds
1-16   **Figure 9**

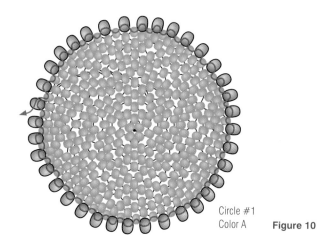

Circle #1
Color A   **Figure 10**

Round 13. Complete the increases: Work flat circular peyote stitch; *using 1A in each stitch, make 2 stitches; using 1A, sew through the next A on Round 12; using 1A, sew through the next A added on Round 12, completing the increase; using 1A, make 1 stitch. Repeat from * 5 more times for a

Circles #2 & #3: Make 2 circles using color B in place of color A, following the instructions for Rounds 1 through 17 (Figure 11).

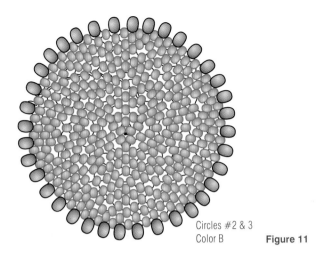

Circles #2 & 3
Color B   **Figure 11**

Circles #5 & #6: Using 5 feet (1.5 m) of prepared thread for each circle, make 2 circles using color D in place of color A, following the instructions for Rounds 1 through 11. When complete, finish each circle by working one round of flat circular peyote stitch; using 1G in each stitch, make 24 stitches; step up into the first G added in this round (Figure 12, Circles #5 and #6). Weave off the tail thread and trim. Reserve the stitching thread for later use. Set aside.

Circle #4: Using 2 feet (61 cm) of prepared thread, make 1 circle using color C in place of color A, following the instructions for Rounds 1 through 11. When complete, finish this circle by working 1 round of flat circular peyote stitch; using 1G in each stitch, make 24 stitches; step up into the first G bead added in this round (Figure 12, Circle #4). Weave off the tail thread and trim. Reserve the stitching thread for later use. Set aside.

Circles #7 & #8: Using 2 feet (61 cm) of prepared thread for each circle, make 2 circles using color E in place of color A, and following the instructions for Rounds 1 through 13.

When complete, finish each circle with 2 rounds of flat circular peyote stitch; for the first round, use 1E in each stitch, make 30 stitches; step up into the first E bead added in this round.

For the second round; use 1G in each stitch, make 30 stitches; step up into the first G added in this round (Figure 13). Weave off both threads and trim. Set aside.

Circle #4
Color C

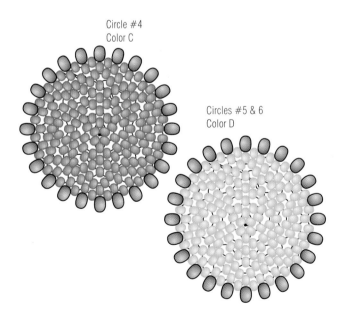

Circles #5 & 6
Color D

Circles #7 & 8
Color E

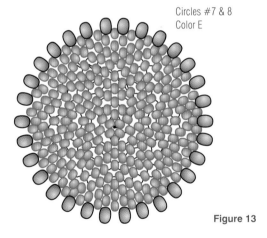

Figure 13

Figure 12

Circles #9 & #10: Using 3 feet (91.4 cm) of prepared thread, make 2 circles using color C in place of color A, following the instructions for Rounds 1 through 11. When complete, finish each circle by working 1 round of flat circular peyote stitch; using 1G in each stitch, make 24 stitches; step up into the first G added in this round (Figure 14). Weave off both threads and trim. Set aside.

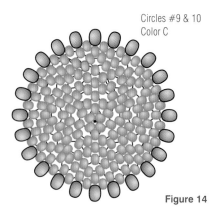

Circles #9 & 10
Color C

Figure 14

Circles #11 & #12: Using 2 feet (61 cm) of prepared thread, make 2 circles using color A, following the instruction for Rounds 1 through 8. When complete, finish each circle by working 1 round of flat circular peyote stitch; using 1G in each stitch, make 18 stitches; step up into the first G added in this round (Figure 15). Weave off both threads and trim. Set aside.

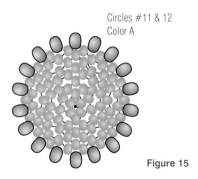

Circles #11 & 12
Color A

Figure 15

Circles #13 & #14: Using 18 inches (45.7 cm) of prepared thread, make 2 circles using color B in place of color A, following the instructions for Rounds 1 through 6. When complete, finish each circle by working 1 round of flat circular peyote stitch; using 1G in each stitch, make 12 stitches; step up into the first G added in this round (Figure 16). Weave off both threads and trim. Set aside.

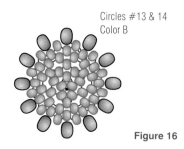

Circles #13 & 14
Color B

Figure 16

Circles #15 & #16: Using 18 inches (45.7 cm) of prepared thread, make 2 circles using color D in place of color A, following the instruction for Rounds 1 through 4. When complete, finish each circle by working 1 round of flat circular peyote stitch; using 1F in each stitch, make 12 stitches; step up into the first F bead added in this round (Figure 17). Weave off both threads and trim. Set aside.

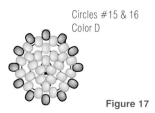

Circles #15 & 16
Color D

Figure 17

The Button for the Necklace Closure

Button Circle #B1: Using 3 feet (91.4 cm) of prepared thread, make 1 circle using color A following the instruction for Rounds 1 through 11. When complete, finish this circle by working 1 round of flat circular peyote stitch; using 1G in each stitch, make 24 stitches; step up into the first G added in this round (Figure 18). Weave off the tail thread and trim. Reinforce the outer edge of the button to stiffen; reserve the stitching thread for later use. Set aside.

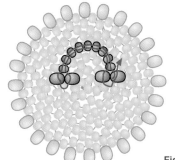

Figure 18

Create the bead loop on circle #B1: Weave the thread to exit any A bead on Round 3. String 1G, 9F, and 1G; look across the center of the circle and find an A bead opposite the one the thread is exiting; sew through that bead. String 1G; sew back through the 9F on the loop; string 1G and sew through the same A bead on Round 3 of the circle as in Figure 18 (red thread). Reinforce the loop; weave off this thread and trim.

Button Circle #B2: Using 2 feet (61 cm) of prepared thread, make 1 circle using color B in place of color A, following the instruction for Rounds 1 through 6. When complete, finish this circle by working 1 round of flat circular peyote stitch; using 1G in each stitch, make 12 stitches; step up into the first G added in this round (Figure 19). Weave off the tail thread and trim. Reserve the stitching thread.

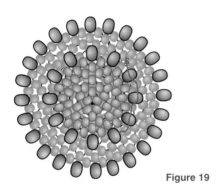

Figure 19

Attach button circle #B2 to circle #B1: Center circle #B2 on top of circle #B1 as shown in Figure 19. Using the thread that is exiting a G bead on Circle #B2, sew the G beads on Circle #B2 to A beads on circle #B1, keeping Circle #B2 centered on Circle #B1 (Figure 19). Weave off the thread and trim.

Create the Loop for the Button Connection on the Necklace
Lay the necklace out in a circle in front of you, smoothing the tube so not twisted and the working end looks like Figure 20 (on the left, red thread) and the starting end looks like Figure 20 (on the right, blue thread).

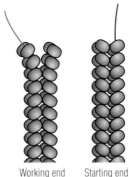

Working end   Starting end   **Figure 20**

Step 1: Place a needle onto the tail thread, attached to the starting end of the tube, string 1G; sew down through the next G bead, sewing through the closest G that is part of the other stitch (Figure 21, red thread). Sew up through the next G bead; string 1G, sew down through the next G (Figure 21, blue thread). Step up through the next G and the first G added (Figure 21, green thread).

Figure 21

Note: These 2 G beads are sitting on top of 1G from one stitch and 1G from another, in order for the loop to lie flat when the necklace is on your work station and with the working end of the necklace still looking like Figure 20, on the right.

Step 2. For one side: String 13F; form a loop by sewing through the same G bead the thread is exiting, as in Figure 22, red thread; shape the loop and then reinforce the loop.

Figure 22

Note: Make sure that you are stitching so that when the necklace is laid down on your work surface, the loop will lie flat. Continue stitching for 2 inches (5.1cm cm).

Figure 24

Step 3. For the other side: Weave the thread to exit the other G bead added in Step 1 (Figure 22, blue thread). Repeat Step 2 here for the second loop. Reinforce the loop, and then weave off this thread and trim.

Attach the button with beaded jump rings: Using 12 inches (30.5cm cm) of prepared thread, string 15F; sew through the 2 loops on the end of the necklace plus the loop on the button; even up the threads; overhand-knot (p. 17) the beads into a ring (Figure 23). Weave off each thread in the loop, sewing through beads in opposite directions. Trim both threads.

To test the fit, fold the strip over to meet the remaining stitch on the end of the necklace. Sew down through the aligning G bead on the end of necklace; sew up through the next G bead on the necklace and the G bead on the last stitch of the strip, zipping the stitches together (Figure 25). Test the fit over the buttonf all is well, reinforce the join then weave off the thread, half-hitch (p. 16) every few beads then trim. If the loop is too big or too small, disconnect the zipper and adjust the strip length.

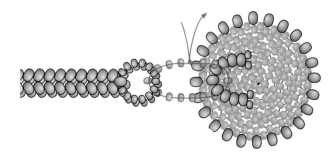

Repeat for 1 more beaded jump ring.

Figure 23

Add the bead loop to the other side of the herringbone necklace: The loop is a single herringbone stitch that is extended off of the working end of the necklace, making a long strip that is then zippered to the other herringbone stitches on this end of the necklace.

String 2G; sew down through the next G on the same stitch; step up through 2G and adjust the tension (Figure 24).

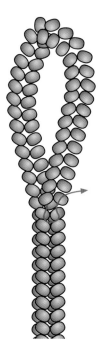

Figure 25

Putting It All Together

Now, we are down to some sewing. This is easy! You can refer to Figure 33 (p. 166) for a visual of the attached circles.

Attach Circles #1 & #4

Place Circle #4 on top of Circle #1 about ¼ inch (6 mm) down from Round 1 (center) of Circle #1, as in Figure 26.

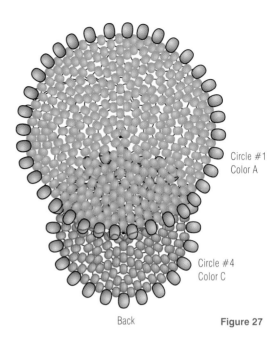

Circle #1
Color A

Circle #4
Color C

Back **Figure 27**

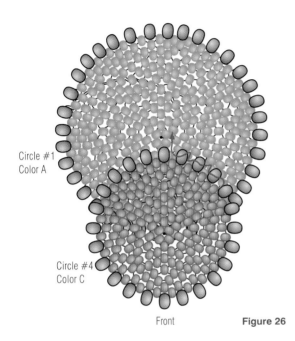

Circle #1
Color A

Circle #4
Color C

Front **Figure 26**

Attach Circle #1 to Circle #2

Place the #2 and #3 Circles down on your work surface about ¼ inch (6 mm) apart, being mindful of the G beads, as it would be best if the circles had G beads in the same locations, mirror imaged, as it were. Place the #1 Circle on top of Circles #2 and #3 about ¼ inch (6 mm) down from the top edges of Circles #2 and #3 (Figure 28).

On the front, and using the thread attached to Circle #4, which is exiting a G bead on the last round of this circle, sew the G beads (on Circle #4) that are overlapping onto Circle #1 to any A beads on Circle #1 that look good, and keep the circles centered with each other (Figure 26).

On the back, and using the same thread as for the front, sew the G beads on Circle #1 that are overlapping onto Circle #4 to any C beads on Circle #4 that look good (Figure 27). Weave off and trim the thread attached to Circle #4.

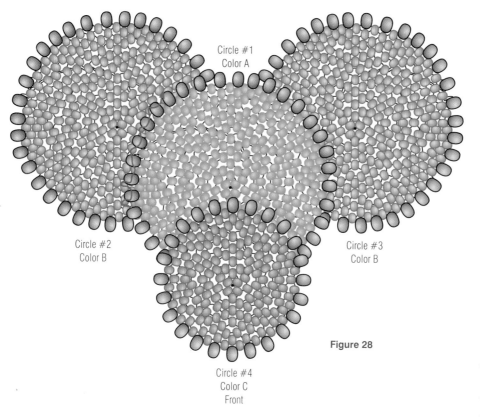

Circle #1
Color A

Circle #2
Color B

Circle #3
Color B

Figure 28

Circle #4
Color C
Front

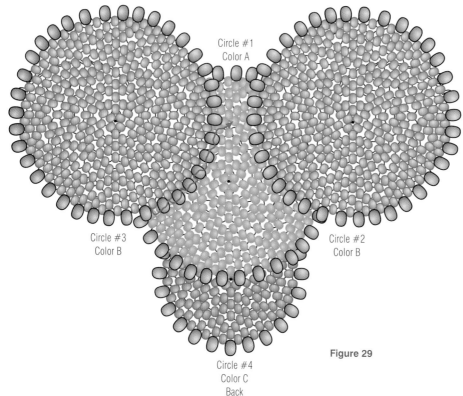

Circle #1
Color A

Circle #3
Color B

Circle #2
Color B

Figure 29

Circle #4
Color C
Back

On the front, and using the thread attached to Circle #1, which is exiting a G bead on the last round of the circle, sew the G beads on Circle #1 that are overlapping onto Circle #2 to any B beads on Circle #2 that look good (Figure 28).

On the back, and using the same thread as for the front, sew the G beads on Circle #2 that are overlapping onto Circle #1 to any A beads on Circle #1 that look good (Figure 29). Weave off and trim the thread attached to Circle #1.

Attach Circle #1 to Circle #3
Repeat the attachment, as done with circle #1 to Circle #2 on the remaining side of Circle #1 (Figures 28 and 29). Set aside.

Right-angle weave Circles #2 and #3 to the herringbone necklace
Close the button and loop closure. Using your index finger, hold up the necklace under the closure, centering the closure on your finger. Mark center bottom of necklace with a pin or needle.

Smooth out the necklace on your work surface with the button and loop closure closed, with the loops made off the ends of the tube lying down flat, while shaping the necklace into a circle. Butt the edges of Circles #2 and #3 up against the necklace (face up),

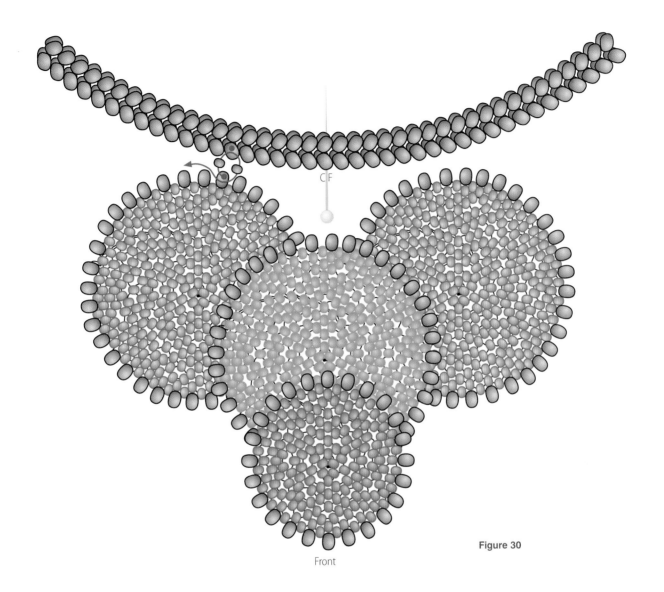

Front

Figure 30

centering the circles on either side of the center marking on the necklace (Figure 30). Weave the thread attached to Circle #2 to exit a G bead on this circle that aligns nicely to a G bead along the top edge of the herringbone necklace, which should be about 6 to 9 G beads to the left of center (Figure 30, red dot beads).

On the front: String 1F, sew through the aligning G bead along the top edge of the necklace; string 1F, sew back through the same G bead on Circle #2, forming a right-angle weave stitch (p. 14 and Figure 30). Reinforce this stitch, ending by exiting the G bead on Circle #2.

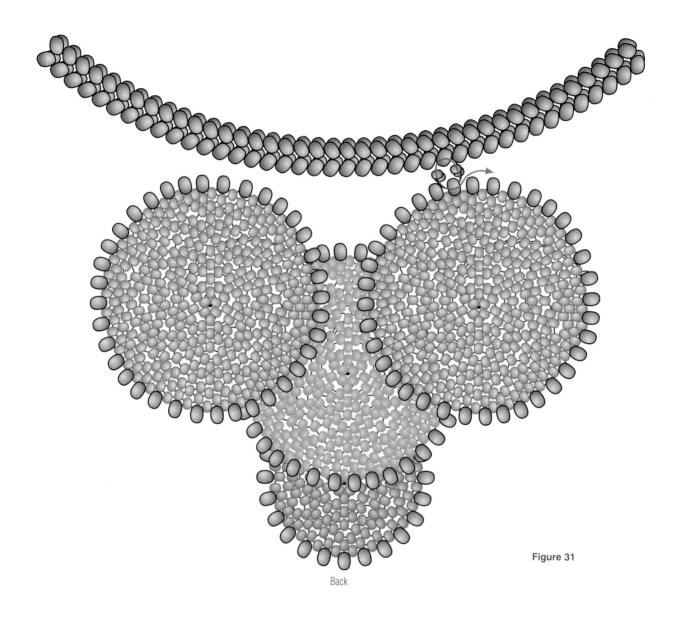

Back

Figure 31

On the back: Turn the necklace over, string 1F, sew through the aligning G bead along the bottom edge of the necklace on the back; string 1F, sew back through the same G bead on Circle #2, forming a right-angle weave stitch (Figure 31). Reinforce this stitch, ending by exiting the G bead on Circle #2; weave off this thread and trim.

Repeat the Circle #2 attachment instructions for Circle #3 (Figures 30 and 31).

Right-angle weave the remaining circles to each other and to the necklace

Step 1. Attach the circles to each other: Place Circle #5 on the left-hand side of the necklace touching Circle #2 and the side of the necklace. Move the thread to exit a G bead on the edge of Circle #5 that touches a G bead on the edge of Circle #2 (Figure 32).

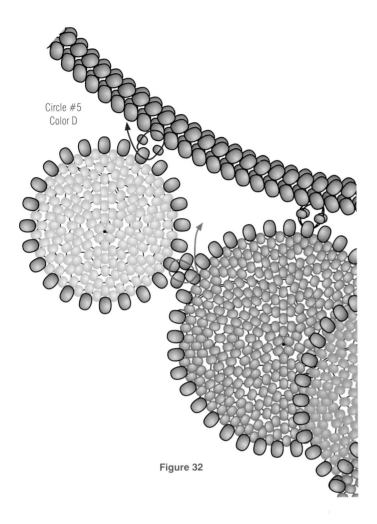

Circle #5
Color D

Figure 32

Step 3: Attach the circle to the back of the necklace: Turn the necklace over; string 1F, sew through the aligning G bead along the bottom edge of the necklace on the back; string 1F, and sew back through the same G bead on Circle #2, forming a right-angle weave stitch. Reinforce this stitch, ending by exiting the G bead on Circle #2.

You can refer to the guide in Figure 33 (p. 166) for a visual of the attached circles.

Repeat Steps 1, 2, and 3 for Circle #6, placing it on the right-hand side.

Repeat Steps 1, 2, and 3 for Circles #7 and #8.

Repeat Steps 1, 2, and 3 for Circles #9 and #10.

Repeat Steps 1, 2, and 3 for Circles #11 and #12.

Repeat Steps 1, 2, and 3 for Circles #13 and #14.

Repeat Steps 1, 2, and 3 for Circles #15 and #16, but use G beads to attach the circles to the necklace. Weave off the threads and trim.

String 1G; sew through the aligning G bead on Circle #2; string 1G, sew back through the same G bead on Circle #5, forming a right-angle weave stitch (Figure 32, red thread). Reinforce this stitch; then weave the thread to exit the G bead on Circle #5 that best aligns to a G bead along the top edge of the necklace.

Step 2: Attach the circles to the front of necklace: String 1F, sew through the aligning G bead along the bottom edge of the necklace; string 1F, sew back through the same G bead on Circle #2, forming a right-angle weave stitch (Figure 32, blue thread). Reinforce this stitch, ending by exiting the G bead on Circle #2.

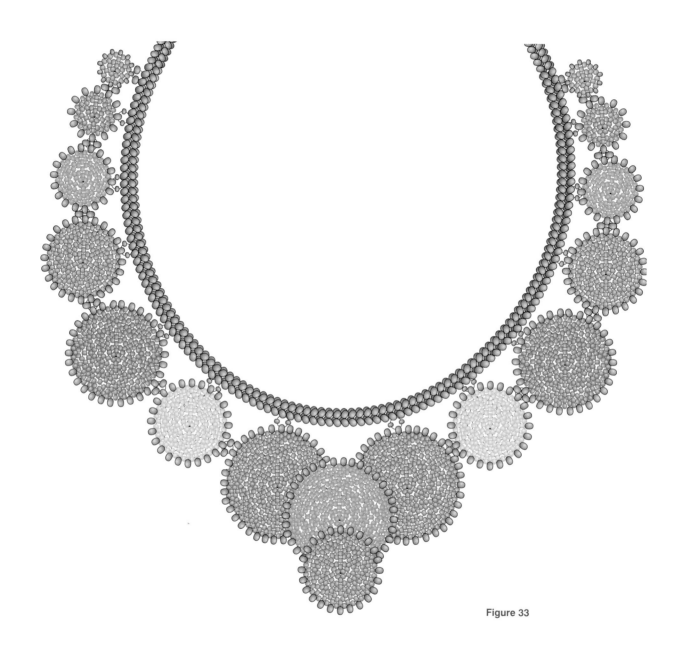

Figure 33

PEARL INLAY EARRINGS

LEAF-SHAPED PEARL EMBELLISHMENTS, mimicking pearl inlays, surround a beaded bezel set with a crystal cup-chain component. The addition of beautiful CZ drops and elegant ear wires add the finishing touches to these magnificent earrings.

Version #1

William Clarke Wontner (1857–1930) was a painter of the neoclassical style, focusing on seductive women posed against beautifully detailed backdrops. Inspired by classical love stories and mythological themes, Wontner had a great passion to paint.

His subject in the 1908 painting *Jade Necklace for an Eastern Princess* shows his skill at setting the stage. A marbled backdrop, sumptuous fabrics, and elegant details surround the lovely princess in what looks Turkish in style.

My focus here is the table. Pearl inlay was at its height of popularity during the time of the Ottoman Empire. Shiny and light-reflective mother-of-pearl (made by some molluscs as the inner layer of their shells), or ivory was cut into shapes and fitted into carved motifs in wood, creating a richly embellished surface. From palace ornamentations on doors and windows to furnishings, as in the Ottoman-style table shown here, the result of this fine work is striking.

As always, I love being inspired by other mediums! There is a challenge there, working in beads and thread, that is hard to describe.

Jade Necklace for an Eastern Princess by William Clarke Wontner

Version #2

Dimensions

1 inch (2.5 cm) wide by 1⅝ inches (4.1 cm) long

Techniques

Peyote stitch, flat circular, even count with increasing

Peyote stitch, tubular, even count

Stitch-in-the-ditch

Skill level

Intermediate

Materials, Version #1

1.5 g aqua gold-lined 15° seed beads (A)

1 g champagne galvanized 15° seed beads* (B)

2 g aqua gold-lined 11° seed beads (C)

1.5 g champagne galvanized 11° seed beads* (D)

14 green iridescent 3-mm crystal pearls

2 clear crystals in gold-toned 8-mm cups (from cup chain**) with 4 holes in the bezel

1 pair of decorative gold-toned ear wires with crystal inlay

2 clear 7 x 30 mm teardrop-shaped CZs with top-drilled holes

Dark beige nylon beading thread

Materials, Version #2

1.5 g aqua violet gold luster iris 15° seed beads (A)

1 g palladium electroplated 15° seed beads (B)

2 g aqua violet gold luster 11° seed beads (C)

1.5 g palladium electroplated 11° seed beads (D)

2 clear crystals in gold-toned 8-mm cups (from cup chain**), with 4 holes in the bezel

1 pair of decorative rhodium-toned ear wires with crystal embellishment

14 white 3-mm pearls

2 amethyst 7 x 30 mm teardrop-shaped CZs with top-drilled holes

Purple nylon beading thread

*I prefer Duracoat galvanized seed beads.
**I use cup chain made by Ezel Findings.

Tools

2 size 12 beading needles

1 glass-headed straight pin

Wire flush cutter

Jewelry chain-nose pliers

Beader's supply kit (p. 5)

Instructions

Create the Base

Flat circular peyote stitch, with increasing, forms a base for these lovely earrings.

Round 1: With 6 feet (1.8 m) of prepared thread (p. 6), string 3A, leaving a 12-inch (30.5 cm) tail; rethread through 2A to form a circle (Figure 1, red thread).

Figure 1

Round 2. Increase: Work flat circular peyote stitch (p. 10); using 2A in each stitch, make 3 stitches; step up through the first A added in this round (p. 12 and Figure 1, blue thread).

Round 3. Complete the increases: Work flat circular peyote stitch; *using 1A, sew through the next A added on Round 2, completing the increase; using 1A, sew through the next A added on Round 2. Repeat from * 2 more times for a total of 6A added; step up through the first A added in this round (Figure 2, red thread).

Figure 2

Round 4. Increase: Work flat circular peyote stitch; using 2A in each stitch, make 6 stitches; step up through the first A added in this round (Figure 2, blue thread).

Round 5. Complete the increases: Work flat circular peyote stitch; *using 1A, sew through the next A added on Round 4, completing the increase; using 1A, sew through the next A added on Round 4. Repeat from * 5 more times for a total of 12A added; step up through the first A added in this round (Figure 2, green thread).

Round 6: Work flat circular peyote stitch; using 1A in each stitch, make 12 stitches; step up through the first A added in this round (Figure 3, red thread).

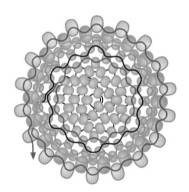

Figure 3

Round 7. Increase: Work flat circular peyote stitch; *using 1A, make 1 stitch; using 2A, make 1 stitch. Repeat from * 5 more times for a total of 18A added; step up through the first A added in this round (Figure 3, blue thread).

Round 8. Complete the increases: Work flat circular peyote stitch; *using 1A, sew through the next A on Round 7; using 1A, sew through the next A added on Round 7, completing the increase; using 1A, make 1 stitch. Repeat from * 5 more times for a total of 18A added; step up through the first A added in this round (Figure 3, green thread).

Round 9: Work flat circular peyote stitch; using 1C in each stitch, make 18 stitches; step up through the first C added in this round (Figure 3, orange thread).

Round 10: Work flat circular peyote stitch; using 1D in each stitch, make 18 stitches; step up through the first D added in this round (Figure 3, purple thread).

The Cup Chain

Prepare the cup chain: The cup chain has metal tabs connecting one crystal cup to another. This style of cup chain has a hole at the base of the metal setting on all four sides, which makes it handy when sewing down the cup chain component to beadwork.

Using the flush wire cutter, cut off the metal tab on one end of the chain, if needed, then cut between the cup chain components for a total of 2 separate cup chain components.

Add the cup chain component to the base: Weave the tail thread to exit any D bead on the edge of the base. Weave the working thread into the base to exit any A bead on Round 5 (Figure 4, red dot bead). Sew through 2 opposite holes on 1 cup chain component. Center the component on the base and sew through any A bead that aligns to the hole of the cup chain component on the opposite side (Figure 4). *Note:* Double-check that the prongs align to D beads on the edge. Sew back through the cup chain component and back through the aligning A bead on the base (Figure 4). Reinforce this attachment.

Figure 4

Weave around in the base to exit an A bead close to one of the remaining holes on the cup chain component. Attach this side of the cup chain component to the base; reinforce.

Stitch-in-the-Ditch to Add the Beaded Bezel

Weave the working thread out to an A bead on Round 6 (Figure 5, red dot bead).

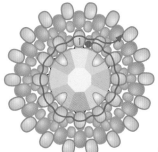

Figure 5

Round 1: Work stitch-in-the-ditch (p. 12); using 1D in each stitch, sew through the next A bead on Round 6. Repeat around the row, keeping this round tight, for a total of 12D added in this round; step up into the first D added (Figure 5 and Figure 6, red thread).

Figure 6

Rounds 2, 3, and 4: Work 3 rounds of tubular peyote stitch (p. 10); using 1D in each stitch, make 12 stitches in each round; step up through the first D added in each round (Figure 6, blue, green and orange threads).

Round 5: Work tubular peyote stitch; using 1B in each stitch, make 12 stitches; step up through the first B added in this round (Figure 6, purple thread). Reinforce if needed to keep this round tight.

Add the Embellishments

These little picots add texture and lead to the little pearl inlay shapes. Weave the thread down the bezel to exit any D bead from Round 1 (Figure 7, red dot bead).

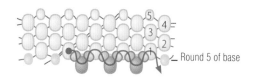

Round 5 of base

Figure 7

Round 1: *Work picots; using 1B, 1C, and 1B, sew through the next D bead on Round 1 to stitch-in-the-ditch, forming a picot; repeat from * 11 more times (Figure 7, red thread).

Round 2. Pearl inlay: Take a look at the prongs on the cup chain component. There are 4 little prongs that hold the crystal within the metal setting. Find one that aligns the best to a Round 1 picot and a D bead on the edge of the base, as in Figure 8, red dot bead, the picot in front of it and the centered prong on the setting of the cup chain component. This spot will now mark the top of the earring. (I marked it temporarily with a straight pin.)

Center top

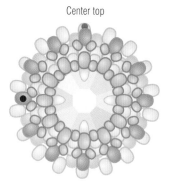

Figure 8

The pearl inlays are added to 7 picots, so the thread needs to be moved to exit the C bead on a picot from Round 1, 3 picots down from the top picot (Figure 8, blue dot bead). This picot also aligns with a prong on the cup chain component (Figure 8).

Step 1: String 11A, and form a circle by sewing through the same C bead on the picot in the same direction as before (Figure 9, red thread).

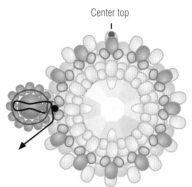

Center top

Figure 9

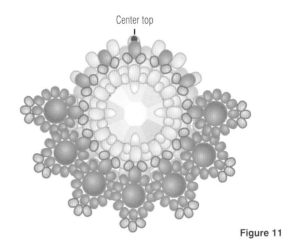

Center top

Figure 11

Step 2: String 1 3-mm pearl, skip the next 5A on the ring, and sew through the sixth A, fitting the pearl within the ring, and sew back through the pearl and the C bead on the picot from the other side (Figure 9, blue thread).

Step 3: Sew through 5A on the ring, string 3B, skip the sixth A, sew through the next 5A and the C bead on the picot, forming a picot at the tip of the embellishment; tighten. Weave forward through the next B bead on the picot, the next D bead on the bezel, the next B and C bead of the next picot (Figure 10).

Side view without embellishments

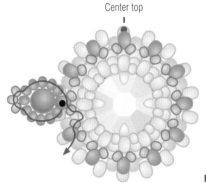

Center top

Figure 10

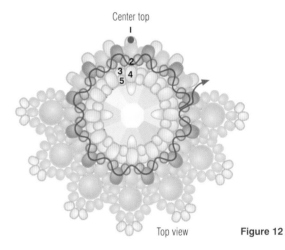

Center top

Top view   **Figure 12**

Repeat Steps 2 and 3 for a total of 7 pearl inlay embellishments (Figure 11). When complete, weave the thread off of the last picot, back into the bezel, exiting any D bead added on Round 2, as in Figure 12, beginning of red thread path on side view.

Add the last row of embellishment: Work stitch-in-the-ditch with picots; using 1B, 1C and 1B, sew through the next D bead on Round 2, forming a picot; repeat around the bezel for a total of 12 picots added (Figure 12, side view and top view). Weave off this thread and trim.

Add the Ear Wire Loop

Weave the tail thread to exit a D bead on the last round of the base, as in Figure 13, beginning of red thread path. *Tip:* The thread should be exiting a D bead right before the center top D bead, with the thread facing the center top bead.

Figure 14

String 1A, 1D, 2A, the teardrop CZ, 2A, 1D, and 1A; skip the next D and sew through the one after that, creating a loop (Figure 14, red thread). Before reinforcing, make sure that the loop is at center bottom.

String 1A; skip the next A bead and sew back through the closest D on the loop, plus the next 2A, the CZ, the next 2A, and the next D bead on the loop. String 1A; skip the next A bead on the loop and sew through the D bead on the base from the opposite side; adjust the tension (Figure 14, blue thread). Reinforce this loop well; then weave off the thread and trim.

Repeat instructions to make the second earring.

Figure 13

String 1B, 1D, 1B, and string the ear wire (making sure it is facing forward), then 1B, 1D and 1B; skip the center top D bead (Figure 13, red dot bead) and sew through the D bead after that, as in Figure 13; tighten. Weave the thread around to reinforce the loop.

Add the Loop for the Teardrop CZ

Find center bottom on the base by looking at the back. It should be a D bead from Round 10 on the base (Figure 14, red dot bead). Weave the thread through the last 2 rounds of the base to exit a D bead on the base right before the center bottom D bead as in Figure 14.

AN ELEGANT LADIES' BROOCH

TWO RINGS OF FIRE-POLISHED BEADS are laced together to bezel around an antique-style cushion-cut CZ, creating a striking central focus to this beautiful brooch. Rounds of netting, along with set CZs and pearls, form a circular shape, ending with a faceted CZ drop and a shaped pin-back connection. Wear the brooch in the eighteenth-century manner by pinning it at the middle bust on a beautiful garment, or pin it on a coat, sweater, or hat for a taste of times past.

Version #1

{ HISTORICAL PERSPECTIVE }

The German neoclassical painter Joseph Karl Stieler (1781–1858) served as the royal court painter of the Bavarian kings and is perhaps best known for his portraits in the Gallery of Beauties at the Nymphenburg Palace in Munich. Among the strikingly lovely ladies of the Gallery hangs the portrait of Nanette Kaula Heine (c. 1829). The young 17-year-old beauty was the daughter of the head of the Jewish community in Munich and exemplified the classical beauty of the time.

Stieler's skill at portraiture excels here, as Nanette is clearly taking center stage. The pillar and landscape backdrop in the painting actually draws your attention to the sitter and to her exceptional beauty. The arrow-style hair ornament and bodice ornament add just the right touch of elegance to her attire.

Eighteenth- and early nineteenth-century bodice ornaments were sewn onto the garment through little eyelets on the ornament itself. As pin backs came to be better made, these ornaments could then be pinned into place. Mostly for enhancing the décolletage, these glorious ornaments could also adorn the shoulder of a gown, serve as a clasp on a cloak, or add a flourish to a headdress. The one shown in this painting is actually a much older style than the date of the painting, so it is probably a family heirloom.

Nanette Kaula by Joseph Karl Stieler

Dimensions

1¾ inches (4.4 cm) wide x 2 ⅝ inches (5.4 cm) long, including the drop

Techniques

Edge-stitching

Netting

Peyote stitch, flat, odd-count technique called step up/step down

Stone setting

Skill level

Intermediate

Materials, Version #1

1 amethyst 14-mm antique cushion-cut briolette CZ

2 amethyst 3-mm round CZs

9 olivine 3-mm round CZs

9 champagne 4-mm round CZs

1.5 g pewter galvanized 15° seed beads* (A)

1.5 g pewter galvanized 11° cylinder beads* (B)

1.5 g pewter galvanized 11° seed beads* (C)

36 soft gold Czech fire-polished 2-mm beads (FP)**

44 dark cream 2-mm Czech glass pearls

1 olivine 7 x 18 mm faceted CZ drop with top-drilled hole

11 sterling silver 3-mm round 6-prong settings

9 sterling silver 4-mm round 6-prong settings

1 silver-toned 1⅜ inch (3.5 cm) long pin back***

Double-sided craft tape, ½ inch (1.3 cm) wide

Dark beige nylon beading thread

Materials, Version #2

1 salmon sorbet 14 mm antique cushion-cut briolette (custom coated)

2 white 3-mm round CZ

9 alexandrite 3-mm round CZ (lab grown)

9 white 4-mm round CZ

1.5 g dark gold galvanized 15° seed beads* (A)

1.5 g yellow gold t galvanized 11° cylinder beads* (B)

1.5 g dark gold galvanized 11° seed beads* (C)

36 rose lumine 2-mm Czech fire-polished beads (FP)**

44 pale rose 2-mm Czech glass pearls

1 champagne 7 x 18 mm faceted CZ drop with top-drilled hole

11 gold-filled 3-mm round 6-prong settings

9 gold-filled 4-mm round 6-prong settings

1 gold-tone 1⅜ inch (3.5 cm) long pin back***

Double-sided craft tape, ½ inch (1.3 cm) wide

Gold nylon beading thread

I prefer Duracoat galvanized seed beads.

**2-mm fire-polished beads are not all the same! There are 2-mm fire-polished beads that are truly 2 mm and 2-mm fire-polished beads that are actually around 2.25 to 2.5 mm. The most common size is the 2.25 to 2.5 mm, and that is what you want to use here.

***I prefer the Japanese pin backs that have holes in the base of the pin back. These holes allow the pin back to be stitched down to the beadwork neatly and tightly, using seed beads.

Tools

2 size 12 beading needles

1 size 13 beading needle (may be needed when embellishing)

1 size 15 beading needle (may be needed when sewing down settings)

2 glass-headed straight pins

Wooden needle case for setting CZs

Small Teflon-coated craft scissors

Jewelry chain-nose pliers

Beader's supply kit (p. 5)

Version #2

Instructions

Bezel the central cushion-cut CZ: This beautiful, antique-style, cushion-cut briolette CZ is quickly bezeled, using 2 rings of fire-polished beads that get laced together with netting.

Creating the Rings

Ring 1: Using 24 inches (61 cm) of prepared thread (p. 6), string 18FP; center them on the thread and overhand-knot (p. 17) the FP beads into a ring. Weave off both threads, trim, and set aside.

Ring 2: Using 6 feet (1.8 m) of prepared thread, string 18FP; leaving a 6-inch (15 cm) tail, overhand-knot the FP beads into a ring (p. 17 and Figure 1). Weave off and trim the tail thread.

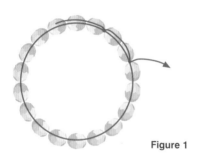

Figure 1

Stitch the Fire-Polished Rings Together

Step 1: On Ring 2, weave forward through 2FP (Figure 2, red thread). *Work netting; using 1A, 1C, and 1A, skip the next FP, sewing through the one after that. Repeat from * 8 more times for a total of 9 nets added (p. 8 and Figure 2, blue thread); step up through the first A and C added (Figure 2, green thread).

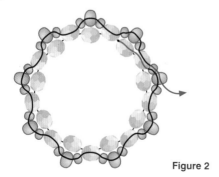

Figure 2

Step 2: Set Ring 1 on top of Ring 2 (Figure 3). Work netting; string 1A, sew through any FP bead on Ring 1 (Figure 3, beginning of red thread); *string 1A, sew through the next C bead on the next net; string 1A, skip the next FP on ring 1, but sew through the one after that (Figure 3); tighten.

Ring 1 —

Ring 2 —

Figure 3

Place the cushion-cut CZ into the bezel. Repeat from * 7 more times; then string 1A and sew through the next C bead on the next net, completing the round (Figure 4). Tighten as you weave forward to secure; end by exiting any of the C beads on the netting (Figure 4, end of red thread path).

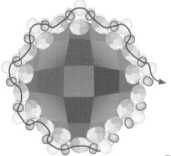

Figure 4

Align the bezel: Take a look at the CZ; pick which side you like the best for the front. Certain stitches need to be in certain places to go any further. Check out Figure 5: the threaded needle marks center top, the remaining needle marks center bottom, and the sides are marked with white head pins. Massage the bezel so that your piece looks like Figure 5.

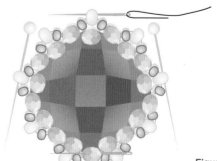

Figure 5

Creating the Front of the Brooch

A variation of netting, along with set CZs creates the circular component for the front of the brooch.

Round 1: *Work netting; using 1A, 1 pearl, and 1A in each stitch, sew through the next C bead on the next net. Repeat from * 8 more times for a total of 9 nets added in this round; step up through the first A, pearl, and A added (Figure 6).

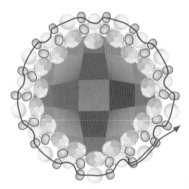

Figure 6

Round 2: *Work netting; using 1A, 1C, and 1A in each stitch, sew through the next A, pearl, and A from Round 1. Repeat from * 8 more times for a total of 9 nets added in this round; step up through the first A, C, and A added on this round (Figure 7).

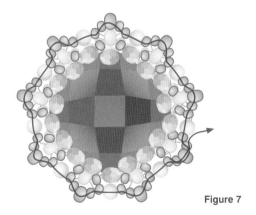

Figure 7

Set the 4-mm CZs: CZs, set into fine metal settings, lend an elegant aspect to this design. They are easy to set; all you need is a bit of patience.

Cut three ½-inch (1.3 cm) pieces of double-sided tape. Place a ½-inch (1.3 cm) square of double-sided tape onto the end of a wooden needle case. Peel off the plastic coating; stick the flat bottom of a 4-mm setting to the center of the tape. Place the CZ onto a solid surface with the flat faceted side down and the point up. Center the prongs of the setting over the back of the CZ; press the setting firmly down over the CZ until the CZ snaps into place within the setting (Figure 8).

Figure 8

Isn't it pretty? Now, you need to check to see if the stone is moving. Using the end of a pair of chain-nose pliers, see if you can wiggle the stone around. If so, close the pliers and gently lower the tips of each of the six prong arms by gently pushing them down close to the CZ, one at a time. Set a total of nine 4-mm CZs.

Round 3. Add the set 4-mm CZs to the beadwork: *String 1A, 1 set CZ as in Figure 9, and 1A; sew through the next A, C, A of the next net, placing the set CZ face up into the space (Figure 9); tighten. Repeat from * 8 more times for a total of 9 set stones added. Step up by sewing through the first A, the setting, and the next A, plus the next A and C (Figure 9, end of red thread path).

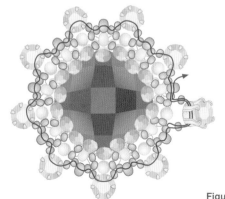

Figure 9

Round 4: *Work netting; using 3A, 3 pearls, and 3A, sew through the next C bead added on Round 2 (Figure 10, red thread). Repeat from * 8 more times for a total of 9 nets added on this round (Figure 10, blue thread); step up through the first 3A added (Figure 10, green thread).

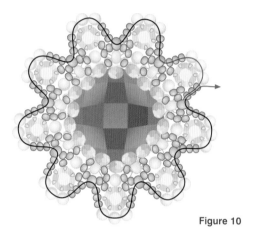

Figure 10

Round 5. Attach the other side of the setting to Round 4:
This round doesn't have any beads added. *Straighten the setting by sewing behind the 2 outside prong arms; sew through the last 3A of this net (Figure 11, red thread), plus the C bead from Round 2 and the next 3A of the next net added on Round 4 (Figure 11, blue thread). Repeat from * 8 more times for a total of 9 settings attached in this round; step up through the 3A, sew through the setting and through 2A of the first net added in Round 4 (Figure 11, green thread).

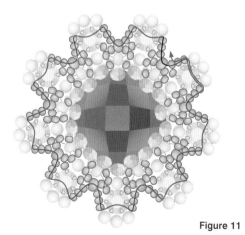

Figure 11

Set the 3-mm CZs: This size of CZ actually sets better when approached in a different way, mainly due to the shape of the setting.

Remove the old tape from the wooden needle case and place a new ½-inch (1.3 cm) square of double-sided tape on it. Peel off the plastic coating of the tape; stick the flat faceted side of a 3-mm CZ to the center of the tape with the point up (Figure 12).

Figure 12

Stick a third piece of tape onto a solid work surface or a piece of paper; peel off the plastic coating; place the back of a setting onto the tape firmly. Center the back of the CZ over the setting (Figure 12); press the CZ gently down over the setting until the CZ snaps into place within the setting. *Tip:* You will have the best results when taking your time and keeping the needle case perpendicular to the table. The setting is top-heavy, so make sure that the setting stays upright while you are adding the stone.

Unlike what I did for the 4-mm settings, I gently lower the tips of each of the 6 prong arms on all of the 3-mm settings, using closed chain-nose pliers, to make sure those little stones stay in place. Set a total of nine 3-mm CZs.

Round 6: Add the set 3-mm CZs to the beadwork: Change the needle to a size 13. *Nestle a set CZ into the space between two 4-mm CZs on the beadwork, and close to your exiting thread. Sew through the 3-mm setting, behind the 2 prong arms that are the closest to the beadwork, as in Figure 13, beginning of red thread. Sew through the 2A, 3 pearls, and 2A of the next net, gently tightening the set stone into place. Make sure the CZ is facing forward!

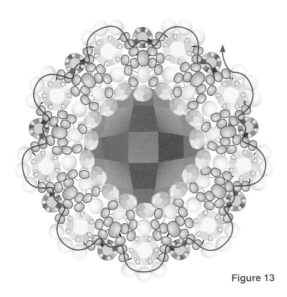

Figure 13

Tip: To keep the thread from catching on the prongs, place your thumb over the closest set CZ while you pull the thread through to tighten.

Repeat from * 8 more times. After adding the last CZ, end the progression by sewing through the next 2A and 3 pearls (Figure 13, end of red thread path). Change the needle back to a size 12.

Round 7: *Work netting; string 5A, sew through the next 3 pearls of the next net; tightening around the outside of the 3-mm set CZ. Repeat from * 8 more times (Figure 14); sewing through 1 pearl on the last repeat (Figure 14, arrow end of red thread); keep the thread.

Add the CZ Drop

Find the center top (green dot A bead marked CT on Figure 14) and center bottom (purple dot pearl marked CB) as in Figure 14. Weave the thread carefully through the pearls added on Round 6 and through the 5A just added to exit an A bead on the left-hand side of center bottom, as in Figure 14, beginning of blue thread path. String 1A, 1C, 1 pearl, 1C, 1A, the CZ drop, 1A, 1C, 1 pearl, 1C, and 1A. Sew through the middle A bead of the next net on the right-hand side of center bottom, as in Figure 14, blue thread turnaround.

Figure 14

String 1A, skip the closest A on the loop, sew back through the next C, pearl, C, A, drop, A, C, pearl, and C. String 1A, skip the next A on the loop, and sew through the middle A bead on the netting, as in Figure 14, blue thread. Reinforce the loop; weave off this thread and trim.

Create the Base for the Pin Back Connection

A peyote-stitch strip forms a base for the pin back, adds a little extension to the sides of the brooch, and hides the pin back from showing through the CZ. This 23-bead-wide, odd-count flat peyote-stitch strip is made using a technique that I call step-up/step-down peyote stitch. This technique makes for a straight strip with clean edges, and with no homeless beads or turn arounds; in truth, it is awesome!

Rows 1 & 2: With 5 feet (1.5 m) of prepared thread, string 24B, leaving a 6-inch (15 cm) tail.

Row 3: Without a bead on the needle, skip the last 2B strung, and sew back through the third-from-last B (Figure 15, red thread). Work flat peyote stitch (p. 9); using 1B in each stitch, make 10 more stitches (Figure 15, blue thread).

Figure 15

Using 1B, sew through the B bead on the tail thread, as in Figure 15, green thread; adjust the tension and your hold on the work. The strip is now odd-count flat peyote stitch.

Row 4: Work flat peyote stitch; using 1B in each stitch, make 11 stitches (Figure 16, red thread). (This is where traditional odd-count, flat peyote stitch is going to be left behind.) Our present form of peyote stitch starts two rows at a time, then goes back and finishes the 2 rows. I will be using two terms to explain the movement of thread. One is to step up and the other is to step down.

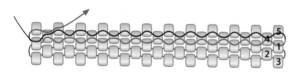

Figure 16

Row 5: Work flat peyote stitch; using 1B in each stitch, make 10 stitches; with 1B on the needle, sew through the next B on Row 4 and the next B on Row 1 (step down) (Figure 16, blue thread). The thread will be in the same B bead as the tail thread. Using 1B, step up through the closest B bead on Row 4 and the next B bead on Row 5 (Figure 16, green thread); adjust the tension.

Rows 6 & 7: *Row 6:* Work flat peyote stitch; using 1B in each stitch, make 10 stitches (Figure 17, red thread). *Row 7:* Using 1B in each stitch, make 10 stitches and step down.

Back to Row 6: Using 1B, make 1 stitch (Figure 17, blue thread). *Back to Row 7:* Using 1B, make 2 stitches and step up (Figure 17, green thread).

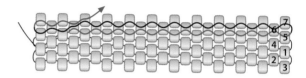

Figure 17

Rows 8 & 9: *Row 8:* Work flat peyote stitch; using 1B in each stitch, make 9 stitches (Figure 18, red thread). *Row 9:* Using 1B in each stitch, make 9 stitches and step down. *Back to Row 8:* Using 1B in each stitch, make 2 stitches (Figure 18, blue thread). *Back to Row 9:* Using 1B in each stitch, make 3 stitches and step up (Figure 18, green thread).

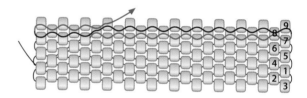

Figure 18

Rows 10 & 11: *Row 10:* Work flat peyote stitch; using 1B in each stitch, make 8 stitches (Figure 19, red thread). *Row 11:* Using 1B in each stitch, make 8 stitches and step down. *Back to Row 10:* Using 1B in each stitch, make 3 stitches (Figure 19, blue thread). *Back to Row 11:* Using 1B in each stitch, make 4 stitches and step up (Figure 19, green thread).

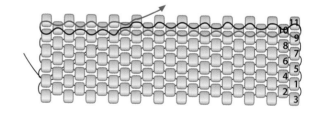

Figure 19

Rows 12 & 13: *Row 12:* Work flat peyote stitch; using 1B, make 7 stitches (Figure 20, red thread). *Row 13:* Using 1B, make 7 stitches and step down. *Back to Row 12:* Using 1B in each stitch, make 4 stitches (Figure 20, blue thread). *Back to Row 13:* Using 1B in each stitch, make 5 stitches and step up (Figure 20, green thread).

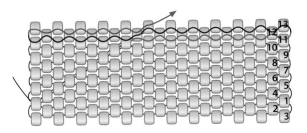

Figure 20

Rows 14 & 15: *Row 14:* Work flat peyote stitch; using 1B, make 6 stitches (Figure 21, red thread). *Row 15:* Using 1B, make 6 stitches and step down. *Back to Row 14:* Using 1B in each stitch, make 5 stitches (Figure 21, blue thread). *Back to Row 15:* Using 1B in each stitch, make 6 stitches and step up (Figure 21, green thread). Weave off the tail thread and trim.

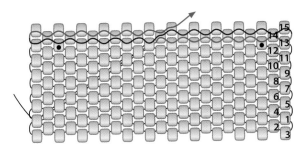

Figure 21

Sew on the Pin Back

I prefer the Japanese pin back as it is well made and the attachment looks best. The pin back has holes in it, so I sew it down to the beadwork with 11° seed beads.

Step 1: Center the pin back over the peyote-stitch strip as in Figure 22; weave the thread forward to exit a B bead that aligns to the hole that is on the top right side of the pin back (Figure 21, black dot bead). Sew through the hole on the pin back (Figure 22, beginning of red thread path).

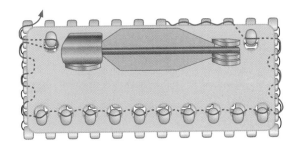

Figure 22

Step 2: String 1C, sew back through the hole, and either sew through the same B bead again or push the needle through the beadwork and then sew through a close B bead. Reinforce this stitch.

Step 3: Weave the thread to exit the first of 10 holes at the bottom of the pin back (Figure 22). String 1C, sew back through the hole, pushing the needle through the beadwork; then sew through a close B bead on the front; tighten.

Step 4: Weave the thread forward, on the front, to align to the next hole; push the needle through the beadwork and through the second hole. Repeat Steps 3 and 4, stitching down all 10 holes of the pin back to the peyote-stitch strip (Figure 22).

Step 5: Weave the thread to exit the last hole on the top left of the pin back. Repeat Step 1; keep the thread (Figure 22). Weave the thread to exit the B bead as in Figure 22, end of red thread path.

Sew the Peyote-Stitch Strip to the Back of the Brooch

Place the pin back onto the back of the brooch, aligning the top edges of the pin back and centering with the two sets of 3 pearls on each side of the brooch (Figure 23). The brooch and the pin back component have a space in between them when sitting on top of each other. Therefore, the space will be bridged with B beads as they are being stitched together.

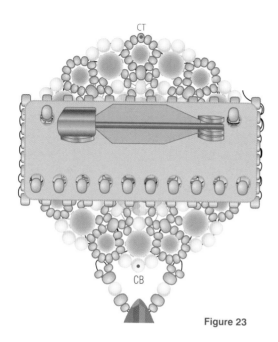

Figure 23

Step 2: Realign the pin back; weave the thread forward 2 stitches (4 beads) in the strip (Figure 24, blue thread). If this bead is sitting on the back of a setting, move the thread forward one more bead. String 1B, stab through the beadwork, tuck around a bead, and then stab back through the beadwork and through the B bead just added, plus through the same B bead on the strip; tighten (Figure 24, green thread).

Step 3: Realign the pin back; weave the thread forward on the strip to exit a B bead right before a fire-polished bead on the brooch; this may be a B bead not on the topmost row (Figure 24, orange thread). String 1B, stab through the beadwork, tuck around a bead, then stab back through the beadwork and the B bead just added plus the same B bead on the strip; tighten.

Step 4: If you can attach to a fire-polished bead, go for it; if not, weave past them and make 3 attachments on the other side, with the last stitch being made as in Step 1, ending by exiting the B bead on the strip as in Figure 24, blue thread.

Step 1: String 1B; tuck the needle through the beadwork right behind the 3 pearls that align to the top edge of the pin back. Loop the thread around and between the middle pearl and the one below it; sew back through the B bead just added and back through the B bead on the strip, as in Figure 24, red thread; tighten. Reinforce this stitch.

Edge-stitch on edge of the strip
*String 1A, tuck the needle under the closest piece of thread on the edge of the strip; tighten. Repeat from * 7 more times with the last stitch sewing through the last B bead on the edge (p. 11 and Figure 25); for a total of 8A added.

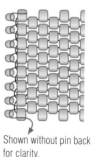

Shown without pin back for clarity.

Figure 25

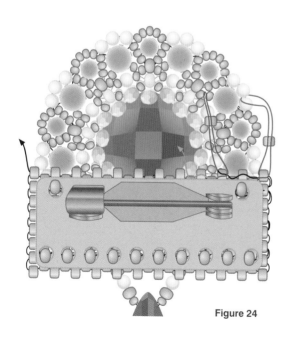

Figure 24

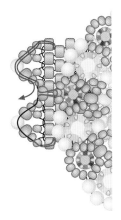

Figure 26

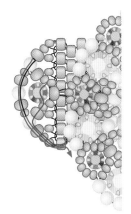

Figure 27

Embellish the edge of the strip

Step 1: Tuck the needle between the closest 2B, pull through, and then sew back through the same B bead just exited and the last A bead just added (Figure 26, red thread). String 1A, 1C, 1 pearl, 1C, and 1A, skip 2A, and sew through the fourth A bead (Figure 26, blue thread).

Step 2: String 1C, sew through the center A bead on the side of the brooch; sew back through the C bead just added and the next A bead on the edge-stitching (Figure 26, green thread).

Step 3: String 1A, 1C, 1 pearl, 1C, and 1A, skip 2A, and sew through the last A bead on the edge-stitching, plus the B bead on the strip. Tuck the needle between the closest 2B; pull through; and then sew back through the same B bead just exited, the end A bead on the edge stitching, the next A, C, pearl, C, and A (Figure 26, purple thread).

Add a 3-mm CZ: Set one 3-mm CZ. Change the needle to a size 13. Nestle the set CZ into the space between the netting on the edge of the strip, making sure the CZ is facing the correct direction.

Sew behind the 2 prong arms of the setting that are closest to the beadwork; sew through the A, C, pearl, C, and A of the net, the A bead on the edge stitching and the B bead on the strip. Tuck the needle between the closest 2B, pull through, and then sew back through the same B bead just exited, and through the end A bead on the edge-stitching, and the next A, C, and pearl (Figure 27, red thread).

Step 4: String 1A, 1C, 1 pearl, 1C, and 1A; sew through the next pearl on the edge embellishment to finish the embellishment on this edge (Figure 27, blue thread). Tuck the needle between the pearl and the C bead, pull through, and then sew back through the netting to get back to the end B bead as in Figure 27, green thread.

Attach the bottom of the pin back to the back of the brooch: Repeat the process as done for the top edge, except make only 2 connections on either side of the fire-polished beads, and don't try to attach the strip to any fire-polished beads.

Edge-stitch and add the embellishment to the second edge of the peyote stitch strip: Repeat the instruction on this edge for the edge-stitching and the edge embellishment. Weave off the thread and trim.

PROJECT RESOURCE GUIDE

Many of the materials and tools that I have used in *Timeless Beadwork Designs* are available at your local bead store. Below you will find a list of online suppliers for the specialty materials that I have used in the book, plus sources for regular beading supplies. If you have any questions regarding materials, or are having a hard time finding materials, please feel free to contact me at info@cynthiarutledge.net

Beyond Beadery
Online only, offering a wide selection of Swarovski crystals and pearls, seed beads and Delica beads
Ph: 800.840.5548
Web: www.beyondbeadery.com

Caravan Beads
Full-service retail bead store and online, offerings include Delica beads and Miyuki pin backs
915 Forest Ave.
Portland, ME 04103
Ph: 800.230.8941
Fax: 207.874.2664
Web: www.caravanbeads.net

Crystal Creations
Full-service retail store and online, offerings include 2-mm Czech pearls
Woodhaven Plaza
4058 Forest Hill Blvd.
West Palm Beach, FL 334406
Ph: 561.649.9909
Web: wwwbeadsgonewild.com

Cynthia Rutledge Studio
Online only, offering a wide selection of CZs, settings, step gauges, Miyuki pin backs, beading supplies, and beading kits
P.O. Box 3666
Crestline, CA 92325
Ph: 909.338.0296
Email: info@cynthiarutledge.net
Web: www.cynthiarutledge.net

Ezel Findings
Online only, offering beautiful ear wires, clasps and cup chain
Ph: 800.977.9904
Web: www.ezelfindings.com

Sonoran Beads
Online only for SilverSilk Capture and SilverSilk Leather
Email: orders@sonoranbeads.com
Web: www.sonoranbeads.com

Whimbeads (AKA Out On A Whim)
Full-service bead store and online, offerings include seed beads and Delica beads
121 E. Cotati Ave.
Cotati, CA 94931
Ph: 800.232.3111
Ph: 707.664.8343
Web: www.Whimbeads.com

ABOUT THE AUTHOR

Cynthia is a contemporary seed bead artist and teacher specializing in peyote stitch and other off-loom weaving techniques, with an emphasis on developing sculptural unsupported shapes in beadwork. As a teacher for more than 20 years, Cynthia shares her expertise on the road for most of the year teaching in the United States and abroad. Her work has been exhibited in national and international shows, and in many books and publications. Among her many accolades, Cynthia has been named as one of *Bead & Button* magazine's top 10 teachers for 2010, as well as the 2011 Designer of the Year for *Beadwork* magazine, along with Carol Wilcox Wells and Kelly Wiese and Sherry Serafini.

ACKNOWLEDGMENTS

Who knew that I was going to write a book? I certainly didn't until I got sweet-talked into it! My excuses had always been my crazy schedule, my lack of beading time already, and a multitude of other reasons. So when I talked to my husband, Mark, about the possibilities, I think he truly thought that I had lost the plot!

The people that I hold most dear are my family, friends, and my amazing support team, as they are the reason that you are holding this book in your hands today. Without them, I never, ever would have been able to accomplish this monumental task.

First and foremost, I would like to thank my husband, Mark, for all of his love and support. He is and always has been the love of my life and my very best friend. During the writing of this book, he picked up the gauntlet by taking over a lot of the duties that I had been doing to give me more time to create and write. Over the time taken to write this book, he has turned out to be a really good cook!

I would like to thank my Mom, Jean Tally-DiVona, for maybe not understanding my creative side, but always encouraging me to explore it. She may have started her conversation with me, when I had some harebrained idea, with the words "no" or "Are you out of your mind?" But she always let me have my head for creating, no matter what it was. For that and many other reasons, I love you, Mom.

Everyone needs a cheerleader to cheer you on when things are tough; to pat you on the back or give you a hug when you have done something good; a listening ear when all you want to do is rant and rave; someone to bounce your ideas off of and give you advice. I found my cheerleader in Carol Wilcox Wells (author of *Creative Bead Weaving: A Contemporary Guide to Classic Off-Loom Stitches* and *The Art & Elegance of Beadweaving: New Jewelry Designs with Classic Stitches*). After working with her at Beads On the Vine for so many years, she has become a very good friend. I thank you, Carol, from the bottom of my heart for your love, kindness and support, my friend.

My friend and illustrator, Bonnie Brooks, in my eyes is a goddess! She is one of the most talented people I know. We have worked together for quite a few years, creating my workshop instruction sheets, and I do believe that she can read my mind and must be my sister. So when it came time to do this book, I was only going to do it if I could work with Bonnie. She has used her amazing skills with graphics here in this book for your viewing pleasure. Bonnie, I thank you so much for your skill, your support and expertise, but most of all, your love and friendship.

I would like to thank all of my beading friends and students for encouraging me to write a book. I have written this book for all of you as a thank-you for your many years of support and kindness, your compliments on my work, and for taking my workshops. When asked about why I travel so much and why I work so hard, I always say that you are the reason for what I do. It is because of you all that I am what I am, and I thank you for that.

Sometimes, I truly think that it takes a village to get things done, what my support team calls "Team Cynthia!" My webmaster, Julie Crocker, has been working with me since the beginning of my Web site and has always strived to make me look good to the rest of the world. She has a listening ear, sound advice, a great sense of style and grace, and I am blessed to have her as part of my team.

Without technical editing, I would be doomed! Thankfully, Mindy Brooks came on board to lend her expertise to this project. We had many hours on the phone, getting "phone ear" while working our way through the projects, with a lot of laughs in between. Thank you so much for your gentle manner and for educating me along the way.

As in the sport of baseball, every team, no matter how good, needs a dependable cleanup hitter. Marlene Blessing came on board to fulfill that role for "Team Cynthia." A well-respected editor and a longtime friend, Marlene went through the entire manuscript, making sure that every detail, no matter how small, fit perfectly from beginning to end. This was a Herculean task, yet Marlene made it all look easy. Her valuable help on this book was very special to me and was the perfect finishing touch.

A big thank-you goes out to Lynne of Lynne Harty Photography for her beautiful photographs of my work, and to the Sterling/Lark team of Marilyn Kretzer, Renee Yewdaev, Diana Ventimiglia, and Jo Obarowski for listening to all of my needs and wants and for understanding how special this project was to me.

INDEX

Note: Page numbers in *italics* indicate projects.